The
Breath Connection

How to Reduce Psychosomatic and
Stress-Related Disorders with
Easy-To-Do Breathing Exercises

The
Breath Connection

How to Reduce Psychosomatic and Stress-Related Disorders with Easy-To-Do Breathing Exercises

Robert Fried, Ph.D.

*Hunter College, City University of New York
and Director, Stress and Biofeedback Clinic
Institute for Rational-Emotive Therapy
New York, New York*

With a Foreword by
Brian L. Tiep, M.D.

 **INSIGHT BOOKS**

Plenum Press • New York and London

Library of Congress Cataloging-in-Publication Data

Fried, Robert, 1935-
    The breath connection : how to reduce psychosomatic and stress
-related disorders with easy-to-do breathing exercises / Robert
Fried ; with a foreword by Brian L. Tiep.
        p.   cm.
    Includes bibliographical references.
    ISBN 0-306-43433-4
    1. Hyperventilation--Psychosomatic aspects. 2. Stress management.
3. Breathing exercises. 4. Medicine, Psychosomatic.   I. Title.
RC776.H9F74   1990
616.2'0048--dc20   89-26738
                                                           CIP

© 1990 Plenum Press, New York
A Division of Plenum Publishing Corporation
233 Spring Street, New York, N.Y. 10013

An Insight Book

Printed in the United States of America

This book is dedicated to
Virginia L. Cutchin, and to Barbara Fried,
Peter M. Litchfield, and Richard M. Carlton,
four unique and exceptional friends.

"Few bodily functions more beautifully illustrate the relationship between thinking and anatomy as does breathing." —Lowry, T. P. (1967):

Hyperventilation and Hysteria.
Springfield: Charles C Thomas.

Foreword

Breathing is basic to life. Throughout the ages, human-kind has somehow understood this—long before we ever conceived of oxygen/carbon dioxide gas exchange. Breathing is life-sustaining and its obvious presence is a sign of life itself; its absence conveys the absence of life. Breathing is commonplace.

Breathing has a variable rhythm which is linked to all metabolic functions and bespeaks physiology and emotion. It becomes tuned to physical activity. Behold the large cat loping across the plain, stalking prey, his inhalation synchronized to his stride; the singer who groups her notes and phrases in discrete breaths for emphasis and strength; the bustling person who sits down with a deep sigh of relief from a busy schedule. Our emotions can be reflected by changes in breathing pattern, rhythm, and style.

Breathing is automatic, thank goodness, and yet easily influenced by changing events or deliberate will. It is simple in its presentation—in, out, repeat as necessary. Breathing is a part of physiology which is always observable. Breathing brings us into intimate communion with our environment. We can think of the lungs as *external organs*, always exposed to the atmosphere.

We are taught to modify our respiratory pattern to improve our performance in singing, playing wind instruments, swimming, running—my violin teacher even taught me diaphragmatic breathing for conveying emotions when playing the violin. Breathing is so approachable; to vary it is to touch all our physiological body processes.

The lungs, a seemingly simple organ system, are really quite complicated. Successful ventilation merely begins with the importation of oxygen and the exportation of carbon dioxide. The ventilation must be matched to the blood flow: Teamwork between the lungs and the circulatory system is vital. If all the blood were to flow to nonventilated air sacs (alveoli) in the lungs, and all ventilation occurred where air sacs had little blood flow, respiration would fail. This is incompatible with life.

In respiration, *breathing* is not the whole story. It is the first step in the respiratory chain of events leading oxygen from the atmosphere to the nucleus of each individual cell. The *red blood cell* must also play a role in respiration since it must "capture" oxygen, carry it to the tissues, and release it in appropriate quantity. Exposure to carbon monoxide, for instance, blocks this transaction. Any break in this chain of oxygen transport will deprive the total body of vital oxygen.

To understand breathing and respiration is one thing. To use breathing as therapy, keeping in mind its complex physiology, is quite another: Many persons have written about the effects of breathing, and breathing retraining, throughout the ages, each bringing new insight, discovery, and excitement to its physiology, psychology, and philosophy.

Dr. Fried has rediscovered breathing and brings a fresh point of view to this complex subject matter. He relates the manner of breathing to respiratory events occurring down the line. He also relates the way in which we breathe to the rest of physiology. He tells us that alteration in breathing mode will bring about changes in the biochemistry of all organ systems and that disordered breathing can cause a variety of problems. The physiological concepts behind these ideas are solidly in place. We know that hyperventilation can cause changes in our delicate acid-base balance and can alter the distribution of blood flow to all organ systems.

We have generally accepted that hyperventilation may occur as a secondary result of such conditions as pain, anxiety, stress, or chemical imbalance. However, Dr. Fried has opened our eyes to the idea that such alterations in breathing patterns may be the primary event in conditions such as migraine, Raynaud's disease, and epilepsy. Whether unconditional acceptance of this point of view will be maintained over the years is almost immaterial. The contribution Dr. Fried makes is that symptomatic relief and possibly etiological control may be achievable simply by modifying breathing. He presents us with case histories in which he describes breathing retraining strategies, and monitoring by instruments that measure the physiological changes in arterial blood oxygen saturation and breath-by-breath carbon dioxide concentration, heart rate, blood pressure, and skin temperature.

Breathing is, by its very nature, inextricably connected to all other body functions in health and disease. Dr. Fried acquaints us with the general body of knowledge relating these processes to each other in a style that is simple and eloquent. He tells us about our physiology, our psychology and nutrition, and continuously relates all this information to the impact of disordered breathing and its modification.

He cautions us not to self-diagnose. Diagnosis is left to physicians. He works with physician colleagues and together they combine their insight for the full care of the patient. But the patient is given a special role.

Too often do we accept the patient as a bystander in his/her own care. In my field, pulmonary rehabilitation, a major component of patient care is patient involvement in day-to-day health management. Patients are taught facts about their body, particularly the lungs, that develop into a working knowledge of breathing. Then, along with exercise programs, they build and maintain endurance, strength, and self-confidence. This also leads to improved self-concept. An integrated program brings about many changes: A patient can look into the mirror now and see an active person—someone in control. Dr. Fried emphasizes this patient-centered approach.

In this book, we learn some of those facts about our anatomy and physiology that relate to the breathing process. There are some surprises as we learn about the various normal and maladaptive bodily states, or conditions that affect, or are affected by, breathing.

Finally, Dr. Fried teaches us a series of exercises, step-by-step, so that we can learn to breathe efficiently and experience the benefits of taking charge.

Brian L. Tiep, M.D.
Medical Director
Pulmonary Rehabilitation Service
Casa Colina Hospital for Rehabilitative
Medicine
Pomona, California

Preface

This book is about psychosomatic disorders and breathing: how breathing relates to health and emotions, and how it may affect them—in short, the psychophysiology of breathing. It also teaches how to do breathing exercises that may contribute to health and well-being.

When my previous book, *The Hyperventilation Syndrome* (Johns Hopkins University Press Series in Contemporary Medicine and Public Health, 1987) appeared, I felt proud of my accomplishment, having reviewed research on hyperventilation pretty thoroughly from about the 1850s to 1986. Few points escaped my attention.

My vigilant, cost-conscious editor at "The Press," Wendy A. Harris, red-penciled over 1000 "superfluous" references. But the book turned out to be exceptionally dense anyway: There are about 120 pages of text and 22 pages of references, with about 20 references each. That comes to about one page of references for each five and one-half pages of text on such items as pulmonary physiology, blood, brain, heart, and cardiovascular physiology, psychopathology, spirometry, plethysmography, and clinical therapeutic practice.

So everybody said "Great! Now why don't you write a book we can read?"

My first reaction was, "What's the matter with these people? The book makes perfect sense to me."

Indeed, the *Hyperventilation Syndrome* is of most use to the clinician working with persons with more or less functional breathing disorders and their sequelae, using treatment methods ranging in technical complexity up to computerized capnography and biofeedback.

But it certainly is no help to the average layperson who has that disorder, and who has little or no training in physiology, yet wishes to learn how to correct it.

I hope that in *this* book I am a little nearer to explaining the relationship between "psychosomatic" disorders and breathing simply enough for most persons to grasp, yet without talking down to my audience, many of whom are widely read and knowledgeable.

Psychosomatic is defined rather more broadly here than would make many of my colleagues comfortable: No one would quarrel with inclusion of anorexia nervosa, ulcers, or asthma. But traditionalists would not include hypertension, for instance.

In recent textbooks, "psychosomatic" disorders has been replaced by *psychophysiological disorders*. This reflects both a shift to a contemporary *psychological and stress-related disorders* approach, and away from the emphasis on *medical* treatment with its overemphasis on drugs.

But I sense that the public, for the most part, still thinks in terms of "psychosomatic" when it comes to those disorders that seem to involve psychological or emotional factors. This book is primarily for the public.

When you finish a book, it is time to express your appreciation to everyone who has helped you. But that acknowledgment seldom does justice to the full scope of the help. A case in point:

When I was Director of Research at the ICD— International Center for the Disabled, New York—Ms. Helen Stonehill, Chief Librarian, was of paramount help to me. She is an exceptionally skilled medical librarian, and exceptionally dedicated to helping. But in the final analysis, albeit exceedingly well, she was at that time doing her job. Now that I am no longer at ICD, she has no such obligation to devote herself to helping me. And yet, in numerous recent instances, she has done no less than she did then.

I am also particularly grateful to Mr. Alan C. Anderson, President of the Lenox Hill Hospital, for granting me access to the Jerome S. Leopold Health Sciences Library there. And I wish also to thank Mrs. Shirley E. Dansker for her patience and help. I must have seemed a strange sight to the staff—obviously too old to be a medical student, and too distraught to be a physician.

A number of people defaced my beautiful manuscript! Just kidding, folks: They corrected grammar, typos, caught factual errors, and made valuable suggestions for text changes. Chief among them is my former editor at the JHUP, Wendy A. Harris, Barbara Fried, Albert Ellis, Ph.D., Richard M. (Richardo) Carlton, M.D., and Brian L. Tiep, M.D., who was kind enough to write the foreword.

There are many other people who have contributed significantly to this book. Endless "discussions" and picking of brains with close friends and professional colleagues, including Peter M. Litchfield, Ph.D., Barbara Peavey, Ph.D., Helen Lowery, and Jan Hoover, shaped many specific thoughts in this book. I would follow them to the ends of the earth just to sit around and talk with them—on two occasions, I actually did.

Chapter 11, on the integration of music in breathing retraining, was conceived in the summer of '88, in the Lewis River Valley, on Ellesmere Island (Canadian Northwest Territories), 82 deg., 5 min. North latitude, while "the gang" were a-breathin' and a-meditatin' only a few hundred miles from the North Pole.

It is there that I tried to record the purest sound of the purest babbling brook to play for my "relaxation" clients. And it is there that, in the serenity of an Arctic morning, the "spirit of the wolves" revealed to me the awesome truth that, to the *objective mind*, the sound made by a babbling brook is indistinguishable from the sound of bacon frying in a pan.

Many a morning brings mail from Herbert Fensterheim, Ph.D., or Dr. Carlton. Then I know that I am in for a valuable new bit of information about hyperventilation or nutrition or whatnot that they have found and are sharing with me.

Now, my friend Dr. Richard M. Carlton is a truly fine physician: We have done many good things together, and we published some of them. Among others, he scrutinized the chapter on nutrition. He always knows everything. Nothing gets by him. He catches every factual error. It is quite infuriating!

Heated arguments with Erik Peper, Ph.D., about whether we do or do not know if there is or is not an ideal breath . . . these are a few of my favorite things.

I wish also to thank Dr. Albert Ellis, Director, and Janet Wolfe, Ph.D., Executive Director of the Institute for Rational Emotive Therapy (IRET), and Ray DiGiuseppe, Ph.D., Director of Training, and other staff of the IRET for their considerable help and support. It was their faith and belief that biofeedback services could complement RET that made the clinic possible and made it work. Dr. Wolfe deserves special thanks for her help in integrating the biofeedback services into the institute.

The board of directors of the IRET granted me the funds with which a portable pulse oximeter was bought for the biofeedback clinic. This is the unit mentioned in Chapter 8, which was used to show significantly reduced levels in my blood oxygen in a commercial aircraft at cruising altitude. Thank you for helping me to establish low blood oxygen (O_2) as a possible trigger of "fear of flying."

No one deserves to be considered a serious student of the physiology of breathing who does not acknowledge the debt this field owes to L.C. Lum, M.D., whose pioneering study of hyperventilation and breathing retraining serves as a model for much of my work.

Finally, the staff at Plenum Press deserves much credit for the production of this book: To Norma Fox, executive editor, who believed in the merit of this book, I owe a special "Thank you." To Frank Darmstadt, editorial assistant, and Andrea F. Martin, production editor, thank you for your help and patience.

The author gratefully acknowledges permission to reprint excerpts from the following:

Dalessio, D.J. (1980). *Wolff's Headache*. Quotes from pp. 56–57 are reproduced with permission of Oxford University Press, Inc., New York, N.Y.

Fried, R., & Golden, W.L. (1989). The Role of Psychophysiological Hyperventilation Assessment in Cognitive Behavior Therapy, *Journal of Cognitive Psychotherapy*, 3:5–14. Reprinted with permission of Springer Publishing Co., New York, N.Y.

Kerr, W.J., Dalton, J.W., & Gliebe, P.A. (1937). Some Physical Phenomena Associated with Anxiety States and Their Relationship to Hyperventilation. *Annals of Internal Medicine*, 11:961–992. Materials from p. 961 are reproduced with the permission of the publisher, the American College of Physicians, Chicago, Ill.

Lewis, B.I. (1957). Hyperventilation Syndrome: Clinical and Physiological Observations. *Postgraduate Medicine*, 21:259–271. Reprinted with permission of McGraw-Hill Publishing Co., Inc., New York, N.Y.

Liddell, H.S. (1956). *Emotional Hazards in Animals and Man*. Quotes from pages 3–6, 10, 12, 15–16, and 63, courtesy of Charles C Thomas, Inc., Springfield, Ill.

Loevenhart, A.S., Lorenz, W.F., Martin, H.G., & Malone, J.Y. (1918). Stimulation of the Respiration by Sodium Cyanid (sic) and Its Clinical Application. *Archives of Internal Medicine*, 21:109–129. Quotes from p. 128, courtesy of the American Medical Association, Chicago, Ill.

Lum, L.C. (1976). The Syndrome of Habitual Hyperventilation. In O. W. Hill (Ed.), *Modern Trends in Psychosomatic Medicine*, 3:96–230.

McClellan, R. (1988). *The Healing Forces of Music*. Amity House, Warwick.

Physicians' Desk Reference. (1988). Excerpts from pp. 772, 985–986, 1216, 1263, 1383, 1528, 1729, and 1902 are reproduced with the permission of the publisher, Medical Economics, Oradell, N.J.

A Cautionary Note to the Reader

Persons may experience breathing difficulties for all sorts of reasons. Some of these are functional disorders such as the hyperventilation sometimes accompanying anxiety. Some are organic pulmonary disorders such as asthma or emphysema. Yet others are organic diseases such as diabetes or hypertension which have breathing disorders as secondary symptoms.

It is unwise for you, and indeed I recommend against your attempting, to follow some of the breathing training methods described in this book unless you have first consulted with your physician or another qualified medical professional, and s/he approves your doing so after establishing that there exists no cause that contraindicates doing so.

For instance, diabetes, as well as some other diseases including kidney disease, produces a condition in the body called "metabolic acidosis." When this condition prevails, the acid-base balance of the body is normalized by compensatory rapid breathing. A change in breathing rate can destabilize you and may result in a life-threatening medical crisis.

And, again, you may have a preexisting condition, or have experienced an accident or recent surgery which could be aggravated by the physical requirements of some of these exercises. Only you know about the existence of such a condition. I recommend against your trying these exercises unless you have first ascertained by medical consultation that you cannot injure yourself by doing them.

Contents

〇〇

Chapter 1. INTRODUCTION 25
Why This Book? 27
What Is the Breath Connection? 30

Chapter 2. WHAT IS A PSYCHOSOMATIC
DISORDER? 35
Introduction 37
The Psychoanalytic Theory of Psychosomatic Disorders .. 38
Cannon's Fight-or-Flight Theory 38
Selye's General Adaptation Syndrome Theory 39
The Somatic Weakness Theory 42
The Evolution Theory 43
Conditioning as the Basis for Psychosomatic Disorders ... 44
Multifactor Theory 44
What Are the More Common Psychosomatic
  Disorders? 47
Illustrative Case: C.M. 49
Why Hasn't Anything Worked for Me So Far? 50
The Breath Connection 52

Chapter 3. BREATHING 53
Introduction 55
How Do You Breathe? 57

19

Respiration 58
The Airway Passages to the Lungs 61
The Lungs 63
The Composition of Air in the Atmosphere and the
    Lungs 64
Breathing Normally 65
Breathing Abnormally 66
The Breath Connection 68

Chapter 4.   THE HYPERVENTILATION SYNDROME ... 73
Introduction 75
Why Do Some of Us Hyperventilate? 76
How Serious Can Some of the Effects of
    Hyperventilation Be? 77
How Can You Tell if You Are Hyperventilating? 80
How Common Is Hyperventilation? 80
Could Your Symptoms Be Hyperventilation-Related? 80
Why Is Medicine Confused about the Hyperventilation
    Syndrome? 85
What if I Am on Medication? 91
The Breath Connection 93
Illustrative Case: V.A. 94

Chapter 5.   PSYCHOSOMATIC DISORDERS, STRESS-
RELATED DISORDERS, AND CONDITIONING 97
Introduction 99
Leading up to the Case of Robert 100
Conditioning 101
We Are Prewired to Conserve Energy 102
The Breath Connection 114

Chapter 6.   NUTRITION AND BREATHING 117
Introduction 119
Eating Your Way to Narrower Arteries 121
Tyramine 121
The Relationship between Hypertension and Breathing .. 130
Foods Implicated in Migraine and Neurological Allergy .. 130

Minerals: Iron, Zinc, Magnesium, Calcium, and
  Potassium—Their Role in Respiration 136
Vitamins 139
The Breath Connection 140
Illustrative Case: N.B. 141

Chapter 7. BREATHING, HYPERTENSION, AND
THE HEART 147
Introduction 149
Breathing and the Cardiovascular System 151
Hyperventilation and Blood Pressure 151
The Heart and Blood Pressure 154
The Relationship between Breathing and Pulse Rate 156
Blood Pressure and Blood Flow through the Arteries of
  the Body 156
The Relationship between Blood Pressure and
  Breathing 158
Arterial Diameter and the Amount of Carbon Dioxide in
  Your Blood 158
Enlarging and Narrowing the Arteries in Your Brain 158
Breathing, Blood Pressure, and Syncope (Fainting)—
  The Vapors 159
The Effect of Hyperventilation on the Heart: You Make
  My Heart Skip a Beat! 160
The Breath Connection 162
Illustrative Case: V.S. 162
Illustrative Case: M.G. 163

Chapter 8. HYPERVENTILATION AND ANXIETY
DISORDERS 165
Introduction 167
Anxiety and Hyperventilation 171
How Does Hyperventilation Cause Psychological
  Problems? 172
The Effect of Low Blood CO_2 on Body Arteries 173
The Effect of Low Blood CO_2 on Brain Arteries 174
The Effect of Low Blood CO_2 on Hemoglobin 174

The Effect of Low Blood CO_2 on Muscles and Nerves 175
The Effect of Low Blood CO_2 on the Nervous System 175
The Psychological Symptoms of Hyperventilation 176
The DSM–III 178
The Psychology of Persons with Breathing Disorders 180
Hyperventilation and Panic Attacks 182
Fear of Flying—Aerophobia 184
The Breath Connection 188
Illustrative Case: R.R. 188
Illustrative Case: M.N. 189
Illustrative Case: F.C. 190

Chapter 9. MIGRAINE, EPILEPSY, AND
RAYNAUD'S DISEASE 193
Introduction 195
Migraine 196
What Is Migraine? 198
Who Gets Migraine? 200
What Causes Migraine? 201
The Role of Low Brain Oxygen in Migraine 201
The Role of Vasoactive Foodstuffs in Migraine 203
Prostaglandins 205
The Epilepsies 206
What Is Epilepsy? 208
Raynaud's Disease 210
Controlling Migraine, Raynaud's, and Idiopathic
  Seizures 212
What Hand Warming Techniques Used in Migraine and
  Raynaud's Disease Teach Us about the Breath
  Connection 214
The Breath Connection 218
Illustrative Case: T.R. 218
Illustrative Case: B.G. 220

Chapter 10. HOW TO INTEGRATE BREATHING AND
NUTRITION TO CONTROL STRESS AND
PYCHOSOMATIC DISORDERS 221
Introduction 223

The Role of Mental Attitude 228
Agreement to Improve My Attitude 229
Alert Rapid Relaxation Breathing Exercise (TM) 230
Preliminary Rapid Relaxation Exercise 232
Abdominal/Diaphragmatic Breathing 235
Breathing Rhythm 238
Integrating Deep-Diaphragmatic Breathing with Other
    Strategies to Control Tension, Anxiety, and Phobias ... 243
Integrating Breathing Exercises into a Program to Control
    Blood Pressure and Heart Disorders 246
Integrating Breathing into a Program to Reduce Migraine,
    Raynaud's and Idiopathic Seizure Symptom Frequency
    and Severity 249
A Note on Breathing and Hand Temperature
    Biofeedback 253
Abdominal Breathing and Hand Temperature 255
The Breath Connection—An Integrative Approach 256
The Breath Connection 271
Illustrative Case: S.N. 271
Illustrative Case: L.V. 274

Chapter 11.   MUSIC AND BREATH: A SOUND
CONNECTION 275
Introduction 277
Drugs, Meditation, and the American Youth Movement .. 278
The Effect of Music on the Mind and the Body—The Role
    of Music in Industry 280
Music, Relaxation, and Other Functions 280
Does Music Affect Human Behavior? 281
The Effect of Music on Learning 289
The Effect of Music on the Autonomic Nervous System .. 289
Brain Functions 293
How To. 295
The Effect of Music on Abdominal Breathing 297
The Breath Connection—Conclusion 297

INDEX 301

CHAPTER 1

Introduction

WHY THIS BOOK?

This book, based on my lectures and workshops, was written for my clients. It contains just about everything that we discuss in the course of our working together.

Besides doing breathing and relaxation exercises, we talk about the best way in which they can help themselves to reduce their suffering by learning everything possible about their condition. Every shred of information is important: It forms part of a total picture of their condition, and it helps them to know what questions to ask me and what answers to expect.

For the most part, my clients suffer from anxiety, stress, and psychosomatic disorders. Usually, they are in therapy with a "primary" therapist who helps them with their emotional or psychological problems. Typically, they are referred to me for help with the somatic aspects of their disorders: tension, insomnia, panic attacks, or with various preexisting medical disorders which are acknowledged to be aggravated by stress and anxiety: high blood pressure, migraine, headaches, hyperventilation, asthma, ulcers/gastritis, colitis, allergies, etc.

Treatment often centers on imagery- and biofeedback-assisted relaxation with deep abdominal (diaphragmatic) breathing training and, as is often necessary, cognitive coping strategies.

It is, therefore, not by coincidence that I practice biofeedback at the Institute for Rational Emotive Therapy (IRET) in New York City. The Institute provides "rational emotive therapy" (RET), a cognitive behavior therapy consistent with the teachings of its founder, Albert Ellis.

Biofeedback complements RET. It is a form of behavior therapy. It is not "cognitive," but teaches clients to reduce their anxiety, stress and pain by adopting rational counterstrategies of self-regulation. Whereas RET asserts that you may be victimized by irrational thinking, we assert that you may be victimized by maladaptive muscle and visceral patterns of stress. Some of these patterns we call "dysponesis." An example of this is the particular configuration of muscle tension, or the partial contraction of the diaphragm observed in persons with chronic pain.

Biofeedback and relaxation therapy follow the principles of "behavioral medicine": The Magazine section of the *New York Times* ran an article (Sept. 27, 1987) by D. Goleman, "The Mind over the Body," with the subtitle, "Behavioral Medicine Grows—In Spite of Detractors." The article defines behavioral medicine as a medical field whose techniques use the mind of the patient to help heal his/her body.

This definition is only partly correct: Most of its techniques do not come from medicine, but from psychology. In fact, much to your disadvantage, the techniques of behavioral medicine are for the most part either ignored or criticized by establishment physicians.

Behavioral medicine is comprehensive, focusing also on the personal, motivational, and social aspects of illness:

- Do you want to be/get well? (motivation)
- Will you adhere to a "behavioral contract"? (compliance)
- What factors contribute to maintaining your disorder? (its social and family context)
- What does the disorder mean to you? (its ideational component)
- What role might the disorder play in your life?
- What secondary problems are created by your coping strategies?

For instance, you may have a long history of migraine and wish to try biofeedback treatment. Although medication helped at first, it no longer does.

After explaining the nature of the disorder to you, and the multifactor approach to its treatment, you may well show up for every training session but will not adhere to the practice exercises and nutritional or other guidelines essential to a satisfactory outcome, despite the considerable pain and misery of this disorder. Some persons simply may not do what is essential to part with symptoms.

Sometimes a symptom may play a vital role in your life. It may be a family rallying point, a source of sympathy or otherwise scarce attention and affection, a means of avoiding unpleasant tasks, etc. If that turns out to be the case, it becomes essential for you to learn coping skills and make life-style changes so that support for the disorder will be neutralized. Conventional medicine lacks the inclination to address such issues. The aim of conventional medicine is to *cure* with medication or with surgery.

Behavioral medicine focuses on the interaction between the individual psychology of the person, his/her social milieu, and physical conditions.

Biofeedback is only one of the methods of behavioral medicine. Biofeedback treatment also requires that we look at you: Your self-image, your family, your symptoms history, how you cope, how you live, what you like and dislike, what you eat, if you exercise, and many other factors, including your hopes and fears. And from all of this information, we try to fashion a strategy of treatment by self-regulation for you.

Self-regulation means that getting well may include methods that you can use yourself. For instance, controlling breathing, or relaxing to overcome muscle tension or high blood pressure; controlling hand temperature, or eating habits, to overcome migraine, or Raynaud's spasms.

There are few conditions that are treated with conventional medication that cannot also be treated with one or more of the self-regulation/biofeedback strategies. But often medication is more rapid, and it certainly is more convenient, though it may have hazardous side effects.

This point is underscored by an article in the *New England Journal of Medicine*: "Risks of Correcting the Risks of Coronary Disease and Stroke with Drugs" (1986:306). Many forms of heart disease and hypertension have been successfully treated with biofeedback, relaxation, and yoga, which entail no such risks.

WHAT IS THE BREATH CONNECTION?

Psychologists in biofeedback practice recognize a two-way relationship between the physiological condition of the body and the brain—the way that the body and brain organs and systems function and interact. It is doubtful that any one of them would stake their reputation on the truth of either of the following statements, (a) "It is the mind that affects the body," or (b) "It is the body that affects the mind."

But biofeedback therapists are trained to know something about both the workings of the body they are helping to train, and the psychology of the person in whom these systems have faltered. They know about the role of learning (conditioning), ideas (cognition), social context, expectations, etc. And now they are learning about the role of breathing: Certain types of breathing can make you ill, others can make you well.

Frequently, when a person's body is disturbed, certain characteristic breathing changes are noted. And conversely, when a person's mental state or mood changes, breathing changes along with it. This has been known for thousands of years and is being rediscovered every day in medical and psychology laboratories all over the world. These breathing changes may become chronic and of their own accord may create new physical or emotional disorders.

I am sure that you have an aunt who, your family whispers, is "neurotic." No family exists without such a skeleton in its closet. But what does *neurotic* mean? Is she "nutty," as Albert Ellis might put it? Is she weird? Phobic? Anxious? Does she have strange unexplainable symptoms such as dizziness—weakness? Shhhh. . . a "woman's disease"? Does she have *hysterical* symptoms, fits of crying, fainting spells (*the vapors*)? Is she known to every physician on the *Avenue*: Her medical file fills an entire cabinet, and she has worn out three seats in the waiting room? I'll bet her ailments are accompanied by some kind of breathing thing: perhaps rapid, shallow breaths, heaving sighs, or, she can't catch her breath.

You may take comfort from the fact that she likely outlived her doctor's office staff—What? It's not an aunt. It's you!

Well, I have spent the past six years studying the role of breathing in psychosomatic, anxiety, and stress disorders. And I believe that I am beginning to understand the role that it plays in these. I have learned that many can be controlled when breathing retraining is incorporated in treatment strategies.

For instance, I have even found, much to my amazement, an early medical account of several persons with chronic "incurable" schizophrenia, of long duration, whose normal mental state was briefly restored with controlled breathing (you can read more about this in Chapter 9).

Much of what we know about breathing comes from yoga practices: Transcendental meditation, shavasan, and Zen all involve breathing. Even modern physical therapy texts now incorporate yoga breathing, though they seldom acknowledge their debt to that venerable ancient practice.

Most of my clients have been told by their physician, at one time or another, "It's all in your mind," and "It's only an emotional problem." As for their breathing, in the absence of lung disease, it is common practice to view it as the hysterical part of their general folly.

"Stop hyperventilating," or "Here, breathe into this paper bag," are common clinical advice given clients showing stress. These were reported to me by persons who were referred to me for breathing retraining.

Disordered breathing is likely to be the best indication of stress and anxiety, for whatever reason. It is part of the mechanisms that rouse you to action in an emergency. It is also part of the mechanisms that rouse you to excitement and pleasure. In short, it reflects many of the body's life adjustment functions. When breathing is abnormal, that may be a warning that there is something going on in your body that you should pay attention to.

Abnormal breathing may have an emotional or a physical basis. Fear and sadness can cause breathing changes, but so can hypertension, kidney disease and diabetes, just to mention a few factors.

This book aims to describe the commoner ways that breathing interacts with stress, emotional, psychological, and psychosomatic disorders, and to teach you some new and powerful techniques that you can use yourself to reduce the suffering and pain that accompany these disorders.

I will teach you an original method—one that I have developed—to correct your breathing and relax by incorporating deep abdominal/diaphragmatic breathing with mental imagery. The method is called the *Alert and Rapid Relaxation Technique*.™

It will help you improve shallow or other breathing difficulty common in hyperventilation, asthma, emphysema, pulmonary fibrosis, and other lung diseases; develop greater lung power (tidal volume) if you are a vocalist; and overcome anxiety and psychosomatic and stress-related disorders.

CHAPTER 2

What Is a Psychosomatic Disorder?

INTRODUCTION

It is likely that you took this little book from the bookstore shelf because it features *stress, anxiety,* and *psychosomatic disorders.*

Based on what we know of the considerable frequency with which such disorders occur in the U.S. population, it is safe to guess that you've already been told that you suffer from at least one, if not more than one, of them. And I'll bet you can't wait to be rid of it.

What are psychosomatic disorders? They are the disorders that are said to result from or be aggravated by emotions or stress.

Psychiatrists used to think that Freud's theories explained how this all comes about. That belief is no longer unanimous. Outmoded psychoanalytic theories are giving way to the more modern views of behavioral medicine.

THE PSYCHOANALYTIC THEORY OF PSYCHOSOMATIC DISORDERS

Freud believed that psychosomatic symptoms are the physical expressions of sexual conflicts, or unexpressed anger. And accordingly, psychosomatic symptoms are specific to unconscious emotional conflicts.

Symptoms with no discernible cause were evidence that you were suffering from *hysteria*, which is what you were said to have if you had symptoms with no discernible cause.

Thus, persons were said to have hysterical this, that, and the other, if no cause could be found. And the very best of hysterical syndromes was "neurocirculatory asthenia, neurasthenia, cardiac neurosis, and effort syndrome," all names that represent the same set of medical textbook symptoms that we now know as *hyperventilation syndrome*.

Hypertension, for instance, might be related to repressed hostility, while asthma might be the expression of an unuttered appeal for parental love and attention. In psychoanalytic theory, it is invariably assumed that there is a symbolic relationship between illness and subconscious conflict.

According to more modern views, the requirements of living in a family, a community, getting along with others on the job, etc., may be stressors that contribute to illness. The price we pay for controlling social interactions may have a nonspecific weakening effect on the body's ability to protect itself from diseases.

Here are some additional theories.

CANNON'S FIGHT-OR-FLIGHT THEORY

W.B. Cannon was a noted American physiologist who postulated that "emotions" are the result of a sudden, involuntary, physiological adjustment of the *autonomic* nervous system to the requirements of survival in a crisis situation.

The autonomic nervous system has two main branches: The *sympathetic* branch arouses us to action, while the *parasympathetic* branch returns us to a pre-action state.

The autonomic nervous system is mostly under the control of a brain center, the hypothalamus, responsible for such processes as emotion, eating, drinking, and sex drives. It automatically adjusts most of your involuntary biological life functions. But it is also affected by the frontal lobes of the brain, and thus influenced by thinking.

The *sympathetic* branch of the autonomic nervous system also orients our attention to environmental changes, some of which may herald danger. This invariably involves *breath holding;* the release of action hormones (adrenaline and noradrenaline) into the blood causing reduced blood flow to the extremities, increased heart rate and blood pressure, automatic muscular blood flow adjustments, and involuntary changes in digestive and other internal organs.

Pavlovian physiologists who studied the way that these autonomic nervous system adjustments could become conditioned to any environmental stimuli, came to the conclusion that *merely eliciting them, for whatever reason, could in itself be stressful.*

SELYE'S GENERAL ADAPTATION SYNDROME THEORY

H. Selye was a Canadian Nobel Laureate who published a book, *Stress Without Distress* (Lippincott, 1974), in which he summarized his theory, now widely accepted, that combines the work of Cannon and of the Pavlovians. He put it this way:

> Mental tensions, frustrations, insecurity and aimlessness are among the most damaging stressors, and psychosomatic studies have shown how often they cause migraine headache, peptic ulcers, heart attacks, attacks, hypertension. . . . (p. 108)

In plain terms, you were not designed to withstand prolonged tension, anger, and frustration—a fact which I am sure comes as no surprise to you as you think about the things in life that you need to cope with. Rather, you seem to be able to function with efficiency—minimal energy expenditure unless otherwise indicated.

But when survival requires it, you are able to rapidly muster, and maintain, high energy output to meet emergency demand in effecting a successful defense or escape from a threatening predator or situation.

Naturally, this increased *arousal* is automatically accomplished by the *sympathetic* branch of the autonomic nervous system and may be observed as vigilance, tension, anger, or rage. When the threat subsides, the arousal dissipates because it becomes inhibited by the opposing action of the *parasympathetic* branch of the autonomic nervous system. This readjustment to prearousal energy expenditure was termed "homeostasis" by Cannon.

What happens if you continue the energy-costly "sympathetic arousal" state is explained by Selye in this way:

> . . .animals exposed to continuous stress for long periods go through the three phases of the GAS [General Adaptation Syndrome]: the initial alarm reaction, followed by resistance and, eventually, exhaustion. . . . (p. 129)

Thus, a particular stressful event may result in nonspecific physical effects in addition to specific ones. And the combination, if chronic, may result in a psychosomatic disorder.

As you can see, according to this theory, there is no rational reason why a symbolic relationship should be thought to connect the symptoms to the stressors. In fact, there is no basis for a rational guess about the source of stress, given the symptoms.

You may of course wonder why Selye, or anyone else, would think that obviously adaptive mechanisms—the very same mechanisms that keep us alive—would contribute to stress and ultimately to disease.

We believe that there has been little evolutionary change that would help adapt us to the modern world. No new behaviors have evolved to deal with trains that do not keep to schedule; unrealistic work demands; family or marital discord; screaming or whining children; health or financial concerns; interpersonal workplace conflicts; sedentary daily routine; fear of technology, computers and modernization; fear of aging and loss of social status, and so on.

And so our tendency is to respond to modern "threats" in the same way that primitive peoples did millions of years ago: We can gasp, tense, snarl, lash out.

Because these automatic orientation and defensive reactions threaten others, we quickly learn to hide their outward expression by voluntary coverup actions: We refrain, wherever possible, from showing frustration, anger, fear, and pain, and even joy, love, and pleasure. And the consequence of this strategy may be that the unseen reactions, breath holding, increased pulse rate and blood pressure, dry throat, etc., persist.

It may be said that we spend much of our time at home or at work, *sitting on the outside and running on the inside.*

THE SOMATIC WEAKNESS THEORY

Another theory proposes that inherited, genetic factors, prior illnesses, nutrition, etc., have a permanently disabling effect which predisposes us to some form of illness or disorder. In other words, the way that you are constructed, the nature and quality of the parts or components that you inherited, your exposure to and history of childhood diseases, pre- and postnatal nutrition, may contribute more to the kind of psychosomatic disorder that you are likely to develop than any psychological or symbolic connection to it.

Although there is considerable similarity between us, there is nevertheless something unique about each of us also. Some persons are really "shook up" by a frightening experience, while others are relatively undisturbed by it. Some persons will not set foot on an aircraft, while others fly loop-the-loops. This apparent fundamental difference in overall reaction patterns has given rise to a *specific-reaction* theory.

For example, persons whose chronic reaction to tension and stress consists of periodic breath-holding by contraction of the diaphragm—a very common reaction, indeed—will reduce the volume of air that they breathe with each breath. To compensate for lower volume, they increase breathing rate.

Increasing breathing rate may cause hyperventilation, a major *cause* of psychosomatic disorders. Prolonged hyperventilation will change the body's acid-base balance, soon reducing the amount of oxygen delivered to body organs and tissues. In a person with an inherited tendency to coronary artery disease, reduced oxygen supply to the heart could prove catastrophic.

THE EVOLUTION THEORY

We believe that the thinking parts of our brain, however, may have undergone a considerable degree of evolution even though the autonomic nervous system is limited to fight-and-flight reaction patterns.

There is a very definite proportional increase in the size of the frontal areas of the brain from lower animal forms to humankind. These are the brain areas just behind the forehead, which function in intellectual activities as well as in some forms of emotion.

Furthermore, the asymmetry in the anatomical structure of our head, with enlargement of the left side, appears to correspond to development of language. The evidence for a "true language" in nonhuman species, especially the apes, is a matter of continuing debate as is also the evidence for their grasp of the concept of "future."

We recognize that nonhuman animal species act in ways that suggest that they have "future." But their actions invariably depend on *experiences* of the moment or of the past.

We, on the other hand, can anticipate the future, or events never previously experienced. This is at the very core of the concept of anxiety, and has required psychologists to postulate *hypothetical* past experiences to which they can attribute a forward projection. The evidence supporting these hypotheses is remarkably fragile.

Philosophers tell us that we tend towards deductive reasoning. And, the rational basis for deductive reasoning is a past condition. Thus, we can explain consequences as following past events.

Our ability to also deduce *irrational* ideas from reasonable past events is a truly unique product of brain evolution: imagined dangers—imagined in the sense that they are not in fact threats to safety—can arouse the same fight-and-flight mechanisms as real ones.

On the brighter side, this ability to break from the confines of rational deductive thinking may also be at the core of poetry, music, and art in its non-representational form.

CONDITIONING AS THE BASIS FOR PSYCHOSOMATIC DISORDERS

The reflex, automatic action of the body, such as withdrawing a finger when touching an unprotected electric wire, is different from automatically salivating when you hear or see the word "lemon." The first reaction is called an unconditioned response because it does not depend on learning. In the second case, a person would not respond by salivating if s/he had never experienced a lemon.

The process by which anything becomes capable of reliably producing a reflex is called classical conditioning. This process is intimately tied to our concept of the formation of psychosomatic disorders.

If you were the child of overprotective parents, it is likely that the chance discovery that you can avoid school by feigning illness would increase in frequency with each successfully faked episode. Here we see the operation of the rewards, avoiding school and getting parental attention, contingent upon a voluntary behavior, faking illness. This is also conditioning. It is called operant conditioning.

MULTIFACTOR THEORY

So far, we have examined different theories of psychosomatic disorders. But in all likelihood, the picture is far more complex. It may well be that all disorders have multiple causes: It is frequently the case that the flu is "going around." And some people get it and others don't. Why is that? One explanation is that stress, or emotional state, affects the body's immune system, impairing the ability to fight off invading germs—viruses or bacteria.

The idea that there is a cause/effect relationship between emotions and illness is not exactly new. The psychoanalytic school, for one, held that view. But the question of which is *cause* and which is *effect* has been debated for some time. For instance, W.F. Evans, in his book, *Mental Medicine*, wrote, as early as 1897:

> Many physicians of extensive experience are destitute of the ability of searching out the mental causes of disease; they cannot read the book of the heart, and yet it is in this book that are inscribed, day by day, and hour by hour, all the griefs, and all the miseries, and all the vanities, and all the fears, and all the joys, and all the hopes of man, and in which will be found the most active and incessant principle of that frightful series of organic changes which constitute pathology. (p. 37)

But Pavlov preferred a purely physiological explanation which has greatly influenced modern medicine:

> My attitude towards the psychiatric material, however, differed greatly from the usual attitude of specialists. . . . I always reasoned on a purely physiological basis and constantly explained to myself the psychical activity of the patients in definite physiological terms. (p. 506)

A more modern view is that stress, emotions, and physiological factors may predispose a person to disease.

In 1967, two researchers, Holmes and Rahe, concluded that there is a strong relationship between selected

Event	Social Readjustment Rating Scale	Score
Death of spouse		100
Divorce		73
Marital separation		65
Jail term		63
Death of close family member		63
Personal injury or illness		53
Marriage		50
Fired from work		47
Marital reconciliation		45
Retirement		45
Change in family member's health		44
Pregnancy		40
Sex difficulties		39
Addition to the family		39
Change in financial status		38
Death of a close friend		37
Change to different line of work		36
Change in number of marital arguments		35
Mortgage or loan over $10,000		31
Foreclosure of mortgage or loan		30
Change in work responsibilities		29
Son or daughter leaving home		29
Trouble with inlaws		29
Outstanding personal achievement		28
Spouse begins or stops work		26
Starting or finishing school		25
Change in living conditions		25
Revision of personal habits		24
Trouble with the boss		23
Change in work hours		20
Change in residence		20
Change in schools		20
Change in recreational habits		19
Change in church activities		19
Change in social activities		18
Mortgage or loan under $10,000		17
Change in sleeping habits		16
Change in number of family gatherings		15
Change in eating habits		15
Vacation		13
Christmas season		12

Score: _____

From Holmes, T.H., and Rahe, R.H. (1967). The Social Readjustment Scale. Journal of Psychosomatic Research, 11:213–218. Reprinted with permission of the authors and Pergamon Press, Elmsford, N.Y.

"life events" and illness. Their study, based on more than 5000 patients, supported a widely held belief that stressful life events are an important contribution to the onset of disease—not only psychosomatic disorders, but infectious diseases and injuries as well. And so, they devised a *Social Readjustment Rating Scale*, which accords numerical values to various common events in ordinary people's lives. The scale is reproduced on the opposite page.

To use this scale, simply check off the items that you experienced within the past year, then add up your score. If you score 300 or better, you would have a 90% chance of developing an illness, with a score of 150, a 50-50 chance, and so on.

Try it. What is your score? Does it correspond to your recent history of illness?

Though the occurrence of disease may require multiple predispositions, predisposition does not condemn you to illness: Preventive measures can be taken to avoid their effects, and we are beginning to learn much about them.

One of the aims of this book is to alert you to a number of such factors, and thereby help you to overcome many of them.

In the *Handbook of Behavioral Medicine* (Guilford Press, 1984) Krantz and Glass report that on the basis of the study of the physiological effect of emotions, it is now generally held that traits, coping dispositions, or personality factors could influence the development and course of disease.

WHAT ARE THE MORE COMMON PSYCHOSOMATIC DISORDERS?

Practitioners recognize the psychosomatic basis of many diseases and disorders. And, a composite of the index of contemporary medical books yields the following list:

- Adrenal disease (Addison's disease, Cushing's syndrome)
- allergy
- amenorrhea (irregular menstrual periods)
- anorexia
- arthritis
- backache
- bronchial asthma
- cancer
- cardiac arrhythmia
- cardiovascular disease
- colds
- Crohn's disease (chronic inflammatory bowel disease)
- diabetes
- dermatitis
- duodenal ulcers
- Epstein-Barr virus (mononucleosis)
- epilepsy
- gastrointestinal pathology
- Graves' disease (hyperthyroidism)
- headache
- herpes virus
- hives
- hypertension
- lupus erythematosus
- migraine
- myositis (lumbago)
- pain
- peptic ulcers
- Raynaud's disease
- rheumatoid arthritis
- sexual organ dysfunction

- suppression of immune response
- ulcerative colitis
- urethritis (bacterial and chronic yeast)

This impressive list is still not exhaustive but it covers most of the things that you are likely to have heard of. Most remarkably, none of the major textbooks cite the *hyperventilation syndrome*, which a number of prominent psychiatrists have attributed to hysteria.

Psychosomatic disorders are not imaginary. You are not malingering if you have one or more of them. They may even "run in families."

Do you recognize any of them? Do you suffer from any of them? If you do, you are in excellent company. Let's look at a particular illustrative case.

ILLUSTRATIVE CASE: C.M.

Ms. C. M. is a 27-year-old divorced administrative assistant of medium height, on the slim side, and well-groomed. She has no children.

She reported experiencing headaches, muscle tension, chest pain and "skipped beats," in addition to bloating and occasional sleeplessness.

These symptoms began several years ago, unconnected to any particular event in her life. They gradually worsened. Headaches became more frequent, and more intense, and she dreaded the skipped heart beats.

I observed, when she first entered my office, that her handshake was limp, her hand cold and clammy, and her posture suggested depression.

She related having seen numerous physicians who told her that she was "fit as a fiddle." Cardiac arrhythmia (*ventricular premature contractions*), which she perceived as "skipped beats," was not thought to be dangerous, and her problems were said to be emotional and she was advised to seek proper psychiatric help.

She then sought help from several different therapists. One, a psychiatrist, gave her medication. Nothing helped and she feared that she would fail with me also.

She reported "every symptom in the book": shortness of breath, dizziness, dry throat and frequent swallowing; blurred vision, faintness; chest pain, heart palpitations, and "skipped beats"; muscle aches, pain, cramps, and twitches; sweating, frequent headaches, chronic indigestion and gas; cold extremities; a fear of dying or going crazy; depression and chronic tiredness.

Her blood pressure was near normal, but her pulse was elevated (112 BPM). Breathing was shallow and rapid—26 breaths per minute (almost twice the normal rate).

Expired breath showed carbon dioxide level depressed to one-third of normal (a typical normal level averages about 5%). And, her hands were exceptionally cold. The left index finger temperature was an uncommonly low 76° F (three degrees F above room temperature). The normal expected value is about 87 to 90° F.

What does this tell us about Ms. C.M.? Her rapid pulse suggests elevated action hormone level; her rapid breathing is due to the shallowness of her breaths, as is common in anxiety and tension patterns with the diaphragm more or less "frozen." Cold hands result from constricted blood vessels (arteries) due to low blood carbon dioxide. A very tense and anxious lady indeed.

Here is a case where numerous "psychosomatic" symptoms are attributed entirely to psychological factors. But stop and think for a moment; if you've never had a "skipped" beat, would you know what it is?—could you produce one? How can one imagine that the "mind" produces symptoms?

WHY HASN'T ANYTHING WORKED FOR ME SO FAR?

This book will show you that, over the past 50 years, highly respected medical publications have documented the fact that certain kinds of mental and physical disorders are associated with common breathing irregularities, especially hyperventilation. Breathing retraining can control them quickly and at litte or no cost.

I have uncovered no evidence of a grand conspiracy to hide this knowledge from you. This is not one of those

"What They Don't Want You to Know About. . ." books. But many things that were common knowledge and practice in the past have been neglected as a consequence of the generally beneficial shift by medicine to reliance on drugs.

In your search for relief you may have consulted numerous doctors and obeyed their instructions faithfully. You probably watch your diet, do aerobic exercises, consume quantities of various medications. Yet you seem to be *treatment proof*. In fact, some among you may be what L.C. Lum, noted British lung specialist, calls "the patient with the fat (medical) folder syndrome." A legend in your own time!

It has perhaps been suggested to you that you may be sabotaging otherwise miraculous treatments and you may blame yourself for their failure and wonder what you are doing wrong.

The gong has sounded the end of round 1. You sheepishly return to your corner wondering what to do next. Round 2 consists of sifting among *self-help* books.

Why are there are so many of them on the market? Logic dictates that they must serve a very important purpose. Well, if the *orthodox* treatments work, why so many *self-help* books?

The preferred explanation is that many persons resist getting well. This is an old ploy which psychologists call *secondary gain*. You are thought to derive some sort of advantage from your disorder.

If you don't benefit from treatment, it is because, (a) you are not motivated to get well because, (b) you derive some benefit from being ill.

It could be that there are some people who do not wish to get well. But the overwhelming majority of persons who suffer from psychosomatic or stress-related disorders do almost desperately want to get well.

THE BREATH CONNECTION

The basic message of this book is that proper oxygen delivery to all parts of your body is crucial to health and well-being. Psychosomatic disorders and stress reactions inevitably are the result of chronic physical "adjust" and "readjust" mechanisms that ultimately deprive the body of oxygen as it is burned up in these futile mini-emergencies.*

That is why your doctor recommends exercise— "aerobics."

Aerobic exercise increases the body's available oxygen and therefore promotes wellness: The Prudential Life Insurance Company has shown, in a recently published report, that where it is not contraindicated because of disability, aerobic exercise promotes health and reduces health care costs.

Delivering oxygen to the body is the responsibility of the respiratory system. Breathing is the process by which air enters the bloodstream, via the lungs. Thus, proper breathing, and correcting common breathing disorders, is the ultimate form of aerobics.

Although there have been popular theories that psychosomatic disorders, unlike stress disorders, are a symbolic manifestation of emotional conflict, there is not a shred of hard evidence to support these theories. In fact, the standard list of psychosomatic disorders is indistinguishable from that of stress-related disorders and this master list is now called "psychophysiological disorders" in professional reference works such as the DSM-III (*Diagnostic and Statistical Manual of the American Psychiatric Association*).

*Thank you, "Kabluna."

CHAPTER 3

Breathing

INTRODUCTION

We identify breathing with life, don't we?

The Book of Genesis tells us: "And the Lord God formed man of the dust of the ground and breathed into his nostrils the breath of life; and the man became a living being." Thus, in Western tradition, all life begins with breath.

It is also perceived to end that way. In The New Testament, "Jesus, crying with a loud voice, said, 'Father into thy hands I commit my spirit!' And having said this he breathed his last" (Luke, 23:46, RSV). Thus, breath is essentially on loan to us: We must return it when we are done with it.

The *Upanishads* represent Indian religious ideas and beliefs. The older of these go back to about 800 A.D. The *Prasna Upanishad* is based on the search for the Supreme Spirit, *Brahman*, by devout students who seek guidance from the sage, *Pippalada*.

According to tradition, the latter offered to answer

their questions if they agreed to study with him for one year. At the end of that time, one of their number, *Kabandi Katyayana*, asked the sage the first of six questions: "Master, whence came all created things?" The sage answered: "In the beginning, the Creator longed for the joy of creation. He remained in meditation, and then came *Rayi*, matter, and *Prana*, life. 'These two, thought he, will produce beings for me.'"

Prana is the basic force of life. We are said to interact with or acquire this force through meditation—a process in which breathing plays a significant and sometimes crucial role.

In the *Svetasvatara Upanishad*, part 2, *Savitri*, the God of Inspiration, instructs us: ". . .and when the body is silent steadiness, breathe rhythmically, through the nostrils with a peaceful ebbing and flowing of breath. . . ."

Zen was introduced in China in the sixth century A.D. Less a religion than a tradition, it focuses on meditation to realize one's true nature. The first four of the "112 ways" are breathing instructions.

In the Chinese tradition, *Qui* (pronounced "chi"), a tripartite entity with both organic and inorganic property is the vital energy of life. Its third component, natural air Qui, is absorbed by the lungs from the air we breathe.

In the Western tradition, common metaphors also arouse our interest in breathing because they reflect our equating breathing with emotions and other passions of life, such as love, anger, joy, and sorrow, and even altruism.

We hold that each human feeling has a specific breathing pattern with which it is associated, and we believe that we can identify that emotion by observing a person's breathing.

Shakespeare, for instance, illustrated regret this way:

When to the sessions of sweet silent thought
I summon up remembrance of things past,
I sigh the lack of many a thing I sought
And with old woes new wail my dear time's waste.

Sonnet XXX

Tolstoy, in describing anger wrote, "His pen is breathing revenge." Thomas Hood, in *The Bridge of Sighs*, tells us that

One more unfortunate,
Weary of breath,
Rashly importunate,
Gone to her death.

This morbid poem contrasts with Sir Walter Scott's well–known patriotic and altruistic paean:

Breathes there the man, with soul so dead
Who never to himself hath said,
This is my own, my native land.

There are of course many other examples—the list is virtually inexhaustible—that tell us much about what we believe about breathing. Let's take a look now and see what we know about it.

HOW DO YOU BREATHE?

Here is a simple test: Are you wearing comfortable clothing that does not confine you or restrict your breathing?

Good! Now sit comfortably back in your chair—preferably, but not necessarily, in front of a mirror.

Place your left hand on your chest, over your heart, and place your right hand on your abdomen, over your belly button. Now pay attention to your breathing. Note what each hand is doing as you are breathing in, and as you are breathing out.

If both hands are rising and falling as you breathe— more or less simultaneously—in a shallow motion, you are *chest breathing*.

If your abdomen moves in, and your chest moves up when you inhale, and the opposite happens when you exhale, you are *reverse breathing*.

Ordinarily, you cannot count your breaths accurately when you focus on them, because that changes them. But try anyway. If you count over 14 breaths per minute (b/min), you are probably breathing too rapidly for someone who is sitting comfortably in a chair!

If the hand on your chest is virtually still, and the hand on your abdomen moves out when you inhale, and moves in when you exhale, you are breathing correctly.

But isn't breathing automatic? How can there be so many different ways to breathe—some even alleged to be associated with stress-related and psychosomatic disorders?

RESPIRATION

Ordinarily, regulation of life functions is automatic. Breathing takes place without your thinking about it. The heart beats, blood is oxygenated and circulated, pressure is regulated, and waste gases are removed, all without requiring your attention.

Metabolism goes on without your attention and so does the removal of various waste products. Many different parts of your body that wear may be repaired or replaced as required: blood cells, stomach lining, and skin tissue, among others. Your hair and nails grow. Various segments of your nervous system automatically maintain you in the upright position and keep you informed about inside and outside temperature and environmental happenings. Tissue water concentration is automatically regulated.

In order to perform these remarkably complex functions, your body relies on an inherited, prewired program of *reflexes* that rely on various sensors to report what is happening at a particular body location. These may be sense organs such as those for vision, hearing, smell, and touch, or the carotid sinus or aortic arch mechanisms that respond to blood pressure (baroreceptors). There are also chemoreceptors which respond to concentrations of various chemicals, including gases such as oxygen (O_2) and carbon dioxide (CO_2).

Muscles and glands are employed by your body to accomplish the best available adjustment.

Thus, one cardinal rule in behavioral medicine is that unless it is interfered with, your body knows exactly what it is doing and always does the best thing to do under the circumstances. Consequently, *if you have a disorder, you may reasonably assume that the disorder itself is the body's best adjustment to the circumstances.*

Contrary to what you may think, your body did not let you down. The disorder is evidence that your body is doing the best it can with what is available. It makes sense, therefore, to ask, "What do I have to do to make it unnecessary for my body to have to make this particular adjustment that we call a disorder?"

Breathing is the *only* vital life function which we can voluntarily control, and therefore frequently manage to deregulate.

Ordinarily, breathing is under the control of reflexes that respond to information from sensors located at various sites in the body, analyzing blood concentration of oxygen and carbon dioxide, reflexes of the lungs, and brain mechanisms. All of these mechanisms are subject to the influence of the autonomic nervous system, which adjusts body function to expected or actual physical activity.

It is information from the brain, relayed by the two branches of the autonomic nervous system, that adjusts us for environmental demands. The *sympathetic* branch orders the release of adrenaline into the bloodstream and the acceleration of other action-related functions. It is the *sympathetic* branch of the autonomic nervous system that accelerates the heart, constricts arteries, increases blood circulation in the skin, promotes sweating, etc., when we run, for instance. The *parasympathetic* branch restores the physiological balance for energy conservation.

All of these automatic control mechanisms can be readily bypassed only in breathing: Within limits, we can increase respiration rate at will, or hold our breath, pretty much regardless of what the circumstances dictate. But, we cannot increase or decrease blood pressure at will, for instance, or digestion, or sweating.

Thus, we can actually interfere with metabolism. Bear in mind that when we do this, the body has to adjust other processes so that the system is compensated, balanced, or in "homeostasis."

All body functions are breathing related, and they interact in complex ways. Thus it is helpful to know a little bit about the process of breathing.

Breathing is performed by the respiratory system: the mouth and nose, and other airway passages, the muscles of the chest and rib cage, the diaphragm, and the lungs.

Body ventilation requires all of the above systems plus the circulatory system, including the heart and the interconnecting arteries and veins, to transport O_2 to the tissues and remove CO_2.

THE AIRWAY PASSAGES TO THE LUNGS

Contraction of the diaphragm and expansion of the rib cage result in a negative air pressure (partial vacuum) in the chest, which causes air to be drawn into the respiratory system through the nose and mouth, and into the lungs via the trachea, the bronchi, and bronchioles.

Ideally, you should breathe through the nose because it prepares or *conditions* the air for the lungs. The nose, unlike the mouth, which is simply an opening designed to lead to the stomach, is better suited to respiration.

George Catlin, in a remarkable little book, *Shut Your Mouth* (Tubner), written in 1869, proposed that

> The mouth of man, as well as that of brutes, was made for the reception and mastication of food for the stomach, and other purposes; but the nostrils, with their delicate and fibrous linings purifying and warming the air passage, have been mysteriously constructed and designed to stand guard over the lungs—to measure the air and equalize its draughts, during hours of repose.

He further warns that

> The atmosphere is nowhere pure enough for man's breathing until it has passed this mysterious refining process; and therefore the imprudence and danger of admitting it in an unnatural way, in double quantities, upon the lungs, and charged with the surrounding epidemic or contageous infections of the moment. (p. 27)

It is an interesting suggestion, isn't it, that under certain circumstances, if done in a particular way, breathing may be an "unnatural act!" I would remind the reader also that this was written in the 1860s, when the air could not possibly have been more polluted than it is today.

The nose accomplishes this "conditioning" process by means of its various structures: Two cavities leading from the trachea communicate with the outside world through the nostrils. The cavities are separated by the *septum* and lined with a *mucus blanket*.

There is a structure at the upper end of each nasal cavity called the *turbinate*. It narrows the air passage to the trachea. And air drawn through the nose, separated right and left, swirls through nasal hair and past the turbinates, causing the formation of swirling currents that encourage the air filtration process by promoting the removal of coarser airborne particles. Smaller particles, as well as germs, are deposited on the sticky *mucus blanket*, to which they adhere.

Thus the nose helps to filter pollutants from the air before conducting it to the lungs.

But, in addition, it also moisturizes and warms the inspired air: As expired air rushes out past the turbinates, it meets the cooler air in the nose and deposits moisture on the mucus blanket of the turbinates. As inspired air swirls in past the turbinates, it picks up the now-warmed moisture previously deposited on the mucus blanket of the turbinates and returns it to the lungs, thus conserving body water. But, in the approximately 20,000 daily excursions of air through the nose, it is estimated that an additional two quarts of water are supplied by the turbinates.

In addition, air entering the body is rapidly warmed by the turbinates. Even entering at a temperature of 45 deg. F, air will reach body temperature by the time it has passed the turbinates.

The mucus membrane lining the nasal cavity, as well as the trachea, extends all the way down to the bronchi of the lungs. It is populated with cells from which protrude little hairlike structures called *cilia*. These cilia are constantly in motion, moving the mucus blanket, against gravity, up from the lungs.

The mucus blanket has the capability to trap debris

and bacteria, which it can destroy, removing these from the respiratory tract—usually by transport to the stomach.

The little blood vessels in the mucus lining of the nose also help in disinfecting its mucus blanket, by virtue of their rich supply of white blood cells, which are part of the body's immune system. However, the nose also has been shown to have an equally rich supply of infectious germs, including dangerous *staphylococcus*.

Thus, in addition to accommodating the sense of smell, the nose performs a vital function in correct breathing and may reflect various conditions of the body: Under the influence of increased levels of histamine released by the body as a reaction to allergy, the nasal mucus lining will swell and excrete fluid. That's what happens when you have a cold or hay fever.

The nasal lining will also swell under other conditions, including migraine and sexual arousal. In fact, for that reason, sexual arousal makes some persons sneeze and its sustained form results in a painful nasal congestion called "honeymoon nose." We are told that this condition may be readily remedied without medical intervention.

Inspired air enters the lungs through the trachea, a flexible tube made predominantly of cartilage, which divides into the bronchi, which in turn divide into smaller bronchioles, and again into alveolar ducts, which lead to the alveoli of the lungs.

THE LUNGS

The lungs are made of relatively light and porous tissue forming four lobes, two overlapping each other on each side of the chest, lying more or less freely in the chest cavity, and resting on the diaphragm. The chest cavity and

associated rib-cage muscles form a structure, flexible up to
a point, which expands during *chest breathing*.

The lungs are covered by membranes (pleura) and
constantly moistened by a soaplike lubricant (surfactant).
This lubricant reduces friction as the lobes of the lungs
expand and contract, and ride over each other with inspiration and expiration.

The alveoli, at the end of the alveolar ducts, are extremely small spherical sacs where the gas exchange takes
place. Small vents connect adjacent alveoli.

Atmospheric air finds its way, via the air passages, to
the alveoli. There it is separated from the returning
oxygen-depleted blood in small blood vessels by a set of
thin membranes. There are an enormous number of alveoli in the lungs: their surface area, if they were unfolded, would be about 75 square meters in an adult man.

Alveoli form small clusters, like grapes, after which,
parenthetically, they are named. Each of these has its own
blood circulation. Oxygen dissolves through the membranes in the capillaries into the blood, and carbon dioxide
passes from the blood into the alveoli until the pressure of
these two gases is equal in the blood and in the alveolar
air. This gas exchange and equalization process occurs
rapidly and continously. Then blood, stripped of its excess CO_2, and oxygenated, is ready for the return trip to
body tissues via the heart.

THE COMPOSITION OF AIR IN THE ATMOSPHERE
AND IN THE LUNGS

Atmospheric air contains about 21% oxygen, 0.03%
(3/10 of 1%) carbon dioxide, 78% nitrogen, and varying
quantities of water vapor; other gases such as carbon mon-

oxide, methane, helium, argon, neon, etc., and pollut-ants. This is the approximate gas composition of air as it enters the lungs.

The air leaving the lungs during expiration is called *end-tidal air*. It is composed of approximately 14% oxygen, 5% carbon dioxide, 6% water vapor, and 69% nitrogen and other gases.

Our principal concern in this book will be with the two gases most important to us from the point of view of life: oxygen (O_2) and carbon dioxide (CO_2).

The term for lack of oxygen is "anoxia." Reduced oxy-genation of body tissues is called "hypoxia." And, chronic hypoxia is called hypoxemia. None of these conditions is desirable. In fact, they are so undesirable that we will do "aerobic exercises" to avoid them.

Aerobic exercise contributes more oxygen to the body than is required by the activity. It creates, in a sense, an oxygen surplus. But it is only a slight surplus because the body has mechanisms that protect it from excessive O_2: O_2 is a dangerous substance. It causes "oxidation," which means to burn. It is potentially so harmful in excessive doses that it has been jokingly said that were it invented today, it would be a prescription item.

BREATHING NORMALLY

When you are sitting quietly, your breathing rate should be about 13 breaths per minute (BPM). On the average, men breathe a little slower than women: 12 to 14 BPM for men versus 14 to 15 in women.

Breathing rate is typically, though not invariably, re-lated to breathing volume: *minute volume* is the quantity of air going in and out of the lungs during one minute of breathing. The average normal adult has a *tidal volume* (air going in and out with each breath), at rest, of about 500 milliliters (ml). Thus, *minute volume* would be about 500 ml, times 13 BPM, or 6500 ml.

BREATHING ABNORMALLY

Most persons with rapid breathing, in excess of the average breathing rate, have shallow breathing; tidal volume is low. Thus, *minute volume* may be unaffected, or only slightly reduced. In many persons, shallow breathing results from partial contraction of the diaphragm, a part of their stress reaction to the demands of their world.

Partial contraction of the diaphragm is part of the pattern of muscle tension in a stress response and it reduces the space in the chest into which the lungs can expand during the inspiration phase of breathing. Thus, with reduced lung expansion, the average person will tend to increase breathing rate to attempt to maintain a more or less constant *minute volume*—a compensatory mechanism.

However, this attempt to maintain more or less constant *minute volume* may result in an excessive loss of carbon dioxide (CO_2). This loss of CO_2 ultimately results in a shift in the acid-base balance towards alkalinity: CO_2 is a major body component in acid formation.

But a mechanism involving buffers soon restores the acid-base balance (to about pH 7.40). This buffer mechanism is crucial to functioning: Metabolism in each cell in your body is highly dependent on the right acid-base balance. Even small shifts to acid, or to alkaline, create enormous problems for your body cells.

Imagine that the hemoglobin molecules in your red blood cells function like tiny magnets. They can pick up or release oxygen. The degree of their "magnetism" depends on the acid-base balance. At the proper balance, they will pick up oxygen in the lungs and give it up at the tissues where the "magnetic" pull is greater because of the greater density of carbon dioxide, and therefore acidity.

In hyperventilation, so much carbon dioxide may be lost that blood becomes more alkaline (base) than it should be and the "magnetism" of the hemoglobin molecules increases so that it may give up less oxygen to the tissues as it makes the rounds.

You should be aware that shallow and/or rapid breathing are not invariably the outcome of stress. There are numerous physical conditions that may result in such breathing disorders. Among these are pulmonary conditions: chronic obstructive pulmonary disease (COPD), emphysema, interstitial fibrosis, asthma, or allergic reactions, for example. And, there are numerous other conditions as well, ranging from high blood pressure (hypertension), diabetes, kidney disease, heart disease, and hypoglycemia, to lesions in parts of the brain.

There is also a breathing *mode*: chest (thoracic) or abdominal (diaphragmatic). In chest breathing, the rib cage spreads and the chest goes up.

In spite of its dramatic appearance, this breathing mode results in relatively little air entering the lungs. On the other hand, abdominal/diaphragmatic breathing, accomplished by alternately contracting the diaphragm and abdominal muscles, increases the space in the chest into which the lungs can expand to accept air. Thus, a far greater volume of air is exchanged with abdominal than with chest breathing.

Finally, breathing has *rhythm*. The *rhythm* is the relative duration of inspiration and expiration. This is usually called the *I/E ratio*. In deep diaphragmatic breathing, inspiration and expiration are equal in duration. But typically, one of the phases of breathing, inspiration or expiration, may be exaggerated or too brief.

Ideally, in a person at rest, diaphragmatic breathing, through the nose only, should prevail, at a rate of 3 to 5—yes!—3 to 5 breaths per minute—with proportional increase in tidal volume so that *minute volume* will be about normal. The I/E ratio will be about 1:00.

But, in many persons, rapid and shallow breathing results in an increased expulsion of carbon dioxide. This is called hyperventilation, and it is one of the commonest abnormal breathing patterns associated with psychosomatic disorders and stress reaction.

THE BREATH CONNECTION

As we have seen, people ordinarily breathe more or less at about 12 to 15 breaths per minute. And since, on the average, men breathe somewhat less rapidly than do women, the volume of air entering and leaving the lungs is somewhat greater in men. As activity increases, breathing rate, as well as the volume of air entering and leaving the lungs, increases.

When at rest, breathing should be through the nose, and predominantly abdominal, meaning diaphragmatic, with equal inspiration and expiration cycles.

In abdominal breathing, ventilation of the lungs is accomplished in this way: Contraction of the diaphragm creates a partial vacuum in the space between the lungs and the rib cage. The lungs expand into that space while filling with air. The contraction of the diaphragm, above and somewhat behind the viscera, pushes them forward, making the abdomen move forward. This perceived motion of the abdomen is the reason for calling diaphragmatic breathing "abdominal breathing." It should be noted that no air ever enters the abdomen proper.

When the lungs are filled, the distended abdominal muscles contract, causing the viscera to push the diaphragm back into its original place. This squeezes the lungs, expelling the air in expiration.

As activity level increases, other components are added to the breathing process, including chest expansion.

Chest breathing is accomplished by expanding the rib cage. This is observed as the chest rising up during inspiration. Chest breathing is an inefficient form of breathing because the volume of air entering and leaving the lungs is considerably less than that in diaphragmatic breathing. Consequently, chest breathers must breathe more rapidly in order to maintain an adequate minute volume.

Thus, with increased respiration rate, chest breathers are likely candidates for hyperventilation because in the process of faster breathing, they will expel more than the normal amount of carbon dioxide from their body.

Why do people develop chest breathing? They must develop it because diaphragmatic breathing is the way we all breathe as infants. There are many reasons and some are basically indications that there is something wrong with the body.

First, there may be pulmonary problems. These are related to diseases of the lungs. Anything that interferes with (a) air entering or leaving the lungs; (b) gas exchange in the alveoli; or (c) blood circulation through the lungs will cause changes in breathing rate and pattern and may result in additional problems created by the resultant hyperventilation.

Second, there may be metabolic disorders whose

compensatory mechanisms involve breathing. Hypo-glycemia and diabetes, as well as other diseases of the kidneys or liver, may result in "metabolic acidosis." This means that your body's acid-base balance has shifted to-wards greater acidity and must be compensated by more rapid breathing.

Third, other conditions will increase breathing rate: Disorders of the respiratory centers in the brain, metabolic problems relating to pituitary, adrenal or thyroid function, heart disease, high blood pressure, and various forms of anemia will likewise result in breathing changes that may lead to hyperventilation.

Emotional stress and psychological disorders con-stitute a fourth category of known contributors to hyper-ventilation. These typically come about as a consequence of various physical maneuvers that sometimes entail initial breath-holding or unusual shifts to shallow chest breathing.

There is yet a fifth source of unusual breathing which results from adherence to fashion in clothing or appear-ance. I like to think of hyperventilation in that connection as the *Designer Clothes Syndrome*. This means that when you are wearing skintight clothes, or slacks that may be too narrow at the waist, you may actually be forced to chest-breathe because the abdomen cannot expand and so the diaphragm is held back or frozen in place. The same is true in men who adopt a macho posture consisting of the chest-out-stomach-in configuration.

The above by no means exhausts the list, but should give you an indication of the variety of different reasons why you may observe disordered breathing. Because of the very real possibility that hyperventilation may com-pensate metabolic acidosis, as in diabetes, giving a paper bag for rebreathing to someone who is observed to hyperventilate may be hazardous unless the medical history of that person is known to you.

CHAPTER 4

The Hyperventilation Syndrome

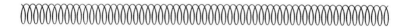

INTRODUCTION

Under ordinary circumstances, when a person is not engaged in any activity requiring movement, breathing should be easy, even, slow, and deep. With increased activity, breathing rate goes up to meet the increased ventilation and metabolic demands of the body.

But in some persons, breathing is rapid even at rest. When this rapid breathing results in an excessive loss of carbon dioxide (CO_2), it is said to be hyperventilation. Hyperventilation has been known for many years to be both the cause and the result of stress, emotional and psychosomatic disorders.

In a "Brief Guide to Office Practice" (*Medical Aspects of Human Sexuality*, vol. 19, 1985), the late Dr. H.E. Walker, Clinical Professor of Psychiatry at N.Y.U. Medical School, New York, wrote:

> Hyperventilation is one of the most misunderstood, under-diagnosed, and frequently overlooked illnesses in medicine and psychiatry.

Even patients who present with hyperventilation in the emergency room and subsequently undergo exhaustive and expensive cardiac and neurological workups often remain undiagnosed and frustrated. Many feel they must have a dire disease and embark on a futile odyssey to find the correct diagnosis and cure. . . .

Because physicians seldom consider hyperventilation as a differential diagnosis, the symptoms, and the search, go on.

WHY DO SOME OF US HYPERVENTILATE?

Hyperventilation may have an emotional basis. Fright, anxiety, panic disorder, agoraphobia, or symptoms of emotion may frequently lead to hyperventilation. Conversely, hyperventilation may lead to these conditions.

Sometimes, hyperventilation may have an organic, or physical basis. It is observed in *all* conditions in which the acid-base balance of the blood shifts towards acid.

To maintain the acid-base balance of the blood, the lungs do an estimated 85% of the work, while the kidneys do about 15%. Any condition that increases its acidity will result in a compensatory increase in breathing rate and expulsion of carbon dioxide (CO_2) from the lungs.

This hyperventilation accompanies disorders of the kidneys or liver; diabetes; cardiac, cardiovascular, and circulatory deficiency, including hypertension (high blood pressure), among other conditions. Rarely, there may be a neurological basis to hyperventilation.

A lesion in any of several brain centers, such as the pons, or medulla, may result in hyperventilation. It is unknown how commonly hyperventilation has a pulmonary basis. Chronic obstructive pulmonary disease (COPD), bronchial asthma, chronic bronchitis and emphysema are among the conditions in which ventilatory problems sometimes lead to hyperventilation. There are other lung problems, in extraordinary cases due to fungi, molds, or to parasitic infections, to fibrosis, etc.

Hyperventilation has, paradoxically, been linked to low blood pressure and fainting spells (syncope), to cardiac arrhythmias, and to idiopathic epileptic seizures (seizures of unknown medical origin). This by no means exhausts the list, as you will see: Hyperventilation has been observed in an extraordinary number of psychological, psychiatric, and physical disorders.

The term "hyperventilation" is commonly attributed to Kerr, Dalton, and Gliebe, who are said to have coined it in 1937 in *Annals of Internal Medicine* (Vol. 11). But in fact, Brody and Dusser de Barenne used the term in a 1932 study showing the same hyperactive reflexes in hyperventilating cats as have been reported in persons who hyperventilate.

HOW SERIOUS CAN SOME OF THE EFFECTS OF HYPERVENTILATION BE?

In "Clinical Application of Blood Gases" (*Yearbook Medical Publishers*, 1982), hyperventilation not due to pulmonary, cardiac or other disease is said to have the following medical characteristics:

> . . .when a person is breathing room air, arterial blood pH is above 7.4, the partial pressure of arterial blood CO_2 is below 30 mmHg. And, oxygen saturation of arterial blood is above minimal normal level.

The pH of a substance is an index of whether it is acid, neutral, or base: 7.0 is neutral. Below 7.0 is acid, and above 7.0 is alkaline (base).

Typically, hyperventilatory breathing shows increased minute volume and rapid breathing. There often may be predominantly chest breathing, with chest heaving, and frequent sighing. The breathing pattern may be irregular, with unequal inspiration and expiration; and there may be spasms, gasps, or breathing interruption (apnea).

Most persons will readily recognize the acute hyperventilation that may arise in frightful situations. But chronic hyperventilation is quite subtle and its effects may not invariably be obvious.

I sometimes find that clients who hyperventilate have rapid breathing, and sometimes grossly exaggerated chest movements. But more typically, breathing is very shallow—with almost imperceptible breathing movements—often accompanied by much sighing.

When some of the symptoms of the hyperventilation syndrome such as shallow breathing, frequent sighing, report of dizziness, a sense of unreality, inability to catch one's breath, etc., are present in a person, but it is not clear that s/he is, in fact, hyperventilating, some clinicians employ a "hyperventilation challenge" procedure:

This consists of having the person breathe deeply and rapidly (20 to 30 breaths per minute) for about 2 to 3 minutes. Parenthetically, I am opposed to the use of this "hyperventilation challenge," even though Prof. Walker recommended it. I consider it hazardous:

As early as 1924, a physician named Joshua Rosett showed that "overventilation" can lead to epileptic seizures. And, more recently, Dr. L.C. Lum, a noted British pulmonary physician, cautioned against its use in persons with chest pain or with neuromuscular disorders because, among other effects, it has been shown to trigger angina and arrhythmias.

Gottstein and colleagues, reporting on the brain in the *Proceedings of the Fourth International Symposium on Regulation of Cerebral Blood Flow* (Pitman, 1970), put it even more strongly:

> . . .one might assume that hyperventilation with a $PaCO_2$ [percentage of arterial blood saturated with carbon dioxide] less than 20 torr and a jugular PO_2 as low as 20 torr will cause an inadequate oxygen supply even in healthy subjects. This should be considered with regard to therapeutic hyperventilation. (p. 172)

This cautionary technical note is a warning to professionals using the "hyperventilation challenge" that it may dangerously reduce delivery of oxygen to body organs and tissues, and especially the heart. The above study, as well as those of other medical investigators, have shown that reduced blood levels of carbon dioxide (CO_2), lost through hyperventilation, cause heart arteries to contract in spasms—sometimes quite violently. This action of low blood levels of CO_2 is said to cause *ischemic heart disease*. A comparable phenomenon, also related to low blood levels of CO_2 in the brain, has been linked to the so-called *transient ischemic attacks* (TIA) associated with stroke, which you probably have read about lately in the newspapers.

A *torr*, parenthetically, is a measure of gas pressure. The normal human adult level of CO_2 in the blood is about 38 torr, or about 5% of the total gases dissolved in it.

Hyperventilation challenge is even used in some therapeutic situations precisely because it will trigger symptoms; and in others, to show the person that the symptoms they experience are due to their hyperventilation.

I prefer to make it a practice to simply tell my clients about the origin of their symptoms without getting them to reexperience them just to prove a point. Then, I teach them how to breathe correctly.

HOW CAN YOU TELL IF YOU ARE HYPERVENTILATING?

I recommend that you determine if you hyperventilate on the basis of the following signs proposed by Dr. Lum, in Hill, *Modern Trends in Psychosomatic Medicine* (Butterworth, 1976):

- Breathing is predominantly thoracic (chest)
- Little use is made of the diaphragm (abdominal movement is minimal)
- Breathing is punctuated by frequent sighs
- Sighing has an "effortless" quality with a marked "forward and upward" movement of the sternum but little lateral expansion
- Normal breathers can imitate the breathing chest movements used by hyperventilators only with difficulty.

Finally, chronic hyperventilators frequently precede speech utterances with a deep sigh: They will even sigh deeply if you just ask them their name.

HOW COMMON IS HYPERVENTILATION?

Hyperventilation is probably the most common of the so called stress-related breathing disorders. There are varying reports of its frequency in the population at large, ranging between about 10 to 25%. And it has been estimated to account for roughly 60% of emergency ambulance calls in major U.S. city hospitals.

COULD YOUR SYMPTOMS BE HYPERVENTILATION-RELATED?

Kerr, Dalton, and Gliebe, in the previously cited pioneering work entitled *Some Physical Phenomena Associated*

with Anxiety States and Their Relation to Hyperventilation, tell
us that:

> During the past several years the world, in general, has
> been undergoing critical social, moral, and economic
> changes; and in the present state of upheaval, an ever-
> increasing number of patients are observed who present a
> symptom-complex which is intimately associated with the
> individual's struggle for security, for independence, or for
> whatever state is presumed to assure the spiritual and ma-
> terial happiness of the individual. (p. 961)

You may note with some amusement that the concerns of patients in 1937 do not appear to be vastly different from yours today. Furthermore, this article, published
in *Annals of Internal Medicine,* addresses symptoms reported by general medical practice patients and not psychiatric patients. It is a fairly recent development that psychosomatic symptoms, the "symptom-complex" cited
above, are thought to be a psychiatric concern.

Kerr et al. continue:

> This symptom-complex is essentially a representation of
> the interaction between emotional and physiological fac-
> tors. While not seen exclusively among persons suffering
> from psychoneuroses, this symptom-complex is frequently
> found in such persons; and its manifestations are desig-
> nated as anxiety states. (p. 961)

In other words, psychosomatic disorders are not the
exclusive domain of the anxiety-neurotic, but they share
with him/her the common factor *anxiety.* Now the question is, of course, "What happens to these persons who
suffer from anxiety-related disorders?" According to Kerr
et al.:

> Patients presenting with the well-known pattern of symp-
> toms *haunt the offices of physicians and specialists in every field of
> medical practice. They are often shunted from one physician to
> another and the sins of commission inflicted upon them fill many
> black pages in our book of achievements.* (p. 961, my italics)

Here, you may recognize the so-called hypochon-driacs, whose complaints are invariably dismissed as being "all in your mind," and those whose identifiable physical symptoms are treated with sedatives, tranquil-izers, and the admonition, "You have to take care of your-self! Relax!" And you will be drawn to the altogether cor-rect conclusion that, apparently, things haven't changed much in 50 years of medical practice, other than in the proliferation of drugs—the newer ones touted as "im-proved."

Here are the symptoms in a few of their cases:

Case 3: Female, age 21.
Chief complaint: convulsive seizures, fatigability, flushing of face and chest, headache, abdominal gas, carpopedal spasms, insomnia.
Physical examination: negative, except "slightly dilated pupils and hyperactive reflexes."

Case 8: Male, age 27.
Chief complaint: grand mal convulsions.
Physical examination: negative, but for Chvostek's sign.

Case 10: Female, age 27.
Chief complaint: precordial pain, weakness, easy fatigability, mus-cle twitches, dyspnea, nausea, right occipital headache with pho-tophobia (light sensitivity).
Physical examination: negative, except for Chvostek's sign and hyperactive reflexes.

But a complete listing of all the different complaints and symptoms reported in the 35 cases they published includes:

Neurological:

- hyperactive reflexes
- headaches
- grand mal seizures
- vertigo (dizziness)

- paresthesia (tingling sensations in hands, feet, etc.)
- nervousness
- irritability

In the head and neck region:

- dyspnea ("can't catch my breath. I feel like I am choking.")
- inability to swallow (constricted throat or throat muscle stiffness)
- headache
- Chvostek's sign
- migraine
- photophobia (light sensitivity)
- puckering sensation about the mouth
- flushing of face
- tinnitus (ringing in ears)

In the chest and abdominal region:

- abdominal gaseous distention
- chest pain
- hypertension
- precordial pain, with or without pain radiating to right or left arm, or to scapula
- tachycardia (rapid pulse)
- palpitations
- angina
- epigastric pain
- colitis
- diarrhea

In arms and legs:

- aching hands and feet

- Raynaud's (cold fingers and toes, with spasms)
- allergic dermatitis
- numbness, stiffness, and/or spasms in hands and/or feet
- tetany
- carpopedal spasms

General:

- easy fatigability

If we look at these 35 cases, we find that there is one instance of each of the following medical conditions: rheumatic heart disease with mitral stenosis and insufficiency, thyroid nodule, splenomegaly, thyroid adenoma, skin lesions, hemorrhoids, and arteriosclerosis with a systolic murmur.

Eight symptoms in 35 cases! But, in 8 of these cases, physical examination revealed *absolutely nothing*! In 24 cases, the only finding was hyperactive reflexes with or without Chvostek's sign.

It would seem that, except that they are very *nervous*, these patients give evidence of fewer *dread* illnesses than one might expect. In fact, it has been shown in a medical study that these symptoms do not lead to an early death. And yet these patients are not well.

WHY IS MEDICINE CONFUSED ABOUT THE HYPERVENTILATION SYNDROME?

Let's look at one particular medical report: It will be an enlightening illustration of the reasons that it has been so difficult to establish the role of hyperventilation in health and disease.

At the time of the Civil War, a military field surgeon named DaCosta first described a number of complaints reported by soldiers. This symptom pattern came to bear his name. It centered on an apparent loss of physical stamina and, consequently, an inability to carry out field duties.

Subsequently, DaCosta's syndrome came to be known variously as "neurocirculatory asthenia," "anxiety neurosis," or "effort syndrome."

Wheeler and colleagues state in the *Journal of the American Medical Association* (vol. 142, 1950) that

> Neurocirculatory asthenia is a state of ill health characterized by a large number of symptoms, including breathlessness, palpitations, chest pain, nervousness, fatigue, headache, dizziness, sighing, attacks or spells, apprehension, trembling and discomfort in crowded places, in the absence of other disease which might reasonably account for these symptoms.

It must occur to you that what is being depicted is anxiety—in the extreme case, panic with agoraphobia.

The emphasis on "disease" in that passage raises the issue of whether a syndrome involving both a psychological and a disease component should be considered a medical rather than a psychiatric problem; because, in its early development, "psychosomatic" was considered in some quarters, and especially by the military, to be tantamount to malingering.

If hyperventilation is a "hysterical" manifestation, as Thomas P. Lowry suggested in 1967 in his book *Hyperventilation and Hysteria* (Charles C. Thomas, 1967), then it is not a medical entity in the ordinary sense of the word. Therefore, all these *medical* symptoms could not possibly be caused by it!

It also deserves comment that in their many references, Wheeler et al. not only fail to cite the previous work by Kerr, Dalton, and Gliebe, whose symptom list is astonishingly similar to theirs, but there is not one single reference to *any* other of the hundreds of medical research articles, previously published, with the word "hyperventilation" in the title. This, in spite of the fact that in a previous study featuring one of these investigators, "abnormal ventilatory index and dyspnea," i.e., poor breathing and inability to catch one's breath, are mentioned.

One might inquire how it is that prominent Harvard Medical School specialists in internal medicine, who first presented their report before the *Section on Internal Medicine, 98th Annual Session of the American Medical Association* (1949), could be totally unaware of pioneering research published in their own journal—*Annals of Internal Medicine*—only eleven years earlier!

Let's read on:

> Signs are not characteristic and consist of slight tachycardia, and tachypnea, tremor of the fingers and overactive deep tendon reflexes. It is probable that the terms neurocirculatory asthenia, anxiety neurosis, effort syndrome, neurasthenia and many others are used in the literature to describe the same disorder . . . . (p. 878)

Translation: slight increase in pulse rate and breathing rate, tremors of fingers, and hyperactivereflexes—just like those reported by Kerr et al. Not a single word about hyperventilation! It boggles the mind. Now, let's take a look at their list of those symptoms experienced by at least 25% of their patients:

- palpitations
- tires easily
- breathlessness
- nervousness
- chest pain

- sighing
- dizziness
- faintness
- apprehension
- headache
- paresthesia
- weakness
- trembling
- breath unsatisfactory
- insomnia
- unhappiness
- shakiness
- fatigued all the time
- sweating
- fear of death
- smothering
- syncope
- flushes
- yawning
- pain radiating to left arm
- vascular throbbing
- dry mouth

Are you beginning to recognize the list? It is always the same symptoms, plus or minus one or two. Can you imagine overlooking rapid breathing (tachypnea)? Did no one think to check breathing? These are, of course, the symptoms of the hyperventilation syndrome.

P.S.: It may interest you to know that neither "effort syndrome," "neurasthenia," nor "neurocirculatory asthenia" appears in the index of the most recent edition of the *Physicians' Desk Reference* (PDR), where "anxiety neurosis" means something different: "Hyperventilation syndrome" is listed under "anxiety neurosis."

Nor can one find these terms in such a standard contemporary textbook as *Internal Medicine* (Stein, J.H., Ed., 1983, Little, Brown & Co.). This text cites "hyperventilation syndrome" under the heading, "Dyspnea Related to Emotional Illness." The symptoms are given as

- dyspnea (breathlessness)
- chest pain
- syncope
- paresthesia
- giddiness
- lightheadedness
- sighing
- gasping
- sensation of smothering

With the exception of the exclusion of "fear of dying or going crazy," this list is identical to that of "Panic Disorder" in DSM-III, the psychiatric diagnostic reference manual which, of course, does not mention hyperventilation!

Psychiatrists, trained in medicine, for the most part do not recognize the medical symptoms of hyperventilation. Is it any wonder your physician is confused?

Let's see what we can learn from other experts in the field: L.C. Lum, the noted British chest surgeon and pulmonary physiologist, listed the following symptoms in connection with hyperventilation:

Gastrointestinal: abdominal distention, constipation, diarrhea, burping
Central Nervous System: twitching eyelids, headache, giddiness, fainting
Cardiovascular: precordial discomfort, palpitation, missed beats

Skeletal System: weak limbs, painful limbs, vague
  pains
General Symptoms: weakness, irritability, insomnia.

An article by Missri and Alexander, in the *Journal of
the American Medical Association* (vol. 240, 1978), provided
the following items thought to be pretty much the standard listing:

General:
  fatigue
  weakness
  exhaustion
Cardiovascular:
  palpitations
  tachycardia (rapid pulse)
  precordial pain (noncardiac chest pain)
  Raynaud's phenomenon (cold fingers and toes,
    spasms)
Neurologic:
  dizziness
  lightheadedness
  disturbance of consciousness or vision
  numbness and tingling of the extremities
  tetany (rare)
Respiratory:
  shortness of breath
  chest pain
  dryness of mouth
  yawning
Gastrointestinal:
  globus hystericus (lump in throat)
  epigastric pain
  aerophagia (burping)

Musculoskeletal:
    muscle pains and cramps
    tremors
    stiffness
    tetany
Psychological:
    tension
    anxiety
    insomnia
    nightmares

This impressive list of symptoms is by no means exhaustive. For instance, B.I. Lewis, at Stanford University School of Medicine, in a report in *Postgraduate Medicine* (vol. 53, 1957), supplies us with the following items:

Neurovascular:
    Central: Disturbances of consciousness, faintness, dizziness, unsteadiness, impairment of concentration and memory, feelings of unreality, "losing mind"
    Peripheral: Paresthesia, numbness, tingling and coldness of fingers, face and feet
Musculoskeletal: diffuse or localized myalgia and arthralgia, tremors and coarse twitching movements, carpopedal spasm, and generalized tetany (infrequent)
Respiratory: cough, chronic throat tickle, shortness of breath, atypical asthma, tightness in or about chest, sighing respiration, excessive yawning
Cardiovascular: palpitations, skipped beats, tachycardia, atypical chest pains, sharp precordial twinges, dull precordial or lower costal ache, variable features of vasomotor instability

Gastrointestinal: oral dryness, globus, dysphagia, left upper quadrant or epigastric distress, aerophagy, belching, bloating, flatulence

Psychic: variable anxiety, tension and apprehension, inappropriate pseudocalmness (hysterical subjects)

General: easy fatigability, generalized weakness, irritability and chronic exhaustion, frightening dreams, sleep disturbances

Did any of your symptoms appear in these lists?

As you can plainly see for yourself, hyperventilation seems to account for the major portion of the so-called "psychosomatic" and "stress-related disorders."

The average medical practitioner and indeed most persons are unaware of the role of hyperventilation in common cardiovascular and circulatory disorders, arrhythmias, hypertension, migraine; musculoskeletal spasms and chronic muscle fatigue; neurological disorders including idiopathic epilepsy; stress–related disorders, including headache; and emotional disorders such as panic attacks and agoraphobia, and depression.

WHAT IF I AM ON MEDICATION?

My colleague Dr. Herbert Fensterheim, a Manhattan-based psychotherapist, recently brought to my attention a list of common prescription medications that may themselves adversely affect breathing.

Persons with chronic hyperventilation may experience a significant increase in frequency and severity of their "psychosomatic" symptoms when their breathing worsens. One of the procedures commonly used by many therapists to demonstrate to their clients that these symptoms are hyperventilation-related is to have them *overbreathe* (this is called the "hyperventilation challenge"). As I have noted, I am, parenthetically, strongly opposed to this procedure because I regard it to be hazardous at least in persons with seizures, unstable blood pressure, or where chest symptoms or a family history of heart disease or stroke is reported.

Some medications may mimic the "hyperventilation challenge" in that they may worsen breathing and also tend to induce some of the symptoms common in hyperventilation, such as lightheadedness, dizziness, a sense of unreality, alteration in consciousness, various strange sensations, etc.—all also common in prolonged anxiety and panic disorder.

It is important, therefore, if you take *prescription* or other medications, that you determine their side effects as well as their main effects. It may surprise you to see how many of these can involve breathing.

I have sampled items from Dr. Fensterheim's list and added a few from a superficial survey of the medications taken by some of my clients. The *Physicians' Desk Reference* (1989), commonly known as the "PDR," tells us the following:

- *Benadryl* (Parke-Davis)–an antihistamine: dryness of mouth, nose and throat, dizziness, thickening or bronchial secretions, tightness of chest. (p. 1528)
- *Bumex* (Roche)—a diuretic: hyperventilation (in 0.1% of cases). (p. 1729)
- *Buspar* (Mead Johnson)—anxiolytic (anti-anxiety): hyperventilation, shortness of breath, chest congestion (between 1/100 and 1/1000 cases). (p. 1263)
- *Cardizem* (Marion)—a calcium channel blocker: breathing difficulty, irregular or fast pounding heartbeat, dizziness or lightheadedness. (p. 1216)

- *Empirin with Codeine* (Burroughs Wellcome)—analgesic, anti-inflammatory, antipyretic (fever reducing): depression of respiration, lightheadedness, dizziness, are said to be among the "most frequently observed adverse reactions to codeine." Chronic use of large doses of aspirin may lead to "salicylism," whose manifestations may include hyperpnea (increased respiration), and hyperventilation. (p. 772)
- *Primaxin* (Merck Sharp & Dohme)—antibiotic: dizziness (0.3%), and psychic disturbance, chest discomfort, dyspnea, and hyperventilation (all less than 0.02%). (p. 1383)
- *Visken* (Sandoz)—a beta-blocker: dyspnea, respiratory distress, bronchospasm, wheezing, palpitations. (p. 1902)
- *Voltaren* (Geigy)—anti-inflammatory, analgesic, antipyretic: dizziness, appetite change, asthma, eczema/dermatitis (rash), urticaria (itch), depression, insomnia, anxiety, irritability, blurred vision, scotoma, palpitation, tachycardia, impotence, dyspnea, hyperventilation, paresthesia (strange skin sensations), memory disturbances, excess perspiration (all less than 1%). (pp. 985-986)

I have not listed medications in which breathing or breathing-related disorders are the result of overdose. For instance: *Mono-gesic* (Central)—non-steroid anti-inflammatory: "Adverse reactions are usually the result of overdosage and may include. . . hyperventilation. . . ." (p. 826).

Where there is a relatively infinitesimal likelihood of experiencing breathing, or breathing-related, disorders I have indicated the published probability. It is not my intent to scare you away from medication, but to alert you to the possibility of breathing-related effects.

THE BREATH CONNECTION

It must be obvious to you, at this point, that it is exceptionally unlikely that hyperventilation syndrome will be correctly diagnosed by the average medical practitioner. Although medicine recognizes it as a disease entity, the hyperventilation syndrome is not well known to most physicians. In those cases where it is recognized, it is frequently ascribed to one's emotional state. That is, you may be accused of hysteria and prescribed tranquilizers—which, parenthetically, sometimes help.

Consequently, if your breathing appears to fit that described here, and if you have any of these symptoms; and if those symptoms could not be explained by your physician and were ascribed to your mind rather than to your body, you may just for once have bought the right book.

Hyperventilation may be relatively simple to control if it is a functional rather than a medical problem. And the last chapter in this book shows you how you can do it yourself. However, please be advised that (1) there are many symptoms that accompany hyperventilation that may not, in fact, be due to hyperventilation: These have to be diagnosed and treated by a competent physician; and, (2) hyperventilation may compensate for a life-threatening metabolic disorder. Therefore, you should never attempt to treat hyperventilation unless you have been assured by a competent physician that it is safe to do so.

Will you agree to that?

ILLUSTRATIVE CASE: V.A.

Ms. V.A. is a 42-year-old married woman, successful in a public relations career. She is of average height and weight, and walks erect, in spite of her chronic fatigue. Her handshake is strong and her hands are warm.

She complained of chronic tiredness and fatigue, which she reported battling more or less successfully each day. But by evening, she is worn out. She has no history of thyroid problems or anemia.

In addition, she reported having had EB virus symptoms some time in the past. I forwarded her to my medical colleague with the suggestion that she be tested for thyroid function and for various anemias. The tests came back negative. And we proceeded on the basis that it might be a recurrence of the EB virus.

Initially, she was chest breathing at a rate of 21 breaths per minute with very low CO_2 (3.52%). This is moderate to severe hyperventilation. But by the end of the first training session, she had good, though brief, control of her breathing: Her rate dropped to 4 1/2 breaths per minute and her CO_2 rose to 4.52%—at the lower end of normal.

She was given nutritional advice and a prescription for multiple vitamins, and she returned for breathing training, once per week for 5 weeks.

Her breathing improved with each practice session and she reported feeling much improved, for the first time in over a year.

On the last session, before terminating treatment, she revealed that she was now practicing breathing regularly, twice per day, and on an ad-lib basis, when she felt tired or tense.

CHAPTER 5

Psychosomatic Disorders, Stress-Related Disorders, and Conditioning

INTRODUCTION

The most acclaimed recent developments in the treatment of psychosomatic and stress-related disorders have been in biofeedback and self-regulation. These advances rely principally on our increasing knowledge of how the nervous system works, and ways in which behavior becomes "conditioned."

It seems entirely appropriate to focus our attention on this and see how it may contribute to the development of psychosomatic and stress-related disorders. It is generally believed that many of the answers to the why's of these disorders may be found here.

Even cognitive behavior therapies that address thoughts and feelings take into account the natural and conditioned triggers of anxiety, anger, frustration, stress, and depression.

It may interest you to know, parenthetically, that the origin of the word "anxiety" is the ancient Greek word that means "to choke." Disrupted breathing has long been recognized to be related to emotions.

LEADING UP TO THE CASE OF ROBERT

In the beginning, medicine and psychology relied mostly on systematic observation of single cases. And that is why these disciplines acknowledge their origin to such astute observers as Aristotle and Linnaeus.

But the discovery by Pasteur and Lister that bacterias cause diseases resulted in a shift to research methods that favored statistical studies of large numbers of persons.

These statistical analyses led to the conclusion, for example, that if a particular drug did not *heal* in a particular case, it was because drugs work only *on the average*: To "cure" a disease requires many factors, and drug effectiveness may be only one of them.

Another is expectation. That is the reason behind *double blind*, controlled, placebo studies, in which no one knows who gets which treatment. This is supposed to isolate the "true medical effects" of the drug in the treatments from these "other" components.

It is now more popular to admit that *most* disorders may also have "other," perhaps psychosomatic, components, in the truest sense of that word: There may be learning, expectation, and psychosocial elements. Those components may be causal, or they may help to maintain the disorder by defeating healing efforts. The autonomic nervous system appears to feature prominently in this scheme.

Every organism, from the very simplest, faces a complex and often unpredictably changing world. It is no more difficult for mankind to survive in a complex industrial world than it is, for instance, for a desert rat which has few choices. And, we share with the rodent the unforgiving obligation of making survival decisions.

A recent Public Service Broadcast (PBS-TV), in fact,

featured a brief story on life on a high-Himalayan plateau, described by the host as inhospitable. Yet, people living there seemed quite healthy despite a diet including only animal products, and an arterial blood oxygen (O_2) saturation of only about 84%, as compared to the normal value of 95 to 98% at sea level.

This blood O_2 level would qualify them for hospital admission here. Who knows how they do it?

CONDITIONING

You may recall from your school days the story of the dog "conditioned" to lift a forepaw when a bell, previously associated with shock to that paw, was rung. Did you know that dogs fall into "types" with regard to how quickly they learn to do this, and how quickly they forget?

In determining these "nervous system types," the Pavlovians studied different parts of the dogs' response: How long does it take before it is observed (latency), how much of it is there (magnitude), how long does it last (duration), and how often is it observed (frequency)?

That's how they discovered that there are about four different "types" of nervous systems that predict how a particular behavior may be conditioned. And you will not be surprised to learn that behaviors that appeared to the researchers to be related to anxiety and neurosis in these dogs were associated with rapid and long-lasting learning of paw lifting.

Now, let's change things a little: The dog is given food, preceded by the sound of a bell. The sequence is bell → food, bell → food, bell → food. . . . After a number of such sequences, or "pairings," the bell alone is sounded and the dog is observed to make chewing motions and to produce saliva. This eating behavior as a response to the bell is taken as evidence of conditioning.

It should be noted that the conditioned response to the bell, i.e., eating, is similar to the unconditioned response to the food, also eating; but it is not identical to it. When the dog salivates in response to the bell, it is to a degree less than his salivation to food. It takes longer for saliva to be produced (latency), less is produced (magnitude and duration), and it is not invariably produced (frequency). Nevertheless, conditioning is a powerful way of altering the "natural" function of reflexive activity. This process may be helpful, or it may prove a hindrance.

Numerous psychologists, beginning with J.B. Watson, usually thought to be the founder of the modern advertising industry—*Madison Avenue*—have shown the role of conditioning of these reflexive behaviors in neurotic and psychosomatic disorders.

WE ARE PREWIRED TO CONSERVE ENERGY

Now, a dog with wires taped to its forepaw is presented with the sound of a buzzer. Its response is a slight startle and head-turn in the direction of the sound. Just checkin' it out.

Then, after the buzzer is sounded again, it is followed by a brief electric shock to the forepaw. The dog jumps violently as it reacts to the shock. This procedure is repeated a number of times.

What would you expect the dog to do when the buzzer alone is sounded? Of course you would expect it to jump. And you would be quite correct. But, interestingly, if you were to continue to repeat that many, many times, the dog would soon stop jumping and would simply withdraw its leg when the bell is sounded.

Lesson 1: Even in the face of what may be presumed to be excruciating pain, behavior tends to be limited to whatever reduces energy expenditure.

Reflexive attempts to evade shock are not voluntary; violent jumping when a limb is shocked is not a voluntary action. Yet, it becomes modified, in fact simplified, over repeated exposure to the shock.

Liddell mentions a particular instance in his book *Emotional Hazards in Animals and Man* (Charles C Thomas, 1956) where a sheep had been subjected to the bell and shock-to-the-forepaw sequence. Now, it was given the bell only: ". . .and by the thirtieth bell the sheep was visibly disturbed. Meanwhile, numerous small tic-like movements of her foreleg were noted during the pauses between signals. These characteristic nervous movements, as we knew from previous experience, clearly indicated that an experimental neurosis had been precipitated" (p. 63).

Notice that the sheep was "visibly disturbed," and twitching. This passage shows quite clearly that the repetition of a "no longer threatening" signal did not make matters better.

This observation strongly supports the idea that once you become fearful in a given situation, that fear may never disappear. It may in fact lead to the pathological behaviors that psychologists call "neurotic": they are not adaptive, and they are stereotyped or repeated without variation no matter what the circumstances.

Lesson 2: Simply repeating a learned fear response may prove hazardous in itself!

Corollary: Observing distress, unadapative and stereotyped behaviors may be the only evidence of the existence of inner turmoil.

Do you begin to get a picture of how your nervous system functions in fear and stress?

Looking only at the paw, what do you suppose would

happen in most instances, if we were repeatedly to expose the animal to the sound of the bell only—without shock to the forepaw? Correct again. The animal would soon stop lifting it at the sound of the bell.

Would you conclude that it has "forgotten" about the shock previously associated with the sound of the bell? Certainly not, if Liddell's observations are correct!

Don't we frequently overlook many indications of distress because we are too narrowly focused on our expectations and assumptions about how we react to the world? We always expect specific reactions to specific situations. Yet frequently, the reactions are generalized unadaptive and stereotyped behaviors—psychosomatic disorders, perhaps?

Few people would argue today that high blood pressure, ulcers, and migraine, for instance, are not of psychosomatic *origin*—meaning physical manifestations of stress or emotional problems. Yet, we accept these as generalized reactions, aggravated by stress.

Even your physician, who tells you that "it is all in your head," meaning stress or emotions, treats these organs as though they were, in fact, the *cause* when s/he prescribes ergotamine, antihypertensives, diuretics, and histamine (H2) blocking agents.

Let us suppose that our sheep ceases to withdraw its leg after many presentations of the buzzer only. This does not mean that there is nothing happening inside it, as would probably be the case if the buzzer had never been associated with shock.

You would say, so what? It doesn't appear to be responding in any case. So what does it matter?

What if your nervous system made you capable of learning to suppress your overt reactions, but not your covert ones? Aren't emotions internal, i.e., covert, reactions not necessarily accompanied by overt behavior? Isn't that why we ask you what you *feel*, when we don't see what you *do*?

Many stress reactions are of this nature, aren't they? Frequently one is not aware that blood pressure is elevated until it is discovered on a routine visit to the doctor.

Let's weave an example from Liddell's demonstration, just as it might have taken place. Imagine, if you will, that you are sitting back in one of those narrow, uncomfortable, hinged wooden row-seats in a lecture room at "Old Ivy Hall" (college of your choice).

Great cathedral windows with grimy, tinted panes admit streams of sunlight, piercing gaps in the dense foliage of a great maple tree outside, giving spectacular life to the disturbed, billowing dust in the hall. Dimly lighted incandescent globe fixtures hang overhead, many yards below the vaulted ceiling.

At the front of the room there is a podium on which stands a lectern which has a brass and green glass-shaded reading light mounted on it. Behind the lectern hangs a blackboard, on which are partially erased formulas and diagrams.

To one side, there is a tripod which supports a faded, creased cardboard-backed map of the Balkans, circa 1878. A broken rubber-tipped pointer rests on the chalk-track of the tripod.

Dark worm-eaten wood panelling surrounds the room, reaching midway up the drab green walls, on which are mounted, well above eye level, three massively framed portraits of past college presidents protected by flyspecked glass—the bland and somber expressions on their faces in harmony with the surroundings.

The room is packed with students, all eagerly anticipating a stimulating lecture. There is much shuffling of notepads and muffled whispering as Prof. Liddell enters the room. The class comes rapidly to order and another lecture is about to commence.

"Today's lecture," announces the professor, "concerns a seemingly normal Shropshire ram, three years of age, named Robert."

> He is comfortably restrained within a wooden box about the size of a piano box with the front removed. This demonstration box is mounted upon a movable table. The only restraint of the animal is provided by a web strap about the chest fastened to a vertical rod. Although prevented from kneeling he has free use of his limbs and can shift position at will. (p. 3)

It should be noted that as Robert is wheeled into the room,

> he is alert but seemingly unperturbed. He glances at the spectators but when a bucket of oats is placed before him he eats at once and continues while the electrodes are fastened to his foreleg. When the food is removed he continues to stand quietly and does not appear to be disturbed by conversation among the spectators or the arrival of latecomers. (p. 4)

The scene is set; now comes the good part:

> His breathing is slow and regular at 41 per minute. He does not bleat and exhibits almost no movement of limb, head, or ears. One gets the impression that in these strange surroundings he is too quiet and composed. (p. 4)

Note also that the assessment of Robert's "mental state" was based initially on his breathing rate. This is not a coincidence. Physiologists and, parenthetically, lovers, the world over, have long known that breathing is the most reliable and ready evidence of arousal and excitement.

It is then determined "electrically" that Robert's heart rate (pulse rate) is 60 to 78 beats per minute (BPM). And:

The demonstrator proceeds to elicit a well established conditioned response. The metronome starts clicking once a second. At the first click Robert abruptly raises his head and pricks up his ears. Then he deliberately lowers his head and slightly crouches with forelegs extended. At the third or fourth metronome beat he executes a small, precise flexion of the right foreleg followed by a series of unhurried flexions of increasing amplitude and vigor. Coinciding with the 11th beat of the metronome a brief electrical stimulus is delivered to the rhythmically flexing foreleg. In response to this electrical startle stimulus Robert executes a brief but vehement flexion of the foreleg reminding one of the withdrawal of the hand at the bite of an insect. Following this rapid, perfunctory flexion, our "patient" immediately resumes his quiet, alert pose. (p. 5)

So far, Robert is behaving as we would expect.

I am certain that in all of the stories that you have read in college textbooks or in the popular press, the emphasis was always on the leg jerk—as in, "When you shock the leg, it jerks away. That's a reflex action." But you are virtually never told what else happens—as if nothing else happens.

At this point, the metal clips are removed from the ram, and you are encouraged to come forward, hold the cloth electrodes, and experience the 6-volt shock. You discover to your amazement that you can't feel a thing! Yet someone in the room will react as Robert did because the threshold for shock stimuli is variable and unpredictable.

Lesson 3: Not everyone is equally sensitive. Something may cause a strong reaction in one individual and none in another. Even in the same person, the threshold will vary from time to time.

Corollary: Anxiety created in a particular person by an event cannot be gauged from its apparent manifest threat to you. What may appear to be relatively harmless to you may frighten someone else.

Twenty minutes have elapsed and now the electrodes have been reattached to Robert's foreleg.

> . . .the respiration rate has increased from 40 to 56 per minute. The respirations are visibly deeper. The metronome is now set at 120 beats per minute. When the rapid clicking begins, the "patient" raises his head and pricks up his ears as before. As the clicking continues for 10 seconds, however, he stands rigidly with head raised but with no movement of the limb. This signal is *not* followed by shock. (p. 6)

But how does Robert react when anticipated (conditioned) shock does not occur?

> Two telltale signs indicate that he is not quiescent during this auditory experience even though there is no withdrawal of the leg. His breathing becomes rapid and labored in addition to which a marked cremasteric reflex can be clearly observed. (p. 6)

The "cremaster" is a muscle which descends into the scrotum with the spermatic cord and draws the testicles upwards. Now, the doorbell is rung. Robert reacts by a "brusque raising of the head and tensing of the motionless limbs with *labored respiration*." In spite of the precision of the positive and negative motor responses it was clear that all signals elicited emotional reactions and the negative signals were the more disturbing even though no shock followed.

Lesson 4: The absence of something disturbing that is expected may cause greater anxiety than its presence, even if it is painful.

It seems that we can reduce anxiety better when we can *do something*. Doesn't this remind you of many of the explanations given for stress and psychosomatic disorders: unexpressed anger, unassertiveness, "eating yourself up," "sitting on the outside and running on the inside."

The demonstration has now lasted about 30 minutes and as Robert awaits what is to follow, "he no longer gives the impression of imperturbability which we noticed half an hour earlier":

> His respiration rate has now increased from 40 to 90 per minute. Breathing movements are labored and audible. He occasionally sighs or yawns and there is much nose licking. During the previous buzzer signal grinding of the teeth was clearly audible and from now on is to be listened for at every conditioned stimulus, positive or negative. However, there is little movement of head or limbs during the intervals between signals.

A series of similar tests, several minutes apart, are successfully passed by Robert. The last is a negative signal, metronome clicks at 72 BPM, and Robert again successfully refrains from flexing his foreleg. But now, for the first time during the demonstration, the pause between signals is *only one minute*. The metronome is sounded at 60 clicks per minute and, for the first time during the hour or so of demonstration, Robert flunks the test. He fails to interpret the signal—the only signal which for three years has always meant shock!

> As the clicking begins at once he freezes with forelegs stiffly extended and with signs of respiratory distress. . . . Robert's reaction to this mild unconditioned stimulus is quite unusual. He leaps violently upward with both forelegs in the air but then immediately resumes a tense pose. (p. 10)

The demonstration is over and the "patient" is dismissed. The murmur in the hall soon dies down and Prof. Liddell now addresses the class:

> Let us now attempt to interpret certain details of the apparently ordinary behavior of this seemingly normal, three-year-old ram which we have just been observing. These

proposed interpretations will suggest for later discussion definite implications for psychiatry. [p. 10]

First consider our animal's apparent imperturbability as he was wheeled in for the demonstration. His deportment did not suggest his confinement within the testing cabinet was of itself a stressful experience apart from the conditioned stimuli which followed. It should be noted in passing that he has been thus confined for several hundred test periods during his three years of training.

"Professor Liddell," one student now asks, "what are the indications that this 'self-restraint' may be harmful?"

"Two simple experiments show that this seemingly innocuous, self-imposed restraint is notably stressful," he replies, and goes on:

> For the first experiment the animal is brought to the laboratory at 10 A.M. and placed in the demonstration cabinet but nothing further is done. His respiration at the end of 5 minutes is 45 per minute but within the hour excitement steadily mounts as indicated by frequent and abrupt movements of the trained foreleg, occasional grinding of the teeth, and steadily increasing respiration rate. When released at the end of an hour the rate is 102 per minute. The second experiment begins at 2 P.M. The sheep is brought from the barnyard and placed in the demonstration cabinet for another hour without tests. But now respiration at the end of five minutes is 115 per minute, in contrast to 45 per minute at the beginning of the morning session. At the end of this second hour, in addition to increasing frequency of limb movement, breathing is labored and audible. During the last five-minute period the respiratory rate is 142 per minute. Since this animal has not been running or struggling and the time was early June, after the sheep had been shorn, the high respiratory rate at the beginning of the afternoon session can be attributed to neither exercise nor thermo-regulation.

"What this means," continues the professor, "is that":

The sheep's perturbation is clearly a manifestation of anxious expectation which perseverates in the barnyard during the recess between morning and afternoon sessions. What is to happen next? The animal has imposed upon itself an abnormally severe restraint. No matter what impends he can neither fight nor flee. . . . From long experience its present attitude must of necessity be fatalistic. (p. 12)

Lesson 5: Anxiety may be masked by apparent calm, even if you are aware that you are in a situation where crucial choices must be made and followed by the execution of precise and appropriate action to avoid unpleasant consequences. But, if the situation persists, arousal increases and the first clue to this is a change in breathing.

Corollary: Breathing is the most reliable indication that an individual is anxious or calm.

Don't we see this clearly also in the Sisyphean life of the "stressed" account executive, junior law firm associate, assembly line worker, homemaker, and in all of those persons for whom the workload just increases proportionately with the passage of time? There is no way to win—no way to escape. It is of little solace that these conditions may be self-imposed.

Lesson 6: In a situation in which specific acts are associated with anxiety, one may be observed to engage repeatedly in vicarious rehearsal or rehashing of these acts. Such acts may be specific and observable, or they may be nonspecific and covert. But breathing changes invariably accompany them.

We may infer that one source of psychosomatic disorders is the long-term damaging effect of these chronic patterns.

Lesson 7: Repeated acts may become habits outliving their initial value: When removed from a situation where crucial judgments and execution of appropriate actions to avoid consequences were once appropriate but no longer are, there may still be a tendency to repeat those acts in that situation or anything that resembles it.

A psychosomatic disorder may or may not result from *present* stress. It can also result from *habit*.

Corollary: Thwarted attempts to cope may take the form of stereotyped and apparently irrational vicarious actions, accompanied by rapid shallow breathing which reflects the degree of accompanying anxiety.

And as Robert is wheeled out in his wooden box, exit stage left, Professor Liddell concludes:

> In order properly to understand this sheep's responses . . . their biological significance must be explored. We now believe that each and every conditional response. . . whether positive or negative, exemplifies a refinement and elaboration, or even chronic distortion, of the crude fight or flight pattern studied by Cannon in his analysis of the emergency reaction. (p. 15)

Lesson 8: Simply calling up fight-or-flight reactions by a positive or negative stimulus inevitably leads to stress and, ultimately, disability.

In other words, (a) it does not matter if a dog barks at a cat, or if the dog's bark is preceded by a buzzer and the buzzer "barks" at the cat; and (b) simply anticipating the bark may be worse than the bite.

Every game teaches about life. We also sometimes must behave like Robert. When we do, we might perchance respond like Hamlet as he was handed the skull of his childhood pal, Yorick:

> Let me see. . . . Alas, poor Yorick! I knew him Horatio: a fellow of infinite jest, of most excellent fancy: he hath borne me on his back a thousand times; and now, *how abhorred in my imagination it is! My gorge rises at it.. . .*" (Act V, Scene 1) (my italics)

What we still haven't resolved is whether (a) his gorge rises because the thought is abhorred in his imagination, or (b) the thought is abhorred in his imagination because his gorge rises. Prof. Liddell would probably support the idea that the skull is an occasion for anxiety which has, among others, gorge-rising as a consequence. Subsequently, Hamlet perceives his gorge to have risen and consequently experiences revulsion.

In therapy,

- a behavior therapist might have employed a counterconditioning technique such as desensitization by teaching him deep muscle relaxation to an imaginal scene in which he gradually approximates the cemetery scene;
- a psychoanalyst might ask him to free-associate and report whatever comes to mind, no matter how trivial;
- his family physician would have prescribed Valium to relax the throat muscles, and referred him to a psychiatrist;
- and, when I asked Albert Ellis, founder of Rational Emotive Therapy, what he might have told him, he replied, "Stop being such a big baby, and quit awfulizing about Yorick. His death may have been untimely, and certainly regrettable, but not the end of the world. You may well feel very sad about Yorick's demise and about your loss. But if you enrage yourself about it you are grandiosely commanding that deeds that you dislike absolutely must never occur. What's more, you are ennobling yourself so much by your rage that you are covering up the fact that you are behaving quite shittily to Ophelia."

THE BREATH CONNECTION

When there is a perceptible change in the world around us, we automatically orient to it. Orientation to sounds, sights, or other stimuli is not learned. Every change is treated as a threat and our body prepares for fight or flight: Not taking a chance promotes survival.

But there is a price to pay for each of these reactions, even to false alarms: the energy cost of preparing for fight or flight, and the return to a normal prearousal state. And situations that do not ordinarily have the ability to call up fight-or-flight reactions can *acquire* them through repeated association with these reactions.

What the case of Robert illustrates most clearly is that reflexive fight-or-flight reactions may not be functionally different from the mental process of determining whether these reactions are called for. This message speaks to our modern world: Both real and imagined dangers and the process of determining the appropriate response may be just as stressful, because the same autonomic nervous system activities are evoked in either case.

Anxiety mimics the internal state of preparation for action. When action follows, the state dissipates: the *parasympathetic* branch of the autonomic nervous system sees to that as increased blood levels of action hormones and fuel (adrenaline and glucose, for instance) are mostly consumed, as it were, by the process.

But in those cases where there is preparation but no need for action, it takes longer to restore the body.

This is also why learning to "relax" at home, or periodically in the office or other place of employment, is so important: By reducing the action-oriented muscle tension, and blood levels of hormones and fuel, relaxation creates an internal environment that is in harmony with the external environment.

What we also learn from Robert is that action or anxiety can be conditioned to trivial environmental phenomena. These then become our own special master switches and we become their slaves.

By breathing control, we can weaken the action of those same switches.

CHAPTER 6

Nutrition and Breathing

INTRODUCTION

Nutrition plays an important general role in health and well-being and there are many good books written on this topic. But its concern to you is that dietary factors have also been implicated in psychosomatic disorders, most of which show disordered breathing.

Just as it is becoming increasingly apparent that psychosomatic and breathing disorders are related, so is it also increasingly evident that nutrition plays a key role in this interaction. I see this often in my clients.

For instance, three of the more common foodstuffs I have found to be frequently responsible for allergic reactions involving breathing are milk, wheat, and corn. These are also at the top of the lists of foods to which most allergy sufferers respond positively.

Since the 1930s, medical journals have reported that there is strong evidence linking foodstuffs to anxiety, depression, migraine, and even childhood hyperactivity and autism. These findings have generally been neglected by conventional medical practitioners. Here are three good examples:

Clarke, T.W. (1934). Epilepsy of allergic origin. *New York State Medical Journal, 34*:647–51.

Beauchemin, J.A. (1936). Allergic reaction in mental disease. *American Journal of Psychiatry, 92*:1191–1204.

Davison, H.H. (1952). Allergy of the nervous system. *Quarterly Review of Allergy and Immunology, 6*:157–86.

These studies employ research techniques just like those used in modern studies and are just as valid today as they were then.

This chapter will tell you a little about how some nutrient substances found in common foodstuffs may play a positive or adverse role in psychosomatic, stress-related, and breathing disorders.

This section is intended to inform you about what we know about the effect of certain foods on psychosomatic and breathing-related disorders. I do not recommend that you consume or stop consuming any substance without consulting a trained medical specialist. One such specialist whom I would like to acknowledge for his help in my understanding of many of the concepts presented here is Richard M. Carlton, M.D., a New York City (Manhattan) based psychiatrist, and author of pioneering research in medical nutrition. He has been instrumental in determining the nutritional and/or allergic basis of the mental or stress-related disorders of many of my clients.

In addition to physicians, one might also consult a licensed nutritionist for guidance in these areas.

EATING YOUR WAY TO NARROWER ARTERIES

There are substances found in common foods that may promote conditions in your body that favor stress and psychosomatic disorders. They are numerous; but among the better known is tyramine.

Researchers at the National Heart Institute, Bethesda, Maryland, have also long known that common foods contain varying levels of substances that are the very building blocks of the crucial nervous system and brain chemical messengers called *neurotransmitters*: acetylcholine, norepinephrine, serotonin, and dopamine, among others. These substances have the ability to turn processes ON or OFF.

It would be helpful to you to be aware of foods that contain or promote the body's release of these various substances if you have a psychosomatic disorder, or suffer from elevated blood pressure, migraine, asthma, allergies, or any other condition on which they have been demonstrated to have a detrimental effect. All of these conditions, and many more, involve breathing.

TYRAMINE

Tyramine is said to be a *sympathomimetic* substance. This means that by its action in the body, it partly or completely mimics the effects of the *sympathetic* branch of the autonomic nervous system, resulting in varying degrees of "fight-or-flight arousal."

Tyramine, present in certain foods, increases as that food undergoes breakdown by bacteria. Thus, leftovers in your refrigerator have a higher content of tyramine than did the food when it was fresh and first prepared. This fact could be important to you if you suffer from high blood pressure and migraine, both of which are well known to be sensitive to tyramine.

When released into the bloodstream, tyramine constricts blood vessels, which in turn may increase blood pressure. But it is usually rapidly broken down by an enzyme, monoamine oxidase (MAO), limiting its effects.

However, the deactivation of MAO by MAO-inhibitors such as the MAOI antidepressants Nardil and Marplan may prevent the breakdown of tyramine, in turn resulting in an increase in blood pressure leading to a dangerous elevation in blood pressure called a "hypertensive crisis," and even possibly stroke. Alternatively, the blood pressure may fall precipitously instead of rising.

If you have suffered depression and have been prescribed MAO-type antidepressants, you may be well aware of the potential danger of hypertension and will have been cautioned about foods containing even the slightest quantities of tyramine. Tricyclic antidepressants, by the way, do not have this particular effect on MAO or on blood pressure. But those of you who have hypertension; were you told about tyramine by your doctor?

Yet, it was reported in a medical journal that some persons may be naturally deficient in monoamine oxidase. Thus, it is advisable for you to be aware that there are foods that contain substances, not inherently harmful to the ordinary person, whose effects may be of concern to you.

I would remind you of the validity of the ancient Roman admonition, "One man's food is another's fierce poison."

While this need be of only minimal concern to most persons, it is a note of caution for others who may suffer from disorders in which vasoconstriction is a prominent feature:

- Hypertension: Tyramine causes blood vessels to contract, increases pulse rate, blood pressure and breathing rate.
- Angina: Tyramine causes blood vessels to constrict, reducing blood flow and oxygen to the heart (myocardium) and coronary arteries.
- Migraine: Tyramine may cause the initial vasoconstriction, which, coupled with platelet aggregation, results in spasms of the arteries in the head, setting off the attack.
- Raynaud's disease: The mechanism is similar to that in migraine but affects the blood vessels in the extremities, i.e., hands and feet.
- Idiopathic epilepsy (idiopathic: of unknown origin): By its action on the *sympathetic* branch of the autonomic nervous system, tyramine promotes rapid breathing leading to hyperventilation. Hyperventilation causes brain blood vessels to constrict, reducing blood flow and promoting abnormal brain waves and seizures.
- Diabetes: Diabetics have been shown to be magnesium and chromium deficient. This favors constriction of blood vessels and unstable insulin effects. Clumping (aggregation) of red blood cells and platelets further impairs blood circulation to the tissues.

  Diabetes results in (metabolic) acidosis, which is typically *compensated* by hyperventilation. It is, therefore, unwise to slow down breathing in diabetics without a physician's approval.
- Asthma: Certain foods, milk and chocolate, for in-

stance, and inhalants such as industrial pollutants, pollen—even bits of cockroach skeleton lost on the kitchen counter or living room carpet—can trigger release of action hormones and inflammatory mediators in the body that narrow airways in the lungs. Clinical studies have shown that pharmacologic dosages of certain essential nutrients, such as vitamin B6, can diminish the frequency and severity of asthma attacks. Tyramine aggravates the condition.

Which are the foods high in tyramine? The *Mayo Clinic Diet Manual* (1981) informs us that food content of tyramine and other amines (proteins containing nitrogen) may be expected to show considerable variation. Factors relating to preparation, processing, and storage of foods may contribute to tyramine content. The quantity of tyramine in a given foodstuff will also vary with the amount of time it is left unrefrigerated: the longer it is left unrefrigerated, the greater the degree of protein degradation by bacterial action, converting more of the amino acid present (tyrosine) into tyramine. Excerpts from the *Manual*, as well as other sources, suggest the following:

Beverage
Avoid: limit coffee, tea, carbonated beverages to three cups per day.
Allowed: decaffeinated coffee, cereal beverage, artificially flavored fruit drink.
Meat and Cheese
Avoid: aged and processed cheese; pickled herring, dried herring; liver; peanuts and peanut butter; aged meats, including dry sausage, hard salami, pepperoni,

and summer sausage—any meats prepared with meat tenderizer or with soy sauce

Allowed: cottage cheese; soft or semidry sausage, cured meat

Fat

Avoid: sour cream; avocado

Allowed: cream cheese

Milk

Avoid: chocolate milk; yogurt

Allowed: all others

Starch

Avoid: fava beans

Allowed: all beans, including broad beans other than fava beans; all other starches

Vegetables

Avoid: sauerkraut

Allowed: all others

Fruit

Avoid: canned figs; raisins; raspberries

Allowed: all others

Soup

Avoid: commercial canned soup; any soup made with soup cubes or meat extracts

Allowed: all others

Desserts

Avoid: any made with chocolate

Allowed: all others

Sweets

Avoid: any containing chocolate

Allowed: all others

Miscellaneous

Avoid: meat tenderizer; meat or yeast extracts: canned soups, soup cubes, brewer's yeast; soy sauce; chocolate; beer and wine, and other alcoholic beverages.

Allowed: all others including baker's yeast as a leavening agent in bakery products.

You might bear in mind that these recommendations, as well as those to follow, were compiled by various dietetic study groups because these foods are shown to increase blood pressure and therefore may be harmful to persons with borderline elevated blood pressure, or hypertension; cardiovascular, circulatory, and vascular problems.

Missing from the above list is the caution to avoid smoked or cured meats (e.g., bacon, lox, and corned beef) and pickled vegetables. You should also be aware of the fact that the riper a given fruit, the greater the content of tyramine.

I have always found it amazing that despite the evidence (many hospitals distribute the list to "heart patients"), dietary recommendations by the average medical practitioner to persons with hypertension seldom mention anything other than "low sodium." It is well known that tyramine found in foods may in some persons be so slowly converted by monoamine oxidase to its nontoxic form (parahydroxyphenylacetic acid), that its effects on blood pressure may pose a serious health hazard.

Here is another list compiled from such diverse sources as the *Archives of Biochemistry and Biophysics*, and the *Mayo Clinic Diet Manual*:

Beverages

Avoid: alcoholic beverages, wines, beer, ale

Allowed: all others as well as decaffeinated coffee and tea

Bread and Bread Substitutes

Avoid: homemade yeast breads; crackers containing cheese

Allowed: all others

Fats

Avoid: sour cream

Allowed: all others

Fruits

Avoid: bananas; red plums; avocado; figs; raisins

Allowed: orange (limited to one small orange per day, not to exceed 2 1/2 inches in diameter); all others not excluded

Cheese, Meat, and Meat Substitutes

Avoid: aged game (not a serious problem in the "Big Apple"); liver and canned meats; yeast extracts; commercial meat extracts; stored beef liver; chicken livers; salami; sausage; aged cheese: bleu, Boursault, brick, Brie, Camembert, cheddar, Colby, Emmenthaler, Gouda, mozzarella, Parmesan, provolone, Romano, Roquefort, Stilton; salted dried fish (herring, cod or camlin), pickled herring

Vegetables

Avoid: Italian broad beans, green bean pods, eggplant

Allowed: tomato (limited to 1/2 cup daily); all others

Miscellaneous

Avoid: Yeast concentrates, or products made with them; marmite; soup cubes; commercial gravies or meat extracts; anything with soy sauce; any protein that has not been stored properly or has some degree of spoilage, i.e., all but those that have been freshly prepared.

Allowed: fresh homemade gravies, excluding the ingredients not allowed.

There is much overlap of these lists, some items appearing in one and not the other.

N.P. Sen, in the *Journal of Food Science* (vol. 34, 1969), reports tyramine content of various standard items. Orange juice has relatively little tyramine, while the whole

Suspect Foods Checklist

Instructions: Make a mark before the vertical line if you have consumed that item the first week, and after the vertical line if you've consumed it the following week.

	Sun	Mon	Tue	Wed	Thu	Fri	Sat
Milk, ice cream							
Wheat							
Chocolate							
Sugar							
Cheese (aged or processed) . . .							
Spinach							
Corn (or products/Karo S) . . .							
Citrus fruit							
Coffee (and/or tea)							
Alcohol, wine, beer							
Banana							
Red meat							
Yeast/bouillon							
Sausage							
Chinese food (MSG)							
Licorice							
Eggs							
Pork/pork products							

Nuts/peanut butter . . . .
Pickled herring . . . .
Seafood . . . .
Cabbage . . . .
Tomatoes . . . .
Egg plant . . . .
Chicken liver . . . .
Processed foods . . . .
Turkey . . . .
Plums . . . .
Salad bar salad . . . .
Fried foods . . . .
Cola . . . .

Other _____

Insomnia

Mild ( )
Moderate ( )
Severe ( )

fruit is not allowed in one other list given above. Cheese is relatively high in tyramine, but content varies with type and sample taken from each type. Yeast and meat extracts are also quite high in tyramine; and so is salted dry herring. This particular list does not mention pickled herring, nor figs or plums, for instance.

Because of the importance of this food list in migraine, hypertension, and other disorders, I am proposing that you consider tracking what you eat that appears on the preceding checklist. It will give you a good idea of what suspect foods you consume, and how frequently you consume them. This may prove very helpful in determining their possible role in your symptoms.

THE RELATIONSHIP BETWEEN HYPERTENSION AND BREATHING

The release into the bloodstream of action hormones or any substance, such as tyramine, that mimics their effects will increase pulse rate, blood pressure and breathing rate.

The average hypertensive person is seldom aware of his/her high blood pressure—it is a hidden symptom, giving no warning of its presence. Likewise, elevated pulse rate may not be known. But, shortness of breath (dyspnea) and rapid breathing (tachypnea) are usually detected first, and are therefore important clues to the possible presence of these other conditions.

FOODS IMPLICATED IN MIGRAINE AND IN NEUROLOGICAL ALLERGY

There are other foods relatively high in another amino acid: tyrosine, a tyramine building block. Chief among these is bananas, including plantains, and tomatoes, plums, avocados and eggplant.

Other foods, such as turkey, may be relatively high in tryptophan, a serotonin building block which has been linked to migraine, idiopathic epilepsy, and other neurological manifestations of allergic reactions. These reactions have been well documented, although medical research into this aspect of clinical practice is limited to the role of allergy to foodstuffs in childhood hyperactivity (hyperkinetic syndrome).

There have been numerous published reports on food allergy in migraine. One of the best is in the *Lancet* (vol. 2, 1983). It cites tyramine-rich foods as contributing to migraine.

I have combined the *Lancet* list with that of Davison, reported in the *Quarterly Review of Allergy and Applied Immunology*, cited above, and with others.* The items are listed below:

1. Milk, sour cream, yogurt
2. Wheat
3. Chocolate
4. Aged or processed cheese
5. Corn (Karo syrup)
6. Alcohol (wine, beer, etc.)
7. Red meat (beef, etc.), pork (pork products)

---

*Adapted from: Davison, H.H. (1952). Allergy of the nervous system. *Quarterly Review of Allergy and Applied Immunology*, 6:157–86; Egger, J. et al. (1983). Is migraine food allergy? *Lancet*, 2:865–69; Lovenberg, W. (1973). *Some vaso- and psychoactive substances in food amines, stimulants, depressants, and hallucinogens occurring naturally in food* (2nd ed.). Washington: National Academy of Sciences; and Udenfriend et al. (1959). Physiologically active amines in common fruits and vegetables. *Archives of Biochemistry and Biophysics*, 85:487.

8. Monosodium glutamate (MSG, in Chinese and Mexican food)
9. Licorice
10. Eggs
11. Bouillon, soup cubes, soy sauce
12. Nuts (especially peanuts and peanut butter)
13. Pickled or marinated herring
14. Seafood, shellfish
15. Citrus fruit (oranges, grapefruit)
16. Cola drinks
17. Bananas
18. Tomatoes, cabbage, spinach, avocado
19. Canned soup
20. Chicken liver, beef liver
21. Processed foods and smoked or cured meats
22. Plums, prunes, canned figs
22. Raisins
23. Broad beans, lima beans
24. Coffee, tea, cocoa

These are among the better known, though you may be sensitive to other foods. The *New York Times* (January 7, 1986) in a survey of research on food allergy and migraine reported finding that "75% of migraine patients may be allergic to 5 or more foods. . . some to 20 or more foods."

These dietary considerations are seldom brought to the attention of parents who have children who suffer migraine. Most physicians tend to rely on medication which, in fact, may have severe side effects and to which one may habituate, requiring ever-larger dosages with diminishing results. Childhood migraine is far more common than most people think and often goes unrecognized.

As a parent, you are probably aware of the role of "junk" foods, and stimulants such as caffeine found in soft drinks, preservatives, coloring, and additives, in migraine. I am sure that you've read about this in many magazines that report on health issues. But, I would like to direct your attention to an article by J. Egger and colleagues, published in the *Journal of Pediatrics* (114:51-58) as recently as January 1989. This article is entitled "Oligoantigenic Diet Treatment of Children with Epilepsy and Migraine." "Oligoantigenic" means low in *antigens*, substances to which your immune system responds with the production of *antibodies*.

This article points out a connection I mentioned previously, namely, that between migraine and epilepsy: What will trigger one, usually triggers the other; anything that jeopardizes the oxygen supply of the brain, usually.

It must be difficult for you to believe that diet may trigger migraine or seizures. But look at it this way: The body's immune reaction to antigens is stressful, and usually involves release of histamine into the bloodstream. Histamine is a vasoconstrictor, narrowing the arteries and reducing blood flow to all parts of the body, including the brain. Furthermore, through another action of histamine, directly on red blood cells, my clients invariably show a reduction of from 1 to 3% in the level of oxygen in their blood.

Thus, once again, here is a connection between nutrition and oxygen delivery to the body and the brain. In the report, the foods mentioned most frequently are:

• cow milk	• pork
• cow cheese	• chocolate
• citrus fruit	• corn
• wheat	• grapes
• food additives	• tea
• hen eggs	• beef
• tomatoes	• cane sugar

You might consider these items if you decide to consult a physician or nutritionist with a view to reducing them in your diet or in your child's diet. Remember, I recommend against going "cold turkey" on foods. "Elimination" diets should be supervised by a qualified professional. Sudden elimination of foods that trigger symptoms may actually aggravate the condition.

I have treated many migraine sufferers and virtually all had some form of breathing disorder, including, in some cases, hyperventilation. There is little doubt in my mind that sensitivity to some foods contributes to disordered breathing in a number of different ways.

Hyperventilation is a known trigger of epileptic seizures, and I can vouch for the role of both nutritional factors and breathing disturbances in that neurological disorder. For persons with idiopathic epilepsy, migraine, and in some cases, asthma, my preferred list ranks:

- milk
- processed or aged cheese
- wheat
- chocolate
- pickled herring or pickled vegetables
- smoked or cured meats or fish
- corn
- bananas, plums, canned figs
- beef
- pork, turkey
- soy sauce
- nuts
- licorice
- broad beans
- eggplant, tomatoes, spinach
- citrus pulp, raspberries

or anything containing these foods. Just as a reminder,

Yes, you can't have bananas.
You can't have bananas today.
Have rice cakes,
Fresh veggies,
An apple, some seltzer. No pizza or latkes, please!
Yes, you can't have bananas.
They'll give you a headache today.

A list of inhalants suspected of triggering these disorders includes:

- dog, cat dander or hair; bird feathers
- dust
- mold
- pollen
- tobacco
- common household cooking gas (leakage through pilot ignition flame)
- and, believe it or not, tiny pieces of the outer shell (exoskeleton) that fall off cockroaches as they crawl about in your apartment!

These food substances and inhalants do not invariably trigger episodes of a neurological or respiratory disorder. Rather, they have been sufficiently frequently implicated in these disorders to be taken seriously. There is still considerable controversy about which substances act and by what mechanism they act to promote these disorders.

My preferred explanation follows *catastrophe theory*, which attempts to explain when a constant relationship is observed to cause an unpredictable change:

For instance, a constant pressure applied when bending a stick will result in a predictable bowing of the stick, up to a point. Beyond that point, it breaks. This would not be predicted from the initial changes in the stick due to bending. No matter how much information you have about bending sticks, you cannot predict exactly at what point they will break.

By the same token, a gradual increase in the blood level of action hormones or their mimics, recently consumed in food, may not produce a *gradual* increase in symptoms.

There may be a very gradual change in different processes in the body, accompanied by an increase in breathing. Then beyond a certain point, symptoms emerge wih vigor.

There is even evidence to suggest that a similar phenomenon operates in seizure disorder. Several factors may interact until the seizure threshold is surpassed: The action hormone-mimics consumed in foodstuffs add to stress-related, naturally released, action hormones, and breathing quickens.

You begin to hyperventilate, and that may well be the factor that tips the balance.

By the way, the earliest modern—and effective—medical treatment for seizure disorders was the ketogenic diet, plus pyridoxine (B6).

MINERALS: IRON, ZINC, MAGNESIUM, CALCIUM, AND POTASSIUM—THEIR ROLE IN RESPIRATION

This book is about breathing. Its only concern with nutrition is to make you aware of its role in stress-related and psychosomatic disorders. Thus, the mention of the following items is sketchy, and just to get you acquainted with what's what. It is up to you to follow up.

Proper levels of minerals in the body are essential to

proper functioning. There are many forms of mineral deficiency that both impede health and are manifest in breathing disorders.

Iron. Oxygenated blood flows from the lungs, through the left heart, to the body tissues, where it delivers the oxygen and picks up carbon dioxide. It then returns to the lungs, via the right heart, and the cycle repeats—if all goes well.

For the most part, O_2 is carried in the hemoglobin in red blood cells. The quantity of red blood cells in the blood is regulated by iron availability.

If there is an insufficiency of dietary iron available for the formation of red cells, anemia may follow rapidly. This is a condition characterized by pallor, weakness, loss of appetite, and a number of other symptoms, including an increase in breathing rate which frequently leads to hyperventilation.

Zinc. This trace mineral is involved in the body's storage of histamine and is an essential component in a wide range of enzymes, including RNA and DNA enzymes, and carbonic anhydrase, crucial to respiration.

CO_2 in blood is converted, through the action of carbonic anhydrase, to bicarbonate and hydrogen ions. This is part of the carbon dioxide elimination system and part of the process for maintaining the body's acid-base balance. Zinc is not toxic, and excess body zinc is virtually unknown.

Magnesium. This trace mineral is the fourth most abundant metal in the human body. It is essential to the proper function of the nervous system as well as the cardiovascular, vascular, and circulatory systems.

Magnesium has been said to be the "mimic/antagonist" of calcium: It is the natural way that the body prevents excess calcium from entering tissues. While calcium is necessary to proper bone structure, its excess is detrimental to red blood cells, which it makes rigid; and muscle, heart, and nerve cells, which it makes overactive.

Thus, magnesium deficiency has serious consequences. Unlike zinc, magnesium deficiency can occur rapidly and is thought to be quite common. It is linked to hypertension, and to cardiac arrhythmias and seizures: I have reported its role in epilepsy in *Prevention* (vol. 36, 1984).

Calcium. This mineral is found in all parts of the body, but 99% of it is found in your bones. It is essential to blood clotting and the ability of nerves and muscles to respond to stimulation.

Calcium deficiency is far from rare. It is involved in rickets and osteoporosis. It is rapidly lost from the body by inactivity, especially bed rest.

Calcium has been strongly implicated in emotional and psychosomatic disorders. The treatment of depression, for instance, has been shown to increase calcium retention.

Potassium. This is the third major mineral in the body, next to calcium and phosphorus. Together with sodium, potassium regulates the electrical balance of cell membranes. It is therefore critical in the function of the lungs, heart, blood vessels, and nerve fibers. Potassium deficiency, like magnesium deficiency, can be observed in changes in the electrical activity of the heart and in the reduced motility of the digestive tract, especially the stomach: It is a leading cause of chronic indigestion.

Potassium helps to maintain the body's acid-base and fluid balance, which also affect breathing directly.

Other minerals, such as sodium, copper, manganese, etc., are also important, and I urge you to acquaint yourself with their role in your health. Any standard source, such as Pfeiffer's *Zinc and Other Micronutrients* (a Pivot Original Health Book, 1978), will be helpful.

VITAMINS

There is much controversy about the role of vitamins in health and illness, and it usually centers on whether adequate levels can be obtained in the ordinary American diet.

For example, the recommended daily allowance (RDA) for vitamin C is 45 mg/day. But actually, this is only the *minimum average daily quantity that will prevent scurvy.* This says nothing about enhancing health. In fact, your doctor frequently prescribes greater daily doses just to control cystitis (urethral infection)—over 1000 mg/day.

Vitamin C is an essential vitamin. Among others, it helps prevent anemia, and functions as a "free radical scavenger"—mopping up and preventing tissue damage due to dangerous concentrations in the blood of a variant of oxygen, O_3.

One of the vitamins whose essential function in these disorders is just beginning to become clear is vitamin B6.

Vitamin B6 (pyridoxine) deficiency has been linked to neurological, breathing, and psychosomatic disorders, especially those where hyperventilation has been implicated.

There have been reports of the role of vitamin B6 deficiency in panic disorder and agoraphobia, a hyperventilation-related phenomenon. In one study, nutritional control, monitored by a functional vitamin/enzyme testing procedure, resulted in dramatic improvement in these "psychological" disorders. The deficiencies noted were in B1, B3, B12, folic acid, and B6.

This study also suggested that B6 deficiency was due,

in one case, to inadequate breakdown and absorption of B6 by the body. The administration of preformed pyridoxal-5-phosphate, a metabolite of B6, resolved the problem. It also implicated the role of tryptophan in these disorders.

Vitamin B6 is quickly lost when you are stressed. But it may be toxic and cause irreversible nerve damage, when taken in sufficient quantity. Please don't self-prescribe.

In an article entitled "Intracellular Magnesium Deficiency in Epilepsy," abstracted in the *Journal of the American College of Nutrition* (vol. 4, 1983, pp. 429-30), Dr. Richard M. Carlton and I reported that our epileptic clients who hyperventilated and did not respond well to anticonvulsant medication were deficient in tissue levels of magnesium even if blood serum levels were normal.

Our work on tissue magnesium levels in epilepsy was part of a conference on "Magnesium in Biochemistry and Medicine," held by the American College of Nutrition in 1984. The conference participants were cited by the National Institute of Health (NIH) as being "at the forefront of their discipline by attempting to relate data from cell populations to health and disease."

THE BREATH CONNECTION

The body functions best when it is provided with certain essentials, including an appropriate environment, nutrition, and exercise. The repeated or chronic reduction in any of them is stressful. Coupled with an inherited or acquired predisposition, this constant stress will deplete the body more rapidly of nutrients, vitamins and minerals, in some cases causing a critically low level of these constituents.

Thus, while stress may have a psychological component, it is essentially a wearing down of the body that may reach a point where organs are in jeopardy. This is the start of a medical or psychological disorder.

There is a variety of breath connections to nutrition: Hyperventilation may be promoted by tyraminergic foods (containing or promoting tyramine). Other nutritional problems, such as vitamins C, folic acid, and B6 deficiency, and zinc and magnesium deficiency, among others, may lead to anemia, hypertension, or other disorders that show concomitant breathing changes.

ILLUSTRATIVE CASE: N.B.

Nothing illustrates the role of the "food connection" better than the following letter which I received from a client:

November 23, 1983

Dear Dr. Fried,

Thank you. Thank you. Thank you. You have no idea how very grateful I am for what you have done for me.

After having been referred to the ICD, I recall the day I phoned to make my first appointment with you. I remember asking the receptionist what the initial ICD stood for. When she informed me, the word disabled was sort of a shock to me. But when I thought about it I realized that I was in fact disabled to a very great extent.

Over the past eight years or so, I've been on a constant search for a doctor who could help me. I've seen many general practitioners, a respiratory specialist, a head and neck specialist, a psychologist, a cardiologist, I've even discussed it with my gynecologist and as a nurse, any other of the many doctors I'd had the opportunity to discuss it with, but unfortunately, none of them were able to come up with any solution to my strange and mysterious symptoms. Each time I left another doctor's office I became more and more hopeless.

I was really beginning to allow myself to be convinced by these doctors that I did have some very serious psychological problem that required all the tranquilizers and antidepressants they were always so anxious to prescribe for me. But a little voice inside told me they were wrong and fortunately I persisted in trying to find an answer.

When I say that I've had the problem for about the past eight years, I mean that this is when my symptoms really became quite noticable (sic) by myself and others and began to interfere with my everyday activities. But it's possible that I may have had the problem from the time I was born.

Shortly after my birth, the doctor informed my mother that I was allergic to milk, so during infancy I was nourished on a soy product. Then I outgrew my milk allergy but maybe I hadn't.

When I think back to the diet of my childhood it all becomes a little clearer. I had my favorite grilled cheese sandwich every day. I loved cheese ravioli and baked macaroni and cheese. Veal Parmigiano (sic) was my favorite dish when dining out and ice cream was my favorite dessert. (And I ate plenty of it!) I can still recall sitting at the dinner table and gasping for breath while trying to eat. My father always asking why I was doing that. But I didn't know why.

It wasn't until I was about seventeen and a freshman in nursing school that the symptoms began to become significantly worse. I found it increasingly difficult to sit through lectures. I was chronically yawning and gasping for breath. Very often I was unable to catch my breath. And it became a constant struggle just to get enough air in. It was quite exhausting and very annoying! I was always fearful that the teacher might ask me if he or she were boring me but I just couldn't help it.

Then I developed a new symptom, difficulty swallowing. This occurred with both liquids and solid food and was most distressing! At home, although it was a problem, at least I could take all the time in the world to eat and I had to get up and take several breaks and stroll around through the living room and then come back to the table and try to continue to eat (all) I could. But dining out and especially with company it was very awkward to always be excusing myself and sometimes to have to go outside to get some fresh air before continuing. Although dining out has always been one of my great pleasures, it had now become a terribly frustrating and embarrassing experience. Waiters and maitre d's were always looking a little perplexed and wondering if something was wrong with the food I'd been served. Then when I would start to choke and gag on it it would frighten me so much that I'd be too upset to even attempt to eat any more and would usually ask them to wrap it up for me to take home. The people who we usually dined out with stopped suggesting it when they saw what a fiasco it always turned out to be. There is nothing as frustrating as being in a restaurant with a voracious appetite, having a delicious meal before you and not being able to eat it.

Then some new symptoms developed; heart palpitations and trembling. This was getting to be more than I could handle. I am not denying that I tend to be a nervous type of person but this was ridiculous. It got to the point where the mere ringing of the telephone was enough to trigger an episode of these palpitations and tremors. And then there was insomnia—total insomnia. Never in my life had I had any problem sleeping but suddenly I found it was impossible to sleep. And if and when I would fall asleep I was waking up every hour or two throughout the night in a panic state. Usually these panic states were accompanied by episodes of heart palpitations and tremors. But these were only the physical symptoms. There were psychological symptoms as well.

My "panic attacks" as I called them were terribly frightening. If I had one during the night it would be accompanied by morbid thoughts and fears. I would often feel it necessary to awaken my husband to tell him I loved him as I'd fear that I would die before morning. And although each night I managed to survive, the fear was always just as real every time. It's difficult to explain, but I had this impending sense of doom that just wouldn't leave. I also got these attacks during the day which once caused my husband to come racing home from work to take me to the hospital.

Claustrophobia was another problem. I got it in buses that became too crowded and in theaters. I've even had to get up and leave a restaurant before even placing an order. And the worst experience of all was traveling through the Lincoln Tunnel on my frequent trips into Manhattan.

I can't begin to imagine how I could have continued on in this manner for much longer than I did. When I took the biofeedback sessions in your clinic I found them helpful in that it taught me the proper way to breathe but in spite of the sessions something was preventing me from breathing properly. This is where your theory about milk products comes in.

At first, I have to admit, I was very skeptical. Hadn't I already been through this with many of the other doctors? I told them of my allergy to milk at birth and asked if it was possible that milk could still be what was upsetting my system now. They were all so convincing when they told me that in the absence of gastro-intestinal type symptoms they could assure that milk products were not to blame. But when I finally did adhere to the dairy-free diet I was amazed to see all my symptoms subside. Although, at first, I found it very difficult to maintain this diet as all of my favorite foods must be avoided, I feel so much better when I'm on the diet that it is well worth the sacrifice.

I am like a different person now. My mood is so much better and I'm much more relaxed. I haven't had any panic attacks or palpitations or tremors since early September. I can eat and drink without any difficulty, no more choking and gagging and fear. I am sleeping and not waking up until morning. And my claustrophobia has disappeared! The true test was getting stuck in the Lincoln Tunnel last week and it didn't even phase (sic) me.

Tomorrow is Thanksgiving Day and do I have a lot to be thankful for. My husband and I had been considering starting a family for a while now, but I was really afraid to go ahead as in the shape I was in, I couldn't imagine how I would manage to get through the nine months and especially through the labor. But now that I'm feeling so much better, we can confidently go ahead with our plans without all that fear and worry.

What really concerns me are all of those people who may be suffering as I was for so long and going to doctors and not getting any help. And what is even worse, they may also be driven into a drugged existence simply because the doctor doesn't know what the problem is.

I wonder how long it will take for doctors to become more aware of how certain foods can affect the body and the mind. I certainly am very lucky to have come across someone who does and I intend to tell everyone (the doctors especially) of my experience.

Thank you again, Dr. Fried, for helping me to bring about this miraculous change in my life. I will be forever grateful to you.

Sincerely,
N. B.
(quoted with permission)

This letter was written to me when I was Director of the Rehabilitation Research Institute, at ICD—International Center for the Disabled, New York, and Dr. Richard M. Carlton was my Medical Officer—1980 to 1984. Among other things, we experimented with different standard diets which had been shown to have a salutary effect on the frequency and severity of seizure disorders, and we found that they also worked quite well in anxiety and panic disorders.

Some years after this letter was received, when I decided to write this book, I wrote to Ms. N.B. and asked her for permission to print the letter. Permission granted, I asked Dr. Carlton, who had supervised this case to contact her and write a follow-up:

N.B.'s life prior to treatment (diet changes and breathing retraining) had been held in suspended animation. As she described in her original letter, she had been holding back for years from having children, because the daily gagging and choking, along with the daily panic attacks, would make pregnancy and child-rearing very difficult. And she did not want to conceive while on tranquilizers.

Within a few months of beginning treatment, she felt so well that she let her husband know that she was ready to have children. They had their first child without difficulty, and then a second child two years after that. There were no anxiety attacks during the pregnancies, nor *post-partum* depressions after them. Her children are thriving, and she has a high level of life enjoyment now. This is in stark contrast to the anguish and anxiety she had been experiencing all her life, prior to treatment.

Dr. Carlton continues:

Looking back on this case, it is easy to see why others labelled her "neurotic," and how she would at least partially accept that label. After all, on top of all the "anxiety," she'd also been so "neurotic" as to gag all her life whenever eating, at home and in restaurants. It had never occurred to her that *what* she was eating could be provoking the gagging. Milk and cheese had always been an integral part of all her meals, in childhood and into adulthood. And as soon as she stopped these foods, her gagging stopped and her panic attacks went away.

Gagging and choking, along with all her feelings of anxiety and impeding doom, helped fulfill several of the DSM-III criteria for the diagnosis of anxiety disorder and panic disorder.

So it was very understandable that these were the diagnostic labels that had been ascribed to her over the years.

Now we must assert that there most assuredly are many cases of anxiety/panic that have nothing to do with the patient's diet, the condition being neurotic in origin.

But [Ms. N.B.'s] case is an illustrative example of the *many* patients we have seen, where foods are indeed a major precipitant of the anxiety symptomatology, and where a healthy and well-adjusted person emerges from the skelter once the storm of food-induced problems has passed.

It is important that we remember the sage advice of physicians in ancient Rome, *"One man's food is another's fierce poison."* It is also interesting to know that Chinese physicians have been saying the same thing for at least 3000 years, *"Each food has its poison, so balance your poisons."*

Sincerely yours,
Richard M. Carlton, M.D.

CHAPTER 7

Breathing, Hypertension, and the Heart

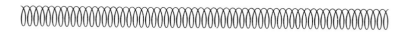

INTRODUCTION

Let us assume that you are a relatively healthy professional man or woman in your middle forties. It has been a routine day at the office and traffic was not exceptionally dense on your return home. You have enjoyed a pleasant dinner with your family and the major feature on the dinnertime news concerned a banal mayoral address to a local civic club.

You are sitting comfortably in your favorite chair now and you are reading or watching TV. You do not smoke.

We would expect your pulse rate to be between 70 and 80 beats per minute (BPM) and your blood pressure about 125/75 mmHg; your breathing rate would be around 12 to 14 breaths per minute (b/min).

End Act I, Scene 1! Cut!

Scene 2: You are sitting in (and slowly sinking into) a soft-leather couch in the waiting room of the executive suite of your firm. The surroundings may best be de-

scribed as posh: Senseless but obviously costly wall dec-
orations and art objects have been collected and dispersed
strategically around the room to give the impression of
"class."

A receptionist, in fashionable drab, not a hair out of
place, sits behind a rosewood desk and shunts incoming
phone calls to various department heads—all vice-
presidents of the company, a position to which you aspire
(note the breathing-related meaning of this term).

This position is as precariously dependent on continuous high-level performance as that of a stunt pilot (with
about equal casualty rates).

In spite of your best efforts, "The Report," which is
your responsibility, is woefully inadequate. You have for
some time been trying to avoid facing the fact that, because of lack of time and inadequate resources, there are
gaps and errors throughout. So your department head, a
man who has gone on record as stating that tact and good-
will are signs of weakness, has requested that you meet
with him.

While you are sitting there, estimating the likelihood
of finding other suitable employment in the geographic
region in which your children attend school, it might not
be unreasonable to suppose that your calm and composed
appearance masks tension and anxiety.

Your blood pressure may rise to 165/95 mmHg, and
your pulse rate to 110 BPM. Your breathing rate may reach
18 or more b/min, with frequent deep sighs.

As time goes by, your hands begin to feel cold and
clammy. You begin to fidget with the folder on your lap
and you can feel your chest pounding. You startle at the
dreaded, though expected sound of, "Mr/Ms Smith? Mr.
Jones will see you now."

BREATHING AND THE CARDIOVASCULAR SYSTEM

The way that you breathe, the rate, rhythm and mode have a profound effect on cardiovascular function—meaning your heart, arteries, and blood flow. Breathing affects the diameter of your blood vessels, your blood pressure, and the work output of the heart (stroke volume). Breathing also affects the timing of the heart beats: its own pacemaker rhythm.

The most commonly observed breathing disorder that is associated with stress or psychosomatic disorders is rapid, shallow chest breathing with hyperventilation.

In this chapter, we will look at the effect of hyperventilation on blood pressure, the heart, and the arteries. You will read about the medical research that concludes that hyperventilation is associated with high blood pressure (hypertension), heart arrhythmias, and angina—all diseases involving the heart or the arteries.

Evidence will be presented to you concluding that breathing control is an effective adjunct and, in some cases, the best method to control these disorders.

HYPERVENTILATION AND BLOOD PRESSURE

Predictable changes in arterial blood pressure occur with changes in breathing and have been reported by many clinical investigators. Many of these changes occur principally as a function of respiration rate: When breathing is within the normal range, blood pressure falls during inspiration. But, when doing slow diaphragmatic breathing, arterial blood pressure drops slightly, with pulse rate, during expiration.

When you hyperventilate, blood flow to the large skeletal muscles increases while blood flow to the hands, feet, and brain decreases. That is one of the reasons for doing slow diaphragmatic breathing during a migraine attack: It restores blood flow to the extremities. Migraine sufferers have notoriously cold extremities, and hand warming with autosuggestion and biofeedback techniques has been shown to be effective in relieving symptoms.

Just as breathing affects blood pressure, blood pressure may also affect breathing: Blood flow through the head may, within limits, vary with blood pressure in the body; but blood flow to the brain decreases as breathing rate increases.

L.G. Tirala, professor of medicine at the University of Munich, published a little book entitled *The Cure of High Blood Pressure by Respiratory Exercises*, in which he sets forth many of these principles. Would you believe that this book was published in 1928?

Thus, the relationship between breathing and blood pressure has been known and understood for a long time. It boils down to this: Elevated blood pressure accompanies those bodily states where rapid, shallow breathing prevails. By altering breathing to a slow diaphragmatic mode, blood pressure decreases.

Elevated blood pressure is a major American health problem. According to the Census Bureau (1987), about 28 million persons in the United States have elevated blood pressure. Women comprise about two-thirds of that number.

Let's take a look at some of the mechanisms that determine, or regulate, your blood circulation and pressure.

Since the description of blood circulation in the human body by Harvey (1628), it has been generally determined that that is how your body transports oxygen and nutrients to your muscles, tissues, and organs, and removes carbon dioxide and other wastes. Before blood was understood to circulate, it was certainly appropriate to refer to blood "vessels."

The blood in the arteries flows from the lungs through the left side of the heart, carrying oxygen held by the hemoglobin molecules in the red blood cells.

The arteries narrow to arterioles, and then to capillaries. As blood goes through the capillaries, some of which have a diameter less than that of a single red blood cell, it gives up much of its oxygen (O_2) and nutrients to surrounding tissues, organs and muscles, and takes on carbon dioxide (CO_2) and other waste products.

But, it can only do so if there is sufficient pressure to help it through the capillaries and into the veins for the return trip to the lungs, pumped by the right side of the heart.

The system of arteries and veins that carries blood to and from your tissues is called the vascular system. Of particular concern to us is the arterial vascular system, which consists of smooth muscle tissue, in the form of tubes or ducts, whose diameter is adjustable by constriction or dilation.

There are numerous physiological factors that affect the strength and the rate of contraction of the heart, and the diameter of arteries, arterioles, and capillaries. These include the action of physiological pressure regulator, chemical and other hormone mechanisms. All of these, interacting in various combinations, result in a given blood pressure.

You can readily feel rhythmic blood pressure pulses in arteries at various points on your body. The wrist is a favorite place to "take" the pulse. You have seen your physician do this many times: With your hand, palm up, the index and middle fingers are placed across your wrist, over the *radial artery*. The pulsations may be timed to give you pulse or beats per minute. There is one pulse for each contraction of the heart. In normal adults at rest, pulse rate will vary between about 70 and 80 beats per minute.

THE HEART AND BLOOD PRESSURE

The heart is a fist-shaped muscle, weighing about 1 pound and containing two pumps—one on the right, and one on the left side. Each pump consists of two chambers which recirculate your total blood volume, an average of about 5 quarts. Ordinarily, this is accomplished under the control of its own automatic pacemakers located in the *sinoatrial* and *atrioventricular* nodes, which determine the rate and patterns of its contractions.

During the course of an average day, at a rate of about 70 beats per minute, your heart will beat over 100,000 times, and pump about 1800 gallons of blood. Quite an undertaking for a fist-sized muscle!

The contractions of the heart are associated with the emission of an electrical current. This current, when it is picked up by little electrode pads on your chest, and amplified, is the basis for the electrocardiogram (ECG), which indicates which phase of the contraction of the heart is in progress. Some components of this current reflect the trigger to contraction, while others are the result of the muscle contraction itself.

Cardiac arrhythmias are deviations in this electrical signal, resulting from various changes in the activity of the heart musculature. They may reflect minor changes in the concentration of essential electrolytes, such as sodium, calcium, magnesium, and potassium; or they may represent life-threatening conditions.

An electrolyte is a substance that facilitates the flow of an electric current through an otherwise nonconducting medium by making it a conductor. For instance, pure distilled water will not conduct an electric current. But, salt dissolved in it will make the water conduct a current. The salt is, therefore, an electrolyte.

The strength of the contraction of the heart—in a sense, the change in its size—determines the amount of blood pumped into the arteries with each contraction. This is called its *stroke volume*. It is the major factor in the *systolic* blood pressure: *Systole* is the contraction and *diastole* is the relaxation phase of the activity of the heart.

The rate and stroke volume are determined by many different factors. The major ones are:

- *Metabolic demand.* The activity of the body influences the frequency and strength of the heart contractions.
- *Sympathetic acceleration.* Stimulation of the heart by the *sympathetic* branch of the autonomic nervous system increases rate and force of contraction, as does release of action hormones (adrenaline and noradrenaline) into the blood.
- *Vagal tone.* Heart rate and force of contraction are slowed under the influence of stimulation by the vagus nerve.
- *Aortic arch receptors.* The aortic arch, a segment of the aorta, the main artery that exits from the heart, contains *baroceptors*. These are cells that respond to the blood pressure, in this case, to the pressure in the left ventricle of the heart (outgoing). An increase in pressure above a certain threshold value causes reflex slowing of the heart, and corresponding drop in blood pressure.
- *Cardiovascular fitness and nutrition.* The health of the

heart muscle depends on regular exercise and the proper balance of nutrients and minerals, as well as the absence from the diet of vasoactive and vasopressor substances.

THE RELATIONSHIP BETWEEN BREATHING AND PULSE RATE

Pulse rate appears to be regular in most persons. That is, heartbeats appear to be more or less regularly spaced over a given time interval. Actually, in persons who are breathing normally, pulse rate rises with inspiration and drops with expiration.

Because it is relatively uncommon to observe this cycle in most persons, it is erroneously called "respiratory sinus arrhythmia" (RSA). It is in no sense of the word an indication of a disorder. In fact, it is most pronounced in children (before they learn to breathe with their chest), in athletes, and in persons who have learned slow, abdominal breathing.

It has been my common experience that my clients almost never show RSA before breathing retraining, and show a restoration subsequently. In fact, I use an RSA of 6 to 9 beats per minute as an indication of improvement.

BLOOD PRESSURE AND BLOOD FLOW THROUGH THE ARTERIES OF THE BODY

The pressure of blood escaping from the artery of a horse was first measured by Hale in 1732. He observed that the blood rose in a glass tube to a height of over 8 feet above the heart of the animal. We don't measure blood pressure quite that way anymore; we use an indirect method.

Blood pressure is ordinarily observed with a pressure cuff. The cuff is usually placed over your left biceps muscle, about two inches above your elbow. It is then inflated until the pressure stops the blood flowing in the *brachial* artery.

A stethoscope is then placed over that artery and air is slowly released from the cuff until a strong thumping sound is heard. This sound indicates restoration of blood flow through the artery. The pressure at which this sound is heard is the systolic blood pressure.

As air continues to escape from the cuff, the sound fades. The pressure at the point where it disappears indicates the diastolic pressure. Although there is some degree of normal variation in the average person at rest, systolic and diastolic pressure should be about 125/75 millimeters of mercury (mmHg), respectively, or as they say, "125 over 75."

Claude Bernard (1852) was the first to show that the diameter of arteries is strongly influenced by the autonomic nervous system. Subsequently we have learned that the medulla in the brain is largely responsible for transmission of nerve impulses to blood vessels. Messages from all parts of the body, but especially from the carotid sinus, aortic arch, and from the respiratory centers of the medulla itself, modify the circulatory system.

- *Vasoconstrictor nerves. Sympathetic* autonomic nervous system impulses cause constriction, or narrowing of arteries.
- *Vasodilator nerves.* Claude Bernard also showed that vasodilation can result from reducing impulses from vasoconstrictor nerves. He cut the *sympathetic* nerve

pathway in the neck of a rabbit and observed dilation of the blood vessel in the ear, on the same side.

- *Vasodilator reflexes.* A rise in pressure in the aortic arch or distention of the carotid sinus leads to vasodilation in skeletal muscles and internal organs.
- *Vasoconstrictor reflexes.* Any painful stimulus, or taking a deep breath, causes reflex vasoconstriction in the skin. A fall in pressure in the aorta, the artery leaving the heart, or in the carotid sinuses in the neck produces vasoconstriction.

THE RELATIONSHIP BETWEEN BLOOD PRESSURE AND BREATHING

When Hale first observed the blood pressure in the artery of a horse, he also noted that it rose and fell, apparently in synchrony with respiration. In persons breathing reasonably normally, blood pressure alternately rises and falls slightly with inspiration and expiration.

ARTERIAL DIAMETER AND THE AMOUNT OF CARBON DIOXIDE IN YOUR BLOOD

The activity of the brain center (the medulla) which controls the diameter of the arteries is affected by the quantity of carbon dioxide in circulating arterial blood. This quantity is affected directly by breathing.

ENLARGING AND NARROWING THE ARTERIES IN YOUR BRAIN

The control of the diameter of the arteries and arterioles in the brain is different from that in the body. In the body, diameter is under the control of the autonomic nervous system, as well as the quantity of carbon dioxide in circulating blood. But, in the brain, the diameter of the arteries forming the *vascular bed of the brain* is determined almost entirely by the amount of carbon dioxide in circulating blood. The autonomic nervous system has been shown to have no direct effect on the diameter of brain arteries and arterioles: *Sympathetic* autonomic nervous system stimulation does not cause dilation of brain arteries.

BREATHING, BLOOD PRESSURE, AND SYNCOPE (FAINTING)—THE VAPORS

When you hyperventilate, you may shortly feel dizzy and faint. If you keep this up, you may even pass out. Several mechanisms combine simultaneously to produce this effect.

First, loss of carbon dioxide results in constriction of brain arteries. The reduced blood flow causes a drop in oxygen delivery to the brain (at this point, your brain waves (EEG) may show the same general pattern as that found during a seizure). In addition, blood pressure may suddenly drop dramatically.

You may wonder why one would expect to see decreased blood pressure in hyperventilation when it has been repeatedly shown to be associated with high blood pressure!

The hyperventilation that is observed in chronic tension and anxiety is associated, in the long run, with high blood pressure, because that form of hyperventilation reflects the driving effects of *sympathetic* autonomic nervous system activity. But, when a person is breathing more or less normally, and is then instructed to breathe quickly (hyperpnea), as in the hyperventilation challenge, blood pressure is usually observed to drop markedly. As previously noted, the impairment in circulation may be sufficient to create a health risk.

THE EFFECT OF HYPERVENTILATION ON THE HEART: YOU MAKE MY HEART SKIP A BEAT!

A number of studies have documented the effect of hyperventilation on the heart. It was reported in 1978 in the *Journal of the American Medical Association* (*JAMA*) (vol. 240), that hyperventilation:

- reduces myocardial oxygen supply (the myocardium is the heart muscle proper);
- causes changes in activity of the heart observed in the electrocardiogram:
  - depression of the S-T segment (the S-T segment represents depolarization and repolarization of the ventricular musculature);
  - flattening and inversion of the T-wave (a T-wave less than 0.5 millimeters is considered evidence of heart disease);
- causes sinus tachycardia (an acceleration of impulses greater than 100 b/min. in a resting person)
- increases cardiac output (increased workload)

Impaired myocardial oxygen supply has also been cited in the medical journal *Circulation* (vol. 52, 1975).

We were alerted by Evans and Lum in 1981 in *Practical Cardiology* to different types of chest pain in hyperventilation. The journal *Chest* (vol. 68, 1975) described in detail the three major types of chest pain experienced by persons hyperventilating:

1. Sharp, fleeting, periodic, originating in the anterior left chest, radiating into the neck, left scapula (shoulder blade) and along the inferior rib margins. Intensity is increased by deep breathing, twisting and bending.
2. Persistent, localized aching discomfort, usually under the left breast (lasting for hours or even for days, not varying in intensity with activity or motion of chest wall). Chest wall is tender at the site of the pain (a local anesthetic provides relief).
3. Diffuse, dull, aching, heavy pressure sensation over the entire precordium or substernum which does not vary with respiration activity (may last for minutes or days and is often confused with angina). (p. 197)

The latter, angina and pseudoangina (Prinzmetal's variant form), have been reported by numerous clinicians in connection with hyperventilation. Some concluded that hyperventilation is a precipitating factor in all forms of angina and angina-like symptoms.

The mechanisms implicated in these symptoms are related to reduced blood flow to the heart tissues and low oxygen content of the blood.

In fact, Levine (1978), in *Postgraduate Medicine*, refers to cardiac manifestations of hyperventilation as "mimics of coronary heart disease."

Systematic investigation of the electrocardiogram in hyperventilation has revealed a number of common signs. But their significance is debated. It has been my experience that clients with "skipped beats" and other forms of trace abnormality have been told by their physician that these are essentially benign. Yet, there is evidence to the contrary.

Christensen, in "Studies on Hyperventilation: II. Electrocardiographic Changes in Normal Man During Voluntary Hyperventilation," in the *Journal of Clinical Investigation* (vol. 25, 1946), concludes that "These electrocardiographic changes are highly indicative of coronary insufficiency" (p. 884). In layman's terms, this means the heart is not getting enough oxygen.

Medical investigators reported in a journal of *The Himalayan Institute* (1979) (devoted to holistic health) the outcome of their study of the breathing patterns found in heart attack patients. They described these patterns for 153 persons in the critical care unit of a hospital in Minneapolis-St. Paul: The breathing patterns were found to consist of predominantly chest breathing in patients with myocardial infarction: 76% showed mouth breathing, compared to 71% in a control group.

THE BREATH CONNECTION

Disordered breathing, and especially hyperventilation, may increase pulse rate and blood pressure and the amount of work required of the heart.

Hyperventilation has been shown to contribute to angina and various forms of cardiac arrhythmia.

ILLUSTRATIVE CASE: V.S.

Mr. V.S. is a 32-year-old professional. He is married and has no children. Well above average in height and of athletic build, he came to see me because of "borderline" hypertension.

He reported mild tension associated with his work schedule, but otherwise appeared to be in good health.

His breathing rate was found to be 18 breaths per minute with low

CO_2 (3.92%). This is a hyperventilation pattern. It came as a surprise to him that he was breathing predominantly with his chest—he'd just never thought about it.

His blood pressure was initially 150/89 mmHg. He was taught deep diaphragmatic breathing and, within minutes, his breathing rate dropped to 4 1/2 b/min with normalized CO_2 (4.88%). At that point, his blood pressure was 137/89 mmHg.

After four once-per-week training sessions, his breathing dropped further to 3 b/min. during training, with normal CO_2 (4.98%), and his blood pressure went from 133/75 mmHg before the breathing exercise to 126/72 mmHg after it.

After the 4th session, there was no further need to see me and he terminated treatment.

ILLUSTRATIVE CASE: M.G.

Mr. M.G. is a 45-year-old contractor. He is married and has two children. He came to see me at the insistence of his psychotherapist because of his many "psychosomatic" symptoms.

M.G. is slightly above average in height, and well built. He was dressed in a business suit, entered my office briskly, spoke clearly and to the point. Although he gave no outward indication of it by his manner or posture, he reported chronic fatigue, tension, anxiety, a mild depression and, in general, stress.

His medical symptoms included "airborne" and food allergies, and "skipped" heartbeats which had been identified for him as ventricular premature contractions (VPC). A number of my clients have this condition, which is described to them by their physician as a "harmless" arrhythmia. But to panic sufferers, who feel the skipped beat, this is not reassuring at all.

At the initial evaluation, his breathing rate was found to be 12 b/min, and CO_2 elevated to 5.67%. I thought at the time that this was an inconsistent observation and made a point to make a note of it. If his CO_2 was that elevated, his breathing rate should have been elevated also as part of an accelerated metabolic reaction. CO_2 elevates only with normal breathing when the individual had previously low blood CO_2 due to hyperventilation.

Subsequently, it turned out that M.G. thought that he should slow down his breathing so that he would "look good on the test"! Inspection of the tracing shows quite clearly slow exhale with a rapid, gasplike inhale—not even a "normal" unnatural pattern.

The cardiogram showed irregular heart beats (VPCs).

M.G. has been in training now for 21 sessions. His breathing is under control, at about 3 to 4 b/min when he is doing slow abdominal breathing exercises. He is much improved and his anxiety and tension are greatly reduced.

The VPCs are essentially gone except on "very bad days." His allergies likewise are lessened following medical nutritional adjustment.

CHAPTER 8

Hyperventilation and Anxiety Disorders

INTRODUCTION

There have been many references in previous chapters to the role of breathing in mental, stress, and psychosomatic disorders. But the often-cited statement by Dulaurens

> Melancholoke folke are commonly given to sigh, because the minde being possessed with great varietie and store of foolish apparitions doth not remember or suffer the partie to be at leisure to breathe according to the necessitie of nature.

written in 1559, serves to remind us that the idea is not exactly new.

In more recent times, the 1930s especially, it began to pick up some momentum. Following the description by DaCosta of the effort syndrome, in the 1870s, through its evolution into "neurocirculatory asthenia," clinicians began to cite breathing disturbances as symptoms more frequently.

In 1935, Christies reported his use of a spirometer in the study of breathing patterns in persons with "neuroses." A spirometer measures the volume and pattern of air moving in and out of the lungs during respiration. The Latin word *spirare* means to breathe.

Christies concluded that there were certain distinct types of "respiratory neuroses," specifically, anxiety and hysteria. He felt that these were essentially respiratory in nature.

Think of it, neuroses brought about by breathing disturbances!

But even more remarkable was a series of studies conducted by Loeventhal, Lorenz, and colleagues, reported as early as 1918 (*Archives of Internal Medicine*, vol. 21), which showed that stimulating breathing could momentarily restore "sanity" in schizophrenic patients.

The study of breathing did not constitute a coherent discipline until 1951, when Clausen reported the following observations of breathing patterns in persons with psychological disorders of the neurotic (anxiety) type:

- inability to "catch one's breath or get enough air" (dyspnea)
- frequent sighing (sighing respiration)
- increased respiration rate (tachypnea or hyperpnea)
- irregularity of breathing (disturbance of inhalation-exhalation coordination)
- sharp transition between inhale and exhale
- prolonged inspiration and curtailed expiration
- principally thoracic respiration
- shallow respiration
- inspiratory shift of median position

Based on these observations, Clausen suggested that a number of technical measures of breathing, such as the inspiration/expiration (I/E) ratio, be used in the assessment of "neurosis" because:

- Neurotic women use a smaller part of the respiration cycle for inspiration than do neurotic men.
- Neurotic men have a significantly more rapid respiration than do normal men (16 vs. 11 breaths per minute).
- In neurotic men and women, a larger part of the respiration cycle is employed for expiration in abdominal than in thoracic breathing.

Finally, Clausen reported that normal men breathe more slowly than normal women, but that sex differences disappear in the breathing patterns of neurotic men and women. Other investigators, using somewhat different measures and criteria, arrived at similar conclusions, Finesinger (*American Journal of Psychiatry*, vol. 100, 1943) among them. He reports the highest abnormal spirogram scores for persons with anxiety.

What do these studies tell us? First, that there are objective, scientific measures of breathing. And second, that they can be used reliably to differentiate breathing patterns in persons suffering anxiety from those not so afflicted. Breathing pattern alone may be a reliable indication of anxiety level.

You might well say, "But breathing reflects *sympathetic* autonomic nervous system activity, doesn't it? Isn't that what you pointed out in Chapter 4?" And I would answer you this way: It isn't simply a matter of breathing rate— how quickly you breathe. It is a matter of other aspects of the pattern, including the relative duration of the inspiration and expiration, and so on.

Others have reported additional measures of breathing that show clearly that specific respiratory changes accompany emotions. The rate, or depth, of breathing increases; sighing increases mostly with anxiety but sometimes in anger or resentment; breathing rate decreases in tension or vigilance; and, breathing may become especially irregular when anger is suppressed.

Breathing changes in depression have been reported in the *British Journal of Psychiatry* (vol. 129, 1976): Breathing rate goes up and carbon dioxide goes down in neurotic depression. Although they don't actually say so, that is an indication of hyperventilation!

Similar findings have been published in connection with grief. Another study in that journal (vol. 119, 1971) compared breathlessness (dyspnea) in persons with obstructive airway disease and those suffering from depression.

Distinct differences between the way the two groups experienced their breathlessness were noted. In persons with depression, breathlessness occurred when they were at rest, with the main difficulty at inspiration:

> They experienced a persistent "heaviness" on the sternum, and their breathlessness fluctuated rapidly and was frequently associated with hyperventilation and sighing respiration. Depressive delusions of imminent death were present. . . . (p. 44)

Such symptoms were not experienced in the group of persons with airway obstruction. Their breathlessness occurred on exertion, with the principal difficulty on expiration. Hyperventilation occurred infrequently.

Thus, other factors equal, *physical breathing disorders may lead to some of the same symptoms as those experienced by persons with anxiety disorders!*

The "depressive delusion of imminent death" reported here and elsewhere in connection with depression has also been reported as the "fear of death" in hyperventilation.

In an article entitled "Psychogenic Hyperventilation and Death Anxiety," in *Psychosomatics* (vol.10, 1969), the authors contend that hyperventilation promotes phobic behavior. But more about phobias later.

ANXIETY AND HYPERVENTILATION

Anxiety states tend to be accompanied by the following breathing changes:

- Breathing becomes irregular (inspiration/expiration ratio shifts).
- Breathing becomes shallow (tidal volume decreases).
- Breathing rate increases (tachypnea).
- The amount of air flowing in and out of the lungs per minute (minute volume) increases.
- End-tidal carbon dioxide decreases (hypocapnia).

In short, hyperventilation.

Among the few exceptions to these changes are certain psychoses.

But which is the *cause*, and which the *effect*? Does anxiety come before hyperventilation, or the other way around? In matters of the body/mind issue, it is well to place the horse before Descartes (pun intended), because therapeutic efforts will depend on that alignment.

If you believe that anxiety causes hyperventilation, then you will treat anxiety to control hyperventilation. But if you think, as I do, that in most cases hyperventilation causes anxiety, then you will treat hyperventilation to control anxiety. Alternatively: Hyperventilation may be a symptom of anxiety. No treatment is therefore required because it will disappear if anxiety is successfully treated. But the overwhelming evidence is that this is seldom the case.

Persons who are anxiety-prone are hyperventilation-prone. This is a *trait* theory: A combination of things go together to form the way a person reacts to the world. Immunizing you psychologically against one should generalize to the other. No evidence to support this position.

You can decrease the likelihood of hyperventilating: Good nutrition, including proper balance of vitamins and minerals, is one way. And, it will also raise the threshold to anxiety reactions.

Can emotions induce hyperventilation? The *sympathetic* branch of the autonomic nervous system can cause hyperventilation at a time of emotion. That would not account for chronic hyperventilation, dyspnea, chest breathing, and sighing respiration.

Looking over all these different theories about hyperventilation and anxiety, I am led to the conclusion that, for the most part, persons with the chronic form of hyperventilation are biologically predisposed to anxiety.

Certainly chronic hyperventilators would not have found the effects pleasurable when they first tried it. They are quite unpleasant and include faintness, dizziness, tingling sensations, vertigo, etc. More likely, they acquired it as a dysponetic response. Dysponesis is a counterproductive pattern of muscle tension and adjustments, such as breath holding, pulling in the stomach, and any of the other efforts that are part of a misplaced coping process.

HOW DOES HYPERVENTILATION CAUSE PSYCHOLOGICAL PROBLEMS?

The psychological disorders that are associated with hyperventilation are due to an insufficiency of oxygen delivery to the brain. In other words, hyperventilation results in varying degrees of what physicians call hypoxia. Hypoxia is a decrease in tissue oxygen.

The anxiety "neuroses" may stem from the fact that the sufferer is experiencing varying degrees of slow and incomplete asphyxiation—a reduction of oxygen to the body and especially to the brain. This is like choking! How come?

Breathing serves at least two major purposes. First, it brings air into the lungs for transportation to the body tissues by the circulatory system. Second, it provides the major means for regulating the acid-base balance of the body. Because breathing is crucial to life, there are all sorts of mechanisms in the body that monitor it.

For instance, there are various specialized-cell mechanisms that are called chemoreceptors that send out information based on such conditions as the amount of oxygen and carbon dioxide in the blood. When these quantities deviate from a given level, automatic correcting actions are called into play. Let's look at some of these.

When you hyperventilate, the amount of carbon dioxide (CO_2) in your circulating blood drops sharply. Low CO_2 is called hypocapnia. Now take a look at the effect of hypocapnia on various tissue systems and organs.

THE EFFECT OF LOW BLOOD CO_2 ON BODY ARTERIES

When CO_2 decreases below normal levels, arteries in the body constrict. This results in reduced blood flow and reduced oxygen delivery to the extremities, i.e., hands and feet. Persons with chronic hyperventilation frequently report cold extremities.

THE EFFECT OF LOW BLOOD CO_2 ON BRAIN ARTERIES

When CO_2 decreases below normal, arteries in the brain constrict, reducing blood flow and therefore O_2 delivery to the brain. Persons who hyperventilate frequently report symptoms associated with low brain blood flow and low brain oxygen: These symptoms include dizziness, faintness, disorientation, vertigo, panic attacks, and such phobias as agoraphobia and "fear of death."

THE EFFECT OF LOW BLOOD CO_2 ON HEMOGLOBIN

Low CO_2 results in an increase in the alkalinity of the blood. This causes hemoglobin to favor retention of oxygen.

Imagine, by analogy, that the hemoglobin molecules are like little magnets. They have to be able to pick up oxygen in the lungs and drop it off in the body tissues. The "magnetism" of the hemoglobin is, within limits, proportional to the acidity of the blood. Within normal limits, a shift towards acidity favors O_2 release.

The red blood cells pick up oxygen in the lungs. But when they get into the tissues, where there is more carbon dioxide due to local metabolism, oxygen is released because the environment in the cells is more acid than the blood. In other words, the "magnetism" of the hemoglobin is slightly reduced.

But when CO_2 is lost in hyperventilation, and blood shifts to greater alkalinity, oxygen is more tightly bound to the hemoglobin in the red cells, and is not released in sufficient quantity. This may result in low tissue oxygen, unfavorable to physical and mental health and well-being.

THE EFFECT OF LOW BLOOD CO_2 ON MUSCLES AND NERVES

When blood CO_2 levels drop, and there is a slight shift towards alkalinity, there is an increase in the amount of calcium entering muscles and nerves. Excess calcium in muscles and nerves makes them hyperactive: They will contract more readily, more rapidly, more strongly, and for a greater duration than they normally would.

THE EFFECT OF LOW BLOOD CO_2 ON THE NERVOUS SYSTEM

Although there are exceptions to it, low CO_2 generally results in increased nervous system activity. This exaggeration of its typical function is usually attributed to increased nerve cell level of calcium.

You may recall from Chapter 3 that Kerr, Dalton, and Gliebe reported that their clients invariably had exaggerated reflexes. The increased calcium may also result in the heart muscle spasms we call angina.

The way that hyperventilation affects the body is poorly understood by many medical practitioners. But were they to understand it, it would be sufficient to explain many of the mental and mood disorders noted in connection with it as effects of low brain oxygen.

Every single one of the effects of low CO_2 that I am describing to you here is well documented in medical books, and is not controversial!

For instance, J.H. Comroe, M.D., professor of medical physiology, states in his book *Physiology of Respiration* (Yearbook Medical Publishers, 1984), in connection with hyperventilation:

Associated with moderate to severe alkalosis are a wide
variety of symptoms. Some are nonspecific, such as fatigue,
headache, irritability, inability to concentrate and lightheadedness. Others are highly characteristic of increased
excitability of nerve and muscle; these include numbness
and tingling of the hands, feet, mouth and tongue, stiffness, aches and cramps of muscles, actual spasms of hands
and feet (carpopedal spasm) and twitching and convulsions. (p. 258)

Comroe continues:

Hyperventilation is also known to decrease cerebral blood
flow because of the reduction in arterial PCO_2; the lightheadedness, convulsions and unconsciousness may be due
in part to cerebral ischemia. (p. 259).

In layman's terms: Hyperventilation reduces blood
flow to the brain because low blood carbon dioxide causes
constriction of the brain arteries. This constrictive reduction in blood flow is responsible for lightheadedness and,
in the extreme case, convulsions and unconsciousness.

Keep these symptoms in mind when we look, a little
later on in this chapter, at the criteria of the American
Psychiatric Association for diagnosing panic disorder.

THE PSYCHOLOGICAL SYMPTOMS OF
HYPERVENTILATION

Most mental health professionals, psychologists, psychiatrists, social workers, or others fail to recognize the
role of hyperventilation in psychological disorders. It is
really not their fault because there is much confusion
about its role in mental and mood problems.

Relaxation techniques used to counter anxiety and
phobic behavior are often claimed to focus on breathing

but in most cases this does not consist of much more than the instruction, "Now take a slow deep breath."

Many instructors are not adequately trained, and from what I have seen of these techniques, their implementation is often an excellent lesson in how to hyperventilate.

It is most commonly the case that hyperventilation goes unrecognized in the clinician's office, and the client's complaint of breathing difficulty, typical in anxiety and other emotional disorders, is often viewed as another one of the symptoms of the disorder rather than a possible *causal factor*.

Despite this lack of recognition by the majority of clinical practitioners, breathing complaints and hyperventilation have been recognized as contributing to psychological disorders for a good many years.

In 1921, for instance, Hofbauer classified hyperventilation under "hysteria" and "neurasthenia" in his book *Atmungs-Pathologie und Therapie* (J. Springer), and said of it, "Diese 'hysterische tachypnoe' ist seit langem bekannt"— "This hysterical tachypnea has been known for the longest time."

The translation of the title of his book is *Respiratory Pathology and Therapy*. In other words, Hofbauer recognized that there were breathing disorders that were of psychological origin.

Freud, that "astute observer," reported a case in the 1890s, in *Studies on Hysteria*, coauthored with Breuer.

A young woman with whom he became acquainted on a trip described attacks consisting of the experience of suffocation, giddiness, closing of the throat, a fear of impending death and other symptoms of the hyperventilation syndrome.

Naturally, he viewed these symptoms to be those of

an anxiety attack resulting from her conflict over an incestuous "approach!"

With a research and clinical history rich in reports of the relationship between breathing complaints and mental and mood disorders, it would be expected that psychology and psychiatry would have made great inroads into diagnosis and treatment. Well, let's take a look and see what these disciplines have to offer.

THE DSM-III

The DSM-III is the third revision of the *Diagnostic and Statistical Manual of the American Psychiatric Association*. It is the standard reference work for all mental health professionals, and the basis for diagnosis of emotional, character, mood, thought, developmental, psychophysiological, and substance abuse disorders. Third-party insurance reimbursement for treatment depends on its categories.

As Ed McMahon might say to Johnny Carson, in that well-known skit, "It's all there. In that book may be found *all* mental problems. . . . Everything you'd want to know about mental problems. . . ." Then Johnny does a slow turn, replying, "You're wrong, Rorschach Breath! There is *no* reference to hyperventilation in the DSM-III."

Neither are there index entries for terms commonly relating to breathing difficulties, such as dyspnea or sighing respiration. Yet "dyspnea" is the first symptom listed under "panic disorder":

1. Dyspnea
2. Palpitations
3. Chest pain or discomfort
4. Choking or smothering sensation

5. Dizziness, vertigo, or unsteady feeling
6. Feeling of unreality
7. Paresthesia (tingling in hands and feet)
8. Hot and cold flashes
9. Sweating
10. Faintness
11. Trembling and shaking
12. Fear of dying, going crazy, or doing something uncontrolled during an attack (p. 231)

These 12 items are the diagnostic criteria for panic disorder: and, none of them is absent from any standard list of hyperventilation symptoms.

Is hyperventilation syndrome synonymous with panic disorder? Clearly, it is possible to have other manifestations of hyperventilation. But in certain persons, the evidence strongly suggests that, for them, it manifests itself as panic disorder, often with agoraphobia.

This brings us back to the notion that psychosomatic disorders are determined by a combination of different factors. The same physical problems may have entirely different expressions in different persons. In one person, hyperventilation may jeopardize oxygen supply to the heart and s/he experiences angina; in another person, there may be artery spasms in the head, with consequent migraine. In yet another person, the symptoms are those of a mental disorder, anxiety and panic attacks, perhaps with phobias including fear of death, or perhaps depression.

Thus, much of the confusion and ambiguity about the role of breathing complaints and physical and mental disorders arises from (a) the diversity of conditions in which it is noted to be present, and (b) our unreasonable expectation that a given set of complaints is invariably the consequence of the same fixed set of bodily conditions.

For the physician trained in differential diagnosis, reason probably dictates that it cannot be the case that hyperventilation causes all these different conditions.

In fact, some authors have remarked about hyperventilation and death anxiety, that one of the problems that has obscured the early recognition of this syndrome lies in the fact that so many different names have been used to designate the chronic form: DaCosta's syndrome, effort syndrome, neurocirculatory asthenia, anxiety state with hyperventilation syndrome and cardiovascular neurosis.

This diagnostic problem was pointed out by Lazarus and Kostan (*Psychosomatics*, vol. 10, 1969):

> The classic textbooks of medicine are equally vague in their clinical descriptions. Although each case must be studied individually, we have found that when the therapist adopts a unified psychophysiological approach to the patient [as outlined above], it is only the exceptional case that does not fit into this description of the hyperventilation syndrome. We would recommend therefore that all of these other terms be dropped, at least until they can be more specifically defined. (p. 21)

Perhaps hyperventilation triggers panic attacks and phobias in panic sufferers in the same way that it will trigger migraine in migraine sufferers. Hyperventilation will not ordinarily trigger migraine in persons who are not subject to it. Other factors must predispose. But, it will cause spasms in arteries just the same.

THE PSYCHOLOGY OF PERSONS WITH BREATHING DISORDERS

I have encountered breathing disorders, dyspnea, or hyperventilation in virtually all of my clients. They seem to share certain common features, but they by no means constitute a distinct personality type. They experience anxiety and they appear to overreact—and they are well aware of that fact. That means that they are well aware of the exaggeration of their anxiety reaction to situations that they recognize might leave other persons undisturbed. Their physiological reactions to certain circumstances are just exaggerated.

Some medical researchers have postulated a type of "life-style" component that hyperventilating clients are alleged to have in common. Dr. Lum described it in these terms:

> The majority of patients studied have shown obsessional and perfectionistic characteristics; a personality type excessively vulnerable to the uncertainties and untidiness of life itself.

In other words, a neurotic person with coping difficulty. What else is new!

Dr. Lum continues:

> The quiet overconscientious secretary with the always tidy desk and immaculate typescript; the houseproud mother or the gifted wife, who finds her own creativity frustrated by the chores of home and motherhood; the executive subject to pressure from directors above and workers below.
>
> Dislike of delegation, difficulty in decision making, dislike of compromise. Frequently, hyperventilators, particularly men, are less tense at work and are most happy when driving themselves hard in their chosen career. It is not uncommon for them to get symptoms at weekends or on holidays and yet be asymptomatic at work. This fits well with the personality type familiar to cardiologists as most prone to cardiac infarction: the aggressive personality, with enhanced competitive drive, inability to relax, addicted to work and tension.
>
> Phobic traits, usually mild, are frequent, particularly claustrophobia.
>
> Hyperventilators, particularly women, are often quiet,

undemonstrative and adverse to the public display of emotions, masking their own anxieties with an outward sem-
blance of tranquility.

No doubt hyperventilators have anxiety in common, and I
have seen a number of these other traits, but not sufficiently often to consider them a hallmark.

HYPERVENTILATION AND PANIC ATTACKS

A British research team headed by D.M. Clark (*Biological Psychology*, vol. 16, 1983) recently reported that the
sensations in panic attacks are similar to those in hyperventilation. They concluded that, in some persons, stress
causes an increase in breathing which results in unpleasant sensations to which these individuals respond with
apprehension.

This position is held very firmly by many experts and
it is best illustrated by the title of the publication by G.A.
Hibbert, "Hyperventilation as a Cause of Panic Attacks"
(*British Medical Journal*, vol. 288, 1984). He contends that
panic of sudden onset may represent the physical form of
anxiety.

This physical predisposition to panic attacks in hyperventilators has been proposed on a number of occasions.
Persons without this predisposition will seldom experience panic attacks in the face of considerable anxiety.
What accounts for this predisposition?

One suggestion involves an intolerance to lowered
blood carbon dioxide and oxygen, because these shift your
metabolism towards its "anaerobic" form—a form not preferred by your body—a form in which there are increased
levels of lactic acid in your blood.

How would it feel to have this happen to you? Well,
breathing would be shallow and rapid and you would feel

out of breath, or unable to catch your breath; and, naturally, you would wonder why.

Your heart might pound in your chest. Are you having a heart attack? Will your heart suddenly stop? You feel very anxious. Your hands shake and you begin to sweat.

Then, you would feel strange, perhaps dizzy. Things around you may seem to be unreal. You may experience coldness and numbness or tingling in your hands and perhaps your toes; and muscle weakness, tremors, and twitches.

You may next figure that you must be "losing it," or that you may die. In any event, you are afraid to move about, even perhaps go outside, convinced that the effort will cause you, at the very least, to pass out. You call your doctor. . . an ambulance. . . . In short, you are experiencing a panic attack.

These are of course the symptoms listed in DSM-III in connection with panic disorder, and they are the very same symptoms that are present in hyperventilation.

There are a number of very provocative research reports that bolster the theory that metabolic changes resulting from hyperventilation lead to panic attacks.

The term "hypoxia" means lack of oxygen, and is usually applied to indicate a severe lack of oxygen. "Graded hypoxia" means hypoxia to a degree less than severe lack of oxygen. This designates a sort of chronic reduction in the amount of oxygen delivered to the brain and other body tissues.

Ordinarily, the body's metabolism is about 93% aerobic: oxygen combining with glucose to provide energy. In persons with chronic, rapid, shallow breathing, poor ventilation of the lungs will reduce body levels of oxygen. When available oxygen decreases, metabolism changes and there may be an increase, even a doubling, in the proportion of metabolism that is anaerobic. In anaerobic metabolism, the body burns substances other than glucose. This results in an increase in the body's production of lactic acid, especially in the brain.

An increase in lactic acid cannot be tolerated by the body, and so it seeks means to restore the acid-base balance. One such method is to increase breathing rate which, by dumping carbon dioxide from the blood, reduces its acid-forming potential.

Thus, if you are a chronic hyperventilator, predisposed to panic attacks, it is simply a matter of time before an acute episode of hyperventilation will be required to compensate the system. Anything that promotes that acute episode will trigger the panic attack as soon as brain levels of lactic acid reach a given level. Panic sufferers have been reported to be more sensitive to brain levels of lactic acid than non-panic sufferers.

Although the reason for the occurrence of panic attacks and agoraphobia is still a matter of debate, there appears to be little doubt that these are breathing related. And, it has been my experience that breathing retraining has helped many persons with such disorders to overcome them.

Numerous publications, including my own in the *Journal of Cognitive Psychotherapy* (vol. 3, 1989), and in *Biofeedback and Self-Regulation* (vol. 12, 1987), have shown the therapeutic effect of breathing training on panic attacks. There is also the *Lancet* (vol. 2, 1984) article on breathing training in agoraphobic patients.

FEAR OF FLYING—AEROPHOBIA

In a complex industrial and geographically decentralized society such as ours, business and professional success frequently depends on the ability to travel.

But have you ever noticed feeling inexplicably tired during, or sometimes after, such a trip? Did you yawn and sigh frequently during the flight? Did you suffer headaches? Did you find it difficult to concentrate on a work task? Was it hard to rise out of your seat, to move about the cabin? Were you surprised by sudden unexplained bouts of apprehension and anxiety, or even fear or panic?

Nothing beats travelling by commercial aircraft to get far, fast—unless you are among the many hapless persons who fear flying—who suffer aerophobia.

Fear of flying, or airplane phobia, is an unusually puzzling phenomenon. What is it the fear of? It is not the fear of airplanes, nor of heights. Neither do aerophobic persons particularly fear that they will die in a crash.

The phobia is more like airplane cabin-claustrophobia. What you may fear most is that the cabin door will close, and then you will have the overpowering urge to leave, and won't be able to do so.

Why should you dread not being able to leave the cabin? Could it be that there is something about the cabin that, perhaps unknowingly, makes you uncomfortable?

Acting on the belief that panic attacks are breathing-related, I set about determining what there might be about the aircraft passenger cabin that would affect breathing. Could it perhaps be the cabin altitude?

The possibility has been largely overlooked that in-flight panic attacks, and a phobic fear of flying, may be related to the way that some individuals react to reduced oxygen in the passenger cabin. Because it *is* reduced!

Cabin pressurization assures that the passenger cabin altitude, ranging between 5000 and 7000 ft, differs from the aircraft cruising altitude, which may range between 25,000 and 40,000 ft. in an average intercontinental passenger jet aircraft. But at 5000 to 7000 ft, reduced barometric pressure results in decreased blood oxygen in most persons who are not adapted to that altitude.

Reduced blood oxygen impairs mental function because, among other things, brain manufacture of chemical messengers is impaired.

Ordinarily, this reduced level of brain oxygen would be expected to have minimal effects. But in persons with a lowered threshold, or who are otherwise predisposed to anxiety and panic disorder, sensations that accompany reduced atmospheric oxygen pressure in the cabin, especially a rapid pulse, may well trigger symptoms.

Panic sufferers are very sensitive to chest and heart sensations.

The psychological consequences of low O_2 have been extensively studied by the military. They are impaired judgment, perception, short-term memory, and ability to carry out complex tasks as altitude increases above 4000 ft. Then, inappropriate behavior begins to emerge at about 8000 ft, and finally, consciousness is impaired.

The military might be expected to have a higher tolerance to the effects of altitude than civilian passengers!

On several recent flights, I used a portable *pulse oximeter* to test the theory that there is a significantly reduced oxygen level in the blood and that this might affect how one feels in an aircraft cabin, perhaps even leading to panic in those so predisposed.

I recorded numerous samples of my blood oxygen saturation, pulse rate, and blood pressure with a probe attached to my right index finger, on two round trips between New York and San Fransisco, and one between New York and Rykjavik, Iceland.

(a) in the (pressurized) aircraft cabin at 5000 ft. and 5600 ft, respectively; and

(b) during deep diaphragmatic breathing, at those altitudes; and

(c) at home, sitting in a comfortable chair, for comparison.

I should add that I am 53 years old, in reasonably good physical condition, and I sometimes (inexplicably) experience mild apprehension during flight. I certainly have no medical condition that would interfere with blood oxygenation. But I did perform this little experiment mindful of the fact that I have some experience with altitude-related hypoxia in an aircraft with an unpressurized cabin at altitudes reaching to over 13,500 ft.

And, since I am quite familiar with aerospace research, being coauthor of a chapter in the book *Physiology of Man in Space* (Academic Press, 1964), I am in a position to affirm that my reaction to cabin altitude is reasonably typical.

I discovered that my average arterial blood O_2 level dropped from my typical 96% to 90.5% (norms range between 95 and 98%), and my pulse rate went from my usual 72 to 96.5.

Astonished by a 6.0% decrease in blood O_2—hardly what I'd expected—I tried abdominal breathing by the same method described in Chapter 10 in this book. To my pleasant surprise, my blood O_2 rose to 95.2% within three breaths. And I immediately felt the difference too. But my pulse stayed in the 90s for some time.

Based on my experience, I would recommend to those of you who experience physical and/or psychological effects from the reduced aircraft cabin altitude, that you consider periodically doing deep diaphragmatic breathing, just a few breaths—three or four—so as not to tire your diaphragm.

This little experiment is entirely consistent with the idea that reduced oxygen is associated with apprehension, anxiety and, perhaps, phobia and panic attacks. It certainly seems to suggest a reason why one might fear not being able to exit a cabin in which one may experience the symptoms accompanying some lack of air.

THE BREATH CONNECTION

Psychological disorders associated with anxiety, including panic disorder, agoraphobia, and depression, are commonly observed in persons who hyperventilate. Because hyperventilation is associated with a reduction in brain blood flow and oxygen availability, it is thought that these conditions may well result from low brain oxygen.

Impaired breathing and hyperventilation, or an equivalent atmospheric reduction in available oxygen, may jeopardize the supply of oxygen to the body and the brain, leading to symptoms, as well as mental, mood, and affect disturbances.

ILLUSTRATIVE CASE: R.R.

Mr. R.R. is a 30-year-old divorced man. He is an insurance executive and devotes a considerable amount of his spare time to physical activity. Although he is shorter than average, he gives the indication of being "in good shape." In fact, his dedication to exercise is partly due to his recent realization that he has frequent episodes of breathlessness.

In addition, he reports many of the symptoms associated with hyperventilation: tension and anxiety, occasional dizziness, and an unsteady feeling, mild and unexplainable panic attacks, and a moderate chronic depression.

His medical complaints consist of low backache, gastritis, low blood sugar, chronic constipation, and coldness of the extremities.

A breathing tracing showed a respiration rate of 16 1/2 breaths per minute, with depressed CO_2 averaging 3.8%. His breathing showed a predominant chest mode. Since there was no report of chest pain, no EKG was done.

Breathing training was initiated immediately, and after a few minutes, he learned deep abdominal breathing. His breathing rate dropped to 4 1/2 b/min and CO_2 rose to 4.26%. Still a little low, but "getting there."

Over the next five sessions, he improved markedly and his symptoms began to decrease in frequency and severity. Before he had been instructed to do so, he reported that he had successfully aborted a number of anxiety and panic attacks by using the breathing technique that he had learned. He was, naturally, very pleased with himself for having thought of this on his own.

After the second session, he was referred to my physician colleague for nutritional counseling and his gastrointestinal and blood sugar problems cleared up as he was getting his anxiety under control.

He remained in training for 14 sessions, the last 10 on a once-every-two-weeks schedule, and treatment with his symptoms mostly under control.

ILLUSTRATIVE CASE: M.N.

Ms. M.N. is a successful artist at 24. Unmarried, she lives alone, but travels abroad frequently. She is above average in height and she is slim.

When she first came to see me, she entered my office energetically, and we shook hands briskly. She reported the following. She experienced tension and moderate anxiety. Her hands were typically uncommonly cold and that interfered with her work. Furthermore, she had been under treatment for some time for abdominal problems, including chronic diarrhea, and she seemed to be developing high blood pressure—all anxiety symptoms, she was told.

Her breathing was of the high chest, rapid (21/min) type, punctuated with sighs. Her CO_2 was not depressed—she was speeding along. Her blood pressure was 130/95—elevated—and at 83° F, in a warm room, her hands were decidedly cold.

Breathing training proceeded rapidly and uneventfully: within 20 minutes, her breathing rate dropped to 2 3/4 b/min, her CO_2 dropped to 4.95%, and her blood pressure to 112/83. Her hand temperature rose to 94° F. Not bad for 20 minutes' work.

Her colitis seemed to me to be somewhat atypical and I suspected lactose sensitivity, food allergy, or folate deficiency. I referred her to my medical colleague. My intuition was correct but my hypotheses were not. The clue was her frequent travels: She had abdominal parasites.

She progressed rapidly and was able to warm her hands reliably by 8 to 10° F in as little as 3 minutes, with abdominal breathing, in 8 sessions.

ILLUSTRATIVE CASE: F.C.

Ms. F.C. is a 30-year-old woman, married, with 3 children. She is, in the traditional sense of the word, a "housewife," bound by expectation to "serve" a tyrranical household in which everyone without exception appears to abuse her mentally and emotionally, and of course takes her for granted.

She was referred to me for stress and "burnout"—an entirely appropriate description of her condition—when she appeared in my office. She came in slowly, and stoop-shouldered. Her expression was sad and her posture suggested depression and lethargy. Her handshake was limp and her hands cold and sweaty.

She slumped into the chair to which I pointed and sighed. Her voice, as she answered my questions, was low, and her tale punctuated by more sighs and chest heaving.

She felt "a wreck," tense, nervous, apprehensive, and anxious. She couldn't catch her breath and felt much of the time as though she were choking. Her husband and children made continuous demands on her for the most menial chores and refused to lend a hand—even cleaning up after themselves. Her husband and one child were both verbally and sometimes physically abusive to her.

She experienced abdominal cramps and diarrhea, and was petrified when her heart "skipped a beat" (ventricular premature contraction), and thought that it was only a matter of time until she had a heart attack and died.

The approach to treatment was multifold. First, her abdominal distress followed a pattern not uncommon in folic acid deficiency. Second, her severe premenstrual syndrome (PMS) suggested vitamin B6 deficiency, as well as a nutritional imbalance involving at least her excessive consumption of sweets. In addition, she was tested for anemia and thyroid function. These tests proved negative. She was given a low sugar diet and prescribed vitamins by my physician colleague.

She came to my office once a week and learned deep abdominal/diaphragmatic breathing with "ocean imagery," muscle relaxation, assertion, and how and when to use each technique.

She learned breathing and relaxation and began to practice assertion and to use "coping self-statements," which are *rational*, positive arguments used to combat anxiety producing thoughts.

Gradually she learned to use breathing to ease her difficulty with self-assertion, and she began to report a lessening of the severity of her symptoms, except on the occasion of a specially "bad day."

As she began to experience reduction of her symptoms, and increased ability to use the breathing to calm herself, it was time for her to return to her primary therapist and resume work on straightening out her family interactions.

CHAPTER 9

Migraine, Epilepsy, and Raynaud's Disease

INTRODUCTION

It may seem curious to find migraine, epilepsy, and Raynaud's disease lumped together in a chapter in a book about breathing, stress, and psychosomatic disorders. Are these disorders psychosomatic? Breathing-related?

You know, of course, that migraine can be brought on by anxiety, tension, and stress. But epilepsy? "Everyone knows" that epilepsy is a brain disorder. Could it possibly be psychosomatic?

That depends. If "psychosomatic" means "caused" by emotional factors, then, no, it is not. But if we broaden the concept to include disorders "brought about," or triggered by such means, then, yes, it is.

Although medical specialists voice the distinction between migraine and epilepsy with confidence, that confidence may not be based in fact.

It is still a matter of conjecture that migraine and epilepsy are entirely different entities. I will make a strong case for the belief that epilepsy is just as much an arterial blood vessel problem as is migraine; and that the distinction between epilepsy and migraine boils down, practically, to *which arteries are affected*—inside, or outside the skull.

It should be noted that epilepsy-like brain waves are usually produced by the *hyperventilation challenge*. This means that there is a connection between hyperventilation and abnormal brain waves which is generally recognized in persons with seizure conditions—another good reason to avoid the procedure, in my opinion.

The *use* of hyperventilation to elicit abnormal brain wave patterns follows logically from the observation that they are invariably spontaneously produced that way. This was known to doctors at the turn of the century who discovered that a good way of finding out if you had epilepsy was to get you to "overbreathe" and produce a seizure!

From a clinical point of view, as well, it is helpful to consider migraine and epilepsy as being one and the same. As you will see, they both respond favorably to breathing training and nutritional management.

MIGRAINE

The history of migraine goes back several thousand years. Aretaeus (first century A.D.) is said to be the first to have singled it out. It was cited by Galen, who is credited with the original designation, "hemicrania," ultimately becoming "hemigraine," or pain of one side of the head; then "migraine."

A brief history of migraine research must mention Wepfer, who recognized the relationship between arterial pulsation, arterial dilation, and pain in the early 1700s.

Subsequently, Parry's compression test demonstrated that pressure on the carotid or temporal artery may relieve migraine, and gave impetus to the belief in the arterial "vascular" basis of migraine, i.e., constriction and dilation of arteries.

Gowers, a giant of 19th century neurology research, noted many similarities between migraine and seizure disorders, especially in regard to the role of hyperventilation; and assigned migraine to the "borderland of epilepsy," the title of his book published in 1907, by Churchill:

> Some surprise may be felt that migraine is given a place in the borderland of epilepsy, but the position is justified by many relations, and among them the facts that the two maladies are sometimes mistaken, and more often, their distinction is difficult. (p. 76)

Gowers noted "alternation" between the two and recognized "premonitory symptoms." But he notes "duration" of the attack as a major distinction. Seizures do not last as long as migraine. He reports arterial compression by ligature, tying a limb, to be successful in aborting seizures.

Virtually every major historic and literary figure has been alleged to have been a migraine sufferer. Included in this list, derived from numerous sources, are Napoleon Bonaparte, Lewis Carroll, Frederic Chopin, Sigmund Freud, Thomas Jefferson, Heinrich Himmler, Leo Tolstoy, and Virginia Woolf. According to one source, at least one in ten persons in the U.S. suffers migraine in one form or another.

Skulls of prehistoric peoples, with trephinations, or burrholes, have been found in Europe and in South America. These burrholes are usually thought to result from religious practices in which "evil spirits" are alleged to be released. It is to the credit of those who performed this "surgery" that those skulls show bone healing—the procedure was not, apparently, intended to be fatal.

If I am permitted speculation, it seems far more likely that these burrholes represent an early attempt to cure headaches, perhaps even migraine.

We tend to patronize cultures that we do not regard as being at least as "advanced" as ours, and attribute all of their rituals to "primitive" religious practice—usually animistic. I have never seen in print, as an alternative to mystical religion, what seems to me to be the obvious explanation for the meaning of the cave drawings found in southern France.

They show, if memory serves me, a bison, a hand with four fingers, a mastodon, and a hand with five fingers. Conlusion: winter basketball tournament, ca. 17,500 B.C.—"Bisons," 4, and "Mastodons," 5.

The winner and new champions! "Mastodons."

Fortunately this one was written on a cave wall. The others, written on trees, were washed away with the rains, or perished with the trees in natural or calamitous circumstances. The "Wolves" lost out in the semifinals. Too bad, they seemed to have had a really good shot at it.

WHAT IS MIGRAINE?

When one speaks about migraine, it is usually understood to mean headache. But, in fact, migraine may take different forms, and headache is only one of them.

Migraine may involve temporary:

- headache—unilateral or bilateral
- nausea/vomiting

- perceptual disturbances:
  - aura—disturbed consciousness/dizziness
  - visual—sensitivity to light, or scotoma: flashing lights or wavy lines
  - smell—hallucination
  - auditory—hallucination
  - sensory—tactual or other hallucination
- paralysis—usually unilateral
- speech impairment—slurring or aphasia

An excellent description of migraine is given by Dalessio, in *Wolff's Headaches*:

> The outstanding feature of the migraine syndrome is periodic headache, usually unilateral in onset, but which may become generalized. The headaches are associated with irritability and nausea, and often with photophobia [avoidance of light], vomiting, constipation, and diarrhea. Not infrequently, the attacks are ushered in by scotoma [a light spot, or scintillating flashes], hemianopia [loss of half the right or left visual field], unilateral paresthesia [sensations in body or limbs], and speech disorder. The pain is commonly limited to the head, but it may include the face and even the neck. . . . Other bodily accompaniments are abdominal distention, cold cyanosed [bluish] extremities, vertigo, tremors, pallor, dryness of the mouth, excessive sweating, and chilliness. (p. 56)

Some persons report feeling exceptionally well the day before an onset, even though changes in arteries may be already apparent then. Sometimes, changes in the nasal mucosal lining which shows a deep reddening may be especially noticeable.

The list of symptoms above is not exhaustive and it is assumed that your migraine has been diagnosed by a competent physician. Headaches are not invariably caused by migraine. According to Dalessio,

A patient with a migraine headache attack looks ill, and often very ill. His features imply dejection and suffering. He may be supporting his head with his hands pressed against the painful region, or against the corresponding side of his neck. His face is occasionally red, but usually it is pale, sallow, with the skin sweaty or greasy. Regardless of superficial color, the temporal, frontal, or suborbital vessels on the painful side appear distended and conspicuous. His extremities are usually cold, he complains of feeling chilly, he smells of stale sweat, and his breath is foul. The patient may be moaning, groaning, or tearful. He looks and acts as though prostrated and speaks slowly, without vigor. If ambulatory, he seems drooped, or lacking in the usual muscle tone. (p. 57)

Migraine may also be characterized by symptoms other than headache, such as recurrent nausea and abdominal cramps (abdominal migraine).

How can you determine if your abdominal cramps might be migraine? Fortunately, or unfortunately, migraine runs in families: If a parent or sibling has migraine in any form, then your symptoms may be suspected of being migraine as well.

WHO GETS MIGRAINE?

Rodolpho Low's excellent book *Migraine* (Henry Holt & Co., 1987) teaches us that:

- the onset of migraine occurs before the age of 10 years in one-third of all cases;
- 56% of migraine sufferers had their first episode by the age of 16 years; and
- the initial episode of migraine occurred before the age of 40 years in 90% of cases.

Dr. Low's book focuses principally on the role of low blood sugar (hypoglycemia) in migraine. Hypoglycemia is well known to precipitate headache and migraine, and has also often been implicated in promoting hyperventilation.

WHAT CAUSES MIGRAINE?

According to the *Merck Manual* (14th edition): "The cause is unknown, but evidence suggests a functional disturbance of cranial [head] circulation" (p. 1299).

Migraine is said to be a "vascular event." This means that migraine depends on disturbance of arterial blood vessels in the head or abdomen. The "event" is, first, constriction, and secondly, dilations of the vessels.

This fact is commonly accepted and standard medical treatments center on it. Thus, the action of ergot derivatives (ergotamine), powerful vasoconstrictors, meaning that they narrow the arteries, lends credence to the theory. Ergotamine reduces the distention in large arteries due to the action of the pulse pressure.

THE ROLE OF LOW BRAIN OXYGEN IN MIGRAINE

"Anoxia" means that there is no oxygen available to body tissue; "hypoxia" means that the supply is curtailed, though not cut off completely. In anoxia, death may follow rapidly. But in hypoxia, depending upon the degree of oxygen reduction, a number of changes in metabolism occur. None of them benefit you.

Many researchers have emphasized the role of low oxygen in migraine. In an article entitled, "Brain Hypoxia: The Turning-Point in the Genesis of the Migraine Attack?"

(*Cephalgia*, vol. 2, 1982), the author proposes that a brief episode of brain hypoxia occurs in *every* attack of migraine.

But these findings are also consistent with a little-discussed, but well–established fact, that the brain wave pattern (EEG) in migraine, almost identical to that in many of the epilepsies, has been strongly associated with hypoxia also: It typically shows abnormalities in the *theta* band of the EEG—between 4 and 7 cycles per second. This is the same pattern as in epilepsy and has led many epilepsy investigators, including the internationally renowned Canadian neurologist, Wilder Penfield, to conclude that hypoxia due to reduced blood flow was responsible for seizures.

The reduced blood flow was attributed by W. Lennox, a noted Harvard neurologist, to the vasoconstrictive effects of low blood carbon dioxide in hyperventilation!

For the most part, the brain wave pattern is directly related to the amount of carbon dioxide in the blood circulating in the brain. And, as the amount of carbon dioxide decreases by hyperventilation, blood flow to the brain is proportionately reduced. Then, the brain wave frequency drops from 12 cycles per second; alpha, the "relaxation brain wave," to 4 to 7 cycles per second, the "seizure brain wave."

These studies teach us that hyperventilation causes constriction of the arteries in the head, thereby reducing blood flow, and oxygen availability to the brain—the breath connection!

I have not seen a single migraine sufferer who did not show hyperventilation and the accompanying brain wave abnormalities. When a combination of breathing retraining and nutritional control reduced the incidence and severity of the migraine attacks, the brain waves always showed the corresponding change.

Such consistently observed low-oxygen-related brain wave patterns have been reported in 30 to 40% of migraine sufferers by a New York research group; and the high incidence of migraine in epileptic seizure sufferers and the comparably high incidence of seizures in migraine sufferers led one doctor to adopt the use of anticonvulsants in the treatment of migraine in children.

THE ROLE OF VASOACTIVE FOODSTUFFS IN MIGRAINE

Amines are proteins. They may be manufactured by the body or ingested in food substances. Those that the body cannot manufacture are called "essential amines." Some among these amines are said to be "vasopressor," and some, "vasoactive" amines.

Vasopressor amines are those that tend to promote increase in blood pressure. Vasoactive amines promote spasm in arteries—alternating constriction and dilation of arteries—as in angina, or migraine. Among these, dopamine, tryptophan and tyramine play a key role in migraine.

There are a number of mechanisms that are activated by these amines. Principal among these is *platelet aggregation*. Platelet aggregation means clumping of blood platelets and results from the release of a *platelet aggregating factor* (PAF) into the bloodstream.

It has been known since at least 1965 that, prior to a migraine attack, blood platelets release a "chemical messenger," serotonin. The *New York Times* reminded us of this breakthrough discovery as recently as October 1988.

Tryptophan, an amine commonly found in many foods, including milk, turkey, and avocado, is a serotonin building block. If you have been advised that supplemental tryptophan may help you to sleep, you should also be advised that it may trigger migraine.

Secondly, the release of serotonin into the blood is accompanied by the release of histamine. As we have seen, histamine is a vasoconstrictor. Thus, blood flow must be impaired to some degree in the face of constricted arteries and clumping blood platelets. This alone would account for some of the reported low brain oxygen level.

Release of platelet aggregating factor in the blood may be precipitated also by tyramine and increased levels of (b-adrenergic) action hormones. That is why your physician may be prescribing such *beta-blockers* as propranolol in the treatment of your migraine.

There are several ways in which you may increase blood levels of these amines and platelet aggregating factor: You can raise your stress level, releasing action hormones, histamine. Or, you can challenge your blood platelets by loading your bloodstream with tryptophan or tyramine.

If your migraine is stress- and nutrition-provoked, and not primarily psychological, you are going to have a hell of a time trying to figure out in therapy why you are "blocking," or hiding the "real reason" for the attack.

Bear in mind also that all of these factors are only operative in persons disposed to migraine—which runs in families. As one group of researchers pointed out, it has been shown that the platelets of migraine sufferers release their serotonin (5-HT) content more readily at all times in response to such agents as tyramine than do the platelets of non-migraine sufferers. A defect in platelet 5-HT uptake and accumulation in migraine sufferers has been reported, in medical research studies, as well as changes in the platelet membrane. Thus, a permanent difference actually exists in the platelets of migraine sufferers.

PROSTAGLANDINS

In 1982, the Nobel Prize in Physiology was awarded to Bergstrom, Samuelsson, and Vane for discoveries concerning prostaglandins. There are several different types of prostaglandins, and they derive their name from the fact that they are found in high concentration in seminal fluid, though they are also found elsewhere in the body. These hormone-like substances are formed from the oxygenation of arachidonic acid—a polyunsaturated fatty acid.

Prostaglandins are not stored in tissue in anticipation of need. They are synthesized within seconds, act in low concentration, and are rapidly destroyed. Prostaglandin E (PGE) is a vasodilator, while the F (PGF) form is vasoconstrictive.

Prostaglandins are of concern in migraine because (a), depending on the type, their release may cause arterial blood vessel vasodilation or constriction; (b) depending on the type, they may promote platelet aggregation; and (c) various food substances and drugs may promote or inhibit their formation.

It was Vane who discovered that aspirin acts by inhibiting the conversion of arachidonic acid to PGE and PGF; and Samuelsson, that an intermediary product of the oxygenation of arachidonic acid, thromboxane, is a potent stimulus for platelet aggregation, strongly implicated in migraine.

Some food substances, grapes, whole grain, for instance, are relatively high in salicylates like those in aspirin. These foods may interfere in the natural formation of protective prostaglandins and they have been shown to promote hyperactivity in children.

This was amply shown in Dr. B.F. Feingold's book, *Introduction to Clinical Allergy* (Charles C Thomas, 1973), which reported the beneficial effects of removing salicylates from the diet of hyperactive children. Excluded were all artificial colors and flavorings, all factory-made soft drinks, candies, cakes, puddings, ice cream, luncheon meats, margarine, many processed cheeses, and such foods as:

- grapes
- raisins
- cucumbers
- cherries
- apples
- apricots
- oranges
- nectarines
- peaches
- plums
- prunes
- tomatoes
- strawberries
- raspberries
- anything flavored with natural mint or wintergreen
- any aspirin-containing medication.

In connection with hyperactive children, the foods may be reintroduced after several weeks if there has been a period of improvement. But you may note that this is the same list of foods as that given in connection with migraine in Chapter 6.

Also implicated in migraine are the kinins. Kinins are powerful vasodilators. They are formed in the active secretion of sweat and saliva, increasing blood flow in body tissues. They are also formed in the skin when it is heated above a certain point, as when it is exposed to the sun. Bradykinin is also implicated in the pain associated with vasodilation.

THE EPILEPSIES

In this section, I am, as they say, "going out on a limb." I maintain that contrary to popular opinion, the epilepsies are not the results of disease of the nervous system. "What?" you say. "Seizures are not due to massive discharge of neurones in the brain?" Right. They are not *due* to it. I have some really convincing evidence to support this otherwise clearly lunatic statement.

While Director of the Rehabilitation Research Institute at the ICD-International Center for the Disabled, New York City, in the period 1980–83, I conducted research aimed at developing behavioral methods of epileptic seizure control.

Some promise had been shown by methods developed by M.B. Sterman in California, and J. Lubar in Tennessee, through "conditioned" brain waves.

After reviewing some 4000 medical research articles and books on epilepsy, I agreed with a minority of "epileptologists" that seizures are due to arterial blood vessel constriction and spasms, just like migraine. The brain electrical discharge observed in seizures, it seemed to me, was the *result* of the seizure, not its cause.

I confirmed, as did many others before me, that hyperventilation preceded each seizure, and devised a method for biofeedback-assisted breathing retraining to reduce the frequency and severity of seizures in persons whose condition did not respond satisfactorily to anticonvulsant medication.

The results of this work were published in 1984, under the title, "Behavioral Control of Intractable Idiopathic Seizures: I. Self-Regulation of End-Tidal Carbon Dioxide," in the journal *Psychosomatic Medicine* (vol. 46, 1984, pp. 315-31). Several other publications on the same topic followed.

There are an estimated 20 million persons in the U.S. who suffer seizures, and the number grows by about 100,000 per year. Most of these persons experience their first seizure at about the time that they should be entering the labor market—18 to 20 years of age. And, most employers have an almost phobic reaction to the word epilepsy.

WHAT IS EPILEPSY?

Epileptic seizures are classified by etiology [cause], manifestations [symptoms], or physiological correlates. Seizures of readily determinable organic origin, such as brain tumors, lesions, or posttrauma, are said to be "symptomatic." Those of unknown origin are called "idiopathic," and may take various forms: petit mal, grand mal, psychomotor, etc., varying in frequency and severity. We shall consider here only *idiopathic* seizures.

In antiquity, persons with epilepsy were either admired or reviled, praised or persecuted. Epilepsy, the "falling disease," the "sacred illness," was often attributed to demonic possession (hence the word "seizure") or to the winds (aura). It was described in detail by Hippocrates and Galen, and a number of references to it may be found in the New Testament (Mark 9.17).

Neurology views seizures as the result of brain cell dysfunction reaching a sort of *critical mass*:

> There seems no doubt, however, that whatever its immediate or remote cause, an epileptic attack is the manifestion of. . . abnormal electrical rhythms in some part of the brain

says one prominent neurologist, aptly named Lord Brain.

Despite the fact that there is no evidence to support it, "there seems no doubt" that seizures result from brain cells going haywire and producing weird patterns.

But we know better, don't we? Seizures are due to low blood oxygen. That's why brain nerve cells go bonkers—the breath connection!

Penfield, probably *the* most respected neurosurgeon in the world, an unquestioned authority on epilepsy, having pioneered its surgical treatment, wrote in *Epilepsy and the Functional Anatomy of the Brain* (Little, Brown, 1954):

> The mechanism whereby hyperventilation elicits changes in the EEG and seizures in epileptic patients is still unknown. It may act by causing a partial ischemia [reduction in blood flow] due to cerebral vasoconstriction, and there may be some increase in excitability accompanying the *lowered CO_2 concentration*. (p. 495, my italics)

And there you have it again, the breath connection. Hyperventilation reduces blood levels of CO_2, causing brain arteries to constrict, and limiting O_2 availablity to brain cells. No wonder they rebel!

Neurologists, who believe the brain-cells-gone-bonkers theory, might have done well to listen to Hans Berger, who discovered brain waves in 1929. He thought that they might come from the arteries in the brain!

Penfield actually observed arteries constricting just before a seizure, during spontaneously occurring hyperventilation in a patient on whom he was operating. But two scientists, Darrow and Graf, observed it earlier in mechanically hyperventilated cats. They must have been astonished by the appearance of the constricting brain blood vessels because they referred to them as having the appearance of "sausage links."

This is an uncommonly graphic description. Penfield referred to "blanching" as the blood drained from the area served by the pulsating, constricting artery.

And so it goes. But why do some persons get seizures and others do not? Why does migraine seem to occur more frequently in persons with seizures, but seizures not as frequently in persons who suffer migraine?

If there is predisposition, what is predisposed? And,

if breathing is involved, why do some persons have the tendency to breathing-related seizures, while others do not? What can we learn from Raynaud's disease?

RAYNAUD'S DISEASE

The coldness and spasms in fingers and toes, first described by Raynaud in 1862, was thought by him to be due to "anxiety neurosis."

The *Lancet* featured an article in 1983 (vol. 2), by Lafferty and colleagues, entitled "On the Nature of Raynaud's Phenomenon: The Role of Histamine." The article also mentions the challenge of the "anxiety neurosis" assumption, by Lewis in 1929, who attributed the spasms to "local fault," meaning some anatomical weakness. The Lafferty group ends the first paragraph thus:

> The exact [reasons] for the condition remains unknown to this day, and although various [blood] and [hormones] have been implicated, no new work has emerged which is likely to overthrow Raynaud's or Lewis' original theories. (p. 313)

What does all this mean? Deutsch et al., in the *Journal of Laboratory and Clinical Medicine* (vol. 26, 1941), reported abnormality in the anatomy of the capillaries in Raynaud's sufferers, and improvement in blood flow with surgical destruction of their *sympathetic* autonomic nerves. This supports Lewis.

In 1946, Hauptmann, at Tufts Medical College, reported finding abnormal capillaries in the fingernail-fold in patients with "neurosis," epilepsy, and migraine.

Now, about predisposition: 88% of "constitutionally neurotic" [chronic anxiety] patients, according to Hauptmann, showed the same capillary abnormality as those with the epilepsy and/or migraine. But only 4% of those who merely had "neurotic reactions" did. The abnormal capillary picture was the same in persons with epilepsy or migraine.

If these studies accurately depict abnormal capillaries that restrict blood flow to various parts of the body in persons with Raynaud's, migraine, or seizures, then that would certainly qualify as "predisposing." And one would have to conclude that histamine (Lafferty et al.) is only an aggravating factor, not a cause.

Hauptmann, meanwhile, also found abnormal capillaries in schizophrenics. In that connection, here is a most amazing study:

In 1918, an article appeared in *Archives of Internal Medicine* (vol. 21). The title of the article is "Stimulation of the Respiration by Sodium Cyanid (sic) and Its Clinical Application."

Pretty straightforward: An early study of breathing in which cyanide was employed, because at the specified sublethal dosage, it actually stimulates breathing.

The investigators injected minute, clearly sublethal doses of sodium cyanide into several "mental" patients. They apparently wished to establish that cyanide, which was a regular part of some then-popular cough mixtures, had been unfairly criticized and thought to be useless.

They established that at the indicated dosage, sodium cyanide is a reliable stimulant, permitting fairly exact control of breathing. In addition to observing the predictable reactions in their patients, whose complaints ranged between various forms of schizophrenia, especially the catatonic, they report that "we have seen. . . a marked improvement in the general condition in many cases." But much more startling is the following revelation:

Evidence of stimulation of the cerebrum [brain] as a whole, especially the psychic centers, was obtained in a number of cases. Thus, several patients who had had eyes closed for a long time, opened their eyes and looked about. In two instances, they yawned quite naturally as though they were awakening from a long sleep. *The most interesting instance of psychic stimulation was observed in case 10. This patient, who had dementia praecox [schizophrenia], entered the hospital June 27, 1917, and up to the time of the injection had not spoken a word, so that no history was obtainable except from the meager statement on his commitment papers. After receiving an injection of 102 cc of fiftieth-normal sodium cyanid within a period of sixty-four minutes, the patient conversed, answered questions and attempted to explain his prolonged silence.* (p. 128)

The italics are mine—and talk about a breath connection!

Unfortunately the patient relapsed after the injection wore off. But think of it: There is sanity hidden beneath the madness. A number of prominent researchers believe that this study gave impetus to the search for a pharmacological means for treating psychosis.

It escaped the attention of psychology and psychiatry that madness may have a physical basis. Could psychosis be related to low brain oxygen? Why not? It has been shown that low brain oxygen interferes with the production of the chemical messengers we call "neurotransmitters," which are crucial to proper mental functioning: exactly the sorts of chemical brain deficits for which people are prescribed various drugs, today.

CONTROLLING MIGRAINE, RAYNAUD'S AND IDIOPATHIC SEIZURES

Let's see if you can "date" this quotation:

The fact is that within a few years every physician who will be expected to be in the race for practice will have to be versed in psychology. He will have to know much concerning the power of thought over organ and functions, and recognize the stupendous fact that within man resides the greatest curative principle, and that it may be directed by the will. (p. 144)

Well, let's see. Could it be ca. 1940, someone addressing the need of psychiatry to focus on the power of the mind in psychosomatic disorders? How about a more recent admonition, let us say 1970, to practitioners to consider a behavioral medicine approach to bolstering the immune system in cancer therapy?

Wrong on both counts! This was written by A.B. Olston who wrote *Mind Power and Privileges* in 1902. And he was addressing *all* physicians.

What makes this book especially interesting is that it is written in the context of "self-hypnosis," but not in the mode of Emile Coué. It was Coué who, you may know, recommended that we tell ourselves, "Tous les jours, à tous points de vue, je vais de mieux en mieux." [Translation: Every day, in every way, I get better and better.]

What Olston was suggesting was that we use mind power to control our vascular system, in order to improve blood circulation:

> We see many instances in which the reflex operations have usurped the office of the will or objective mind, and play all kinds of antics with organs and members. How helpless is that one who thinks and believes that the lower centres are entirely independent of the will. He believes that he must stand aside and watch the caprices of his nerves and trust to their adjustment, and hope that chance will in some way bring the change for the better, or give up in despair and resign himself to his fate. This is only natural from the premise that the will has little or no power over the automatic activities of the system. But incorporate the premise that it *is* the privilege and prerogative of the will to control those activities, and a control will be consummated that is impossible under the negative premise. We need not go

outside the common experiences and observations to find valid evidence of the required and desired facts. We have already spoken of the flushing or pallor of the face caused by an emotion. An emotion is nothing but a thought—a mental process. *If a thought in one way may control the vaso-constriction or dilation of the arteries, it should naturally be expected that a mental process intentionally directed would also be able to do the same.* (p. 147) [These italics are mine.]

Naturally!

And, we now have many more "self-regulation" methods by which we can accomplish these feats, including various conditioning therapies and biofeedback, which have proven helpful in controlling migraine, seizures, and Raynaud's.

WHAT HAND WARMING TECHNIQUES USED IN MIGRAINE AND RAYNAUD'S DISEASE TEACH US ABOUT THE BREATH CONNECTION

Olston tells that he has

. . .a friend who can, by attention, rush the blood to his feet and warm them when they are cold. This is simply a matter of training. The subjective mind has power to dilate the arteries to any part, or to contract them. The success of such efforts depends simply upon the obedience of the subjective mind. That obedience to subjective instruction is acquired by training. (p. 149)

No behavioral scientist today would find that statement particularly surprising, but it must have been sensational, perhaps smacking of the supernatural, in 1902.

In fact, it is this ability—"self-hypnosis"—that led J.H. Schultz (with W. Luthe) to develop *Autogenic Training* (Grune & Stratton, 1959). Autogenic training, a set of postures and relaxation exercises, aims at reducing muscle tension and developing control over the autonomic nervous system. It should not surprise you to hear that most people spontaneously notice a decrease in breathing depth and rate when doing these exercises.

Nor would Olston's report be astonishing to the many thousands of persons who have done "hand warming" by biofeedback as part of the treatment of migraine and Raynaud's. In other words, the self-regulation of blood flow through the extremities has been shown to be a readily learnable task.

There are, as is usual, and perhaps deservedly so, numerous research articles that question this and that methodological procedure; and this and that conclusion; and assert that failure to control this and that creates "artifacts" that make the final scientific interpretation, as stated, doubtful.

Bah! Humbug.

But these arguments in connection with thermal self-regulation of hand temperature by biofeedback do not center on its *effectiveness* in helping persons suffering from migraine and Raynaud's disease. They question whether such factors as placebo, relaxation, expectation, etc., play a determinable role.

What's the point to this, you may ask. Well, we're talking about arteries and blood flow, and delivering oxygen to the brain and other body tissues. Hand warming is supposed to tell us that blood circulates better through the hand. So the hand becomes a way of gauging what's going on in the body, especially the hands and feet.

Of course, we have scientific evidence that shows that this is due to dilation of the arteries, supporting the conclusion that there is now a reduction of nervous activity, reduced blood level of the stress hormones, etc. You see, it all ties in to reducing anxiety.

How do you learn hand warming? Each clinician has a preferred routine. Generally it boils down to trial and error: A temperature sensor is taped to the fleshy part of a fingertip—the right index finger, let us say. It is connected to an electronic device with a readout display of some sort—some are like meters, others are digital—showing numbers. The whole thing acts as a very sensitive thermometer.

By trial and error, you can learn to increase fingertip temperature, getting biofeedback from the readout display. But *savvy* clinicians may teach their clients various relaxation methods which are then included in the trial-and-error activity.

There is an explanation for why all this works. In Raynaud's, dilating arteries makes sense, since Raynaud's appears to be the result of blood vessel constriction on top of "local fault."

In the case of migraine, we also assume artery and capillary narrowing, but we perhaps undeservedly place a greater emphasis on dietary factors.

As someone once pointed out, "If all you have is a hammer, you tend to treat everything as though it were a nail." Thus, the thermometer, electronic or otherwise, has become our hammer in self-regulation by biofeedback.

But the first thing that struck me, when I was trying brain wave conditioning to control epilepsy at the ICD-International Center for the Disabled in New York, some years ago, was the connection between conditioning and breathing.

Psychologists in California reported on the reduction of seizures by the enhancement of a particular brain wave which they named the "sensory motor rhythm" (SMR).

Further work on animals (cats) resulted in the observation that this rhythm—SMR—was observed when the cats seemed to be regulating their pattern of respiration during brain wave conditioning.

I thought that curious—reducing seizure occurs in the presence of a brain wave associated with regulation of breathing. Well, hadn't all the research in the 1930s and '40s, by Lennox, Lennox, Gibbs, and Gibbs, at Harvard, shown that deregulation of the brain followed deregulation of breathing? And, could it be that the brain wave being observed in these more recent studies was simply that which accompanied regulated breathing—which, of course, reduces seizure activity?

Right or wrong, this reasoning led me to look at breathing during that type of conditioning. It came as no surprise to me that the seizure reducing brain wave occurred when there was a notable decrease in blood level of carbon dioxide. Just as had been shown in the late 1930s and early '40s!

Continuing along this line of reasoning, I then decided to focus on biofeedback to teach the clients abdominal breathing which normalizes blood levels of carbon dioxide. It worked quite nicely.

Now, normal levels of carbon dioxide, restored by the breathing biofeedback method I had developed, were also going to other parts of the body—not just the brain. And, since normalizing carbon dioxide in circulating blood results in dilation and restoration of blood flow, there should be a change in fingertip temperature corresponding to a decrease in the brain wave seizure pattern. And guess what? Right on the money, as they say. In as little as three or four breaths!

Naturally, I published these findings as quickly as I could. . . they sank out of sight without making a ripple!

So I decided to write this book, in part, to tell you that deep abdominal/diaphragmatic breathing helps you to relax and increase your fingertip temperature and that is a good thing to do if you have a psychosomatic or stress-related disorder, especially migraine, Raynaud's, or epilepsy. *You can do it faster and more reliably by learning deep abdominal (diaphragmatic) breathing than by thermal biofeedback!*

THE BREATH CONNECTION

Although they are entirely different clinical entities, migraine, Raynaud's disease, and epilepsy appear to share certain common characteristics. They appear to run in families, and to be related to the reaction of the arteries to low tissue oxygen.

Migraine, Raynaud's, and epilepsy appear to be dependent on anatomical predisposition. But other factors may lower the threshold to attacks, including the apparently additive effects of low blood carbon dioxide and oxygen, and foodstuffs which can cut blood flow to brain and body tissues.

These conditions are frequently seen in hyperventilation, and they respond well to behavioral strategies that include diaphragmatic breathing training.

ILLUSTRATIVE CASE: T.R.

Ms. T.R. is a 35-year-old New York City social science teacher. She is unmarried, but has been in a long-term exclusive relationship with the man with whom she is presently living.

She is of average height, but slightly overweight. And, she reports herself to be in very poor physical and emotional shape. During the initial interview, her handshake was limp and her hands ice-cold. She was stooped and gave the impression that she was depressed and that walking itself was an enormous effort. She spoke softly.

As her story unfolded, she stopped several times and sighed deeply. On two occasions, she burst into tears spontaneously. She reported feeling depressed, anxious, and suffering from chronic tiredness, and relatively frequent panic attacks. She expressed hopelessness.

Her physical symptoms included migraine, "psychosomatic pain" (pain of the whole body), TMJ, bouts of EB virus (mononucleosis), frequent hives, frequent thirst, documented hypoglycemia, hay fever and other allergies, muscle spasms, vertigo, periodic involuntary anorexia and weight loss, and inability to swallow food or water. She also indicated that she had had petit mal seizures as a child.

During the initial evaluation, she showed signs of extreme anxiety: Her hand temperature was 78°F in a room at 77°F—one degree above room temperature—in a warm room! Her scalp temperature was 91.5°F.

This discrepancy suggests serious constriction of blood vessels in her hands—Raynaud's. Her breathing rate was 15 b/min with deep chest breaths, and CO_2 elevated to 5.9%, suggesting she was "flying."

Because of the suggestion of elevated metabolism, and the all-over pain, I first suspected a thyroid condition; but because she reported having had petit mal seizures as a child, I thought it equally possible that she was having seizures. Severe and unyielding depression—even suicidal—and panic attacks are well documented in temporal lobe epilepsy. And, if the latter were the case, quite possibly the pain is hallucinated.

For this reason, it was decided to do a simultaneous right and left brain wave analysis: It showed diffuse epileptiform waves on both sides, more on the left side.

A breathing maneuver was employed to see whether she had good control of her diaphragm and if her hand temperature would improve and her EEG would normalize. She was taught abdominal breathing, and the tracing shows a peculiar kind of expiratory spasm on inhale. I had, up to that point, never seen anything quite like this and was at a loss to explain it to her. It seemed almost like small spasms of the diaphragm, or chest muscles—a saw-tooth inspiration pattern.

I have since learned that this breathing pattern is called "diaphragmatic flutter," and is reported by J.B. Harris et al. (*Psychosomatic Medicine*, 1954, 16:54-66) to be a manifestation of "hysteria," and in some instances to be responsible for angina-like chest pain.

She showed some apprehension about relaxing, but by the second session, she breathed abdominally at 3 b/min, with CO_2 at 4.76%. Quite normal.

With continued breathing training, her brain waves showed normalization, although there was still some activity on the right side.

These are all signs of relaxation and normalizing metabolism.

She continued breathing training for several sessions more and derived a measurable degree of relief from it. But her many underlying medical conditions were seen to require more aggressive intervention and she was placed in the care of a physician.

ILLUSTRATIVE CASE: B.G.

Ms. B.G. is a 72-year-old widow. She is retired from secretarial office work and lives alone. She is average in stature but somewhat overweight. She entered my office briskly and energetically and reported that she wished to learn abdominal breathing because she had heard that it might help her to control her blood pressure and her frequent migraine headaches.

She reported frequent transient moderate depression, arthritis, chronic gastritis, and rheumatic pain, in addition to her elevated blood pressure and headaches.

Although her dietary habits were good, she reported a craving for sweets, especially sugar.

At the initial evaluation, her breathing rate was found to be 15 BPM, with low CO_2 (3.68%). Although a breathing rate of 15 b/min is not notably elevated for a person of her age and physical condition, the CO_2 of 3.68% is much lower than one might expect, and arouses suspicion of a low metabolic rate due, perhaps, to a thyroid condition. Headaches are, parenthetically, a common accompaniment of thyroid conditions.

Her blood pressure was 147/83. That is somewhat elevated—she was on antihypertensive medication. During the initial breathing training, she showed remarkably good diaphragm and abdominal muscle control and training progressed rapidly.

At the end of the first training session, her breathing rate was 4.5 b/min, CO_2 at 3.88%. Her blood pressure dropped to 131/77.

She continues periodic training.

CHAPTER 10

How to Integrate Breathing and Nutrition to Control Stress and Psychosomatic Disorders

INTRODUCTION

You have been very patient. You've slogged through nine chapters of sometimes difficult to understand explanations of the role of breathing in many types of stress and psychosomatic disorders. You can be proud of your stamina.

In the previous chapters, I have detailed for you some of the ways that medical science now views the role of predisposition to stress, anxiety and psychosomatic disorders. I have also illustrated for you some of the ways that anxiety may become habitual, resulting in inappropriate or stereotyped tension patterns.

But the physical adjustments of the body during stress and anxiety are, usually, the best way the body has for reacting to threatening situations.

Some of these threats are abstract—fears that come from functioning in a complex social and technological/industrial society. There may be financial worries, social phobias, fear of computers, or any other modern concerns. Repeated anxiety is costly to the body's energy economy:

• You are sitting at the speaker's table and your turn to address the symposium attendees is coming up. You are well rehearsed, yet you fear that you will not remember what you have prepared. Your throat is drying up and you tense as anxiety and apprehension are mounting to almost unbearable levels. Your hands grow cold and begin to sweat and your breath is short and rapid—you can't focus on the group before you—everything is a blur. It is becoming increasingly clear to you that you are bound to stumble and make a complete fool of yourself. . . .

• You are buckling your safety belt. Although some individuals are still putting luggage in the overhead bins, the door of the passenger cabin has closed and the flight attendants are preparing for departure. An overwhelming foreboding of doom is beginning to seep into every fiber of your body. Your throat clamps up and you can't catch your breath. You grasp the armrests in an effort to hang onto something. You feel as though your skin is separating from your body. You feel faint. It is becoming increasingly clear to you that you simply have to escape from this situation because if you do not crash on take-off, you will surely die of a heart attack or stroke caused by the anxiety. Or so the sensations in your chest seem to indicate. You are losing control. . . .

• You are sitting at home, staring into your coffee. You must go to the office. Inexplicably, of late, you feel apprehension, leading to terror, at the prospect of leaving your home. You know that as soon as you even begin to think of going outside, you begin to hyperventilate and feel faint. The sensations in your chest, rapid pounding, suggest a heart attack. And you know that, at the very least, you will not be on the street long before you lose control and pass out. . . .

Very typical and costly situations.

That cost may be one or more stress-related or psychosomatic disorders because you are biologically prepared to ward off all sorts of momentary dangers but you are not prepared to do so on a continuing basis. Danger-coping mechanisms require resources, nutrients, vitamins and minerals, enzymes, neurotransmitters, manufactured as needed or stored in the body, to be expended in relatively enormous quantities—sometimes far greater than the body can afford to sustain indefinitely. This expenditure results in a deficit which, in the long run, may be a major contribution to the disorders that are the central concern of this book.

A case in point: Most persons think that vitamin C deficiency leading to scurvy was predominantly a disease of sailors who, by virtue of long sea voyages, were deprived of nutritional sources of this vitamin. Even your physican was taught this myth.

> Scurvy was at one time a common disorder in seamen on long voyages and many died until it was discovered that it could be prevented and cured by eating fresh fruit or vegetables. The antiscorbutic vitamin ascorbic acid was isolated in 1928 and synthesized in 1933. (p. 247)

This passage, taken from Bell et al., *Textbook of Physiology and Biochemistry* (E & S Livingston, 7th ed., 1968), one of the most respected and widely used medical physiology textbooks, almost certainly studied by your physician in his/her training, is completely misleading.

In fact, though it was indeed a naval physician, James Lind (1716–94), who correctly noted that citrus fruit interfered with its natural course, scurvy was *widespread* (vitamin C was not to be identified for several hundred years).

Up to Lind's time, physicians were at a loss to control what is now generally recognized to have been the *most prominent contribution to mortality rate.* Britain's King Henry VIII is thought to have been a scurvy sufferer. His physical symptoms, swings in judgment and moods, and the propensity of the nobility to avoid consuming vegetables, fit the pattern. But infants were especially vulnerable. Inadequate resistance to infection due to vitamin C deficiency led many to be born "scorbutic."

Lind reported in 1753 in *A Treatise of the Scurvy* (Kincaid & Donaldson) that an orange or lemon consumed daily would *retard the onset of terminal symptoms.* He did not, of course, report that it "cured" scurvy.

It doesn't. In fact, by the time sailors were treated, scurvy was so advanced that nothing could "cure" them and it was invariably fatal—oranges and lemons not withstanding. They would have fared better had they eaten the food of the native peoples with whom they came in contact. Eskimos don't eat lemons and they don't suffer from scurvy.

And of course, it was several centuries before it became known that one could get vitamin C in vegetables. So much for factually accurate medical education.

There are only about 30 or so mg of vitamin C in the average citrus fruit, and that is less than the RDA (recommended daily allowance)! So you can readily see that the nutrition on which you rely to fuel your daily emergencies may be inadequate to the task. Why do you think they sell vitamin C enriched orange juice?

I mention these matters to you because I know that you sincerely believe that you've "taken care" of all the things that should assure your mental and physical health. And, as Molly Goldberg would have put it, "So what's to worry? Here, Jake. Eat some more potatoes. A little schmalz on it. . . some sour cream. It wouldn't hurt!"*

*Thank you, HAL!

Vitamin C loss is not the only factor that has been shown to jeopardize health. Insufficiency of niacin, a vitamin, causes pellagra, which in its early stages includes the following "psychosomatic" mental symptoms: vague headache, irritability, restlessness, apprehension, and, ah! yes, forgetfulness.

Do you have these symptoms, in addition to orgasmic difficulty? Niacin is given to horses to restore orgasm.

Insufficiency of folic acid has been implicated in "psychosomatic" gastrointestinal disorders and, of course, in anemia. And, stress also results in the rapid loss of calcium and potassium. Potassium loss may lead to hypertension and cardiac arrhythmias, or to malabsorption syndrome, both commonly reported by psychosomatic or stress-related disorders sufferers. Anemia has been shown to lead to hyperventilation.

Unusual diets and eating disorders such as anorexia and bulimia often result in nutrient and mineral deficiencies, and jeopardize the body's acid-base balance through "electrolyte" loss.

Thyroid problems figure for their share of symptoms: in mild cases of hypothyroidism, the psychiatric symptoms are typically present before the physical signs appear. In more severe cases, it may lead to myxedema "madness," whose symptoms include disorientation, impaired memory, confusion, and depression.

You will notice that initially, it is always the ubiquitous set of "neurotic," "psychosomatic," or "stress-related" disorders, with a vague suspicion of malingering, attention-seeking, or other "secondary gain." Keep this up long enough and they'll tell you that you are a hypochondriac:

shortness of breath and sighing respiration
chronic tiredness

depression
inability to concentrate
irritability
anxiety
various aches and pains
impaired memory

and so on.

Stress control requires that you manage your resources, conserving them where appropriate, replenishing them where loss is unavoidable. And that includes oxygen.

The addition of deep diaphragmatic breathing, both into a daily routine and on an as-needed preventive basis, is one of the most effective means available to you to help protect and manage your resources.

And, *periodically taking a few abdominal/diaphragmatic breaths is the quickest, easiest, and most effective way of countering anxiety and assuring body and brain tissue oxygenation. It can be done anywhere—in such a way that no one needs to know you are doing it. And it costs nothing to do it.* Integrating a few abdominal breaths, once or twice, into your daily routine may lead, down the road, to its becoming automatic.

THE ROLE OF MENTAL ATTITUDE

A word about "attitude." A thought can initiate or forestall action. Think of the word "lemon." I'll bet you can't do that without just a little bit of salivation. Of course you realize that your reaction to the word "lemon" is due to your having learned something based on your previous experience with lemons.

Science has shown that if you think about moving

your arm, there will be imperceptible contractions of the arm muscles involved. Now, that would not appear to involve learning. If you imagine throwing a dart at a dart board, and it strikes the bull's-eye, this will actually help you to improve that skill, because the imperceptible movements associated with this "covert practice" improve actual performance.

There are thoughts, such as "I CAN DO IT," that help, and there are weakening thoughts, such as "I CAN'T DO IT. IT WON'T WORK." These thoughts function like covert practice whose imperceptible effects affect performance.

Now, let's enter into a contract:

AGREEMENT TO IMPROVE MY ATTITUDE

"I, _____ ,
on this, the _____ of _____ , 19____ , agree that I will take great care to avoid using phrases such as:
"I can't";
"It won't work";
"This is too hard to do";
"I will never get better";
"It will always be like this";
And, if I catch myself making any of these statements, I will say to myself:
"THAT'S NOT RIGHT."
Followed by either:
"I CAN DO IT";
"IF I TRY, IT WILL WORK. MAYBE NOT RIGHT AWAY, BUT WITH PRACTICE IT WILL WORK";
"THIS IS NOT TOO HARD TO DO AND IT IS GOOD FOR ME TOO";
"I WILL GET BETTER";

"IT WASN'T ALWAYS LIKE THIS AND WILL BE BETTER AGAIN";
And each time that I remember to do this, I will say to myself, "GOOD! I REMEMBERED."
Signed: _____

ALERT RAPID RELAXATION BREATHING EXERCISE™

This exercise combines deep abdominal breathing with mental imagery. It was developed over a period of eight years and I have used it as *a part* of the treatment for breathing-, stress-related, and psychosomatic disorders, including the following conditions:

- tension and anxiety
- burnout syndrome
- chronic anxiety disorder
- panic disorder (and agoraphobia)
- simple phobias (social, public speaking, etc.)
- depression
- tension headache
- migraine
- hypertension
- hyperventilation
- Raynaud's disease
- TMJ/bruxism (jaw clenching and teeth grinding)
- asthma
- emphysema
- idiopathic seizures
- gastritis
- irritable bowel/colitis
- ileitis

- hypoglycemia
- heart arrhythmias
- diabetes
- insomnia
- aerophagia

Please note the emphasis on the fact that breathing training is "a part" of the treatment program. A successful treatment program may need to combine "medical management" of the disorders, medication, with nutrition, where necessary, and counseling, cognitive or other behavior modification, biofeedback/self-regulation, and relaxation training, including deep abdominal breathing training.

I have no experience with persons who have a psychosis. In some instances, persons with temporal lobe epilepsy (TLE) may suffer severe depression and report hallucinations and other psychosis-like sensations and symptoms. Except for those cases, I am in no position to speculate about the benefits or possible harmful effects of the breathing exercises on their condition.

A NOTE OF CAUTION: Deep abdominal/diaphragmatic breathing may initially be strenuous for the person who has been holding the diaphragm in partial contraction as part of the physical stress profile. Diaphragmatic cramps are not unheard of. Should they occur and be anything but mild, or should they persist, discontinue the exercise immediately. *IF AN EXERCISE CAUSES YOU TO FEEL PAIN OR DISCOMFORT, STOP IMMEDIATELY.*

SECOND NOTE OF CAUTION: Do not do any exercise if you have any physical condition that would contraindicate its safety or benefits or for which you are not fit by virtue of physical condition or injury.

Among such conditions are:

(a) Any condition involving muscle or other tissue or organ malformation or injury; for example, sprained or torn muscles, torticolis, or fractures; recent surgery, etc.

(b) Any condition in which there is metabolic acidosis, for which hyperventilation may be compensatory (diabetes, kidney disease, etc.). *IF IN DOUBT, CONSULT A PHYSICIAN.*

(c) Deep abdominal breathing may cause a significant decrease in blood pressure. Do not do it if you suffer from low blood pressure, or from any related condition, such as *syncope* (fainting).

(d) If you have *insulin-dependent diabetes*, you should not do this, or any other deep relaxation exercise, without the express approval of your physician, and his/her close monitoring of your insulin needs. In the long run, deep relaxation may be beneficial in the management of diabetes; but the sudden reduction in the blood level of the stress hormones has been demonstrated to reduce insulin dependence. Under certain circumstances, hyperventilation may be the body's protection against diabetic *acidosis*.

PRELIMINARY RAPID RELAXATION EXERCISE*

If I were to teach you relaxation or breathing in my office, you would be sitting comfortably in a high-back chair listening to my instructions, or imagining yourself at the beach or in another relaxing setting. Sometimes the background might be music or ocean sounds.

But before reaching this stage, you would have learned to do sustained abdominal (diaphragmatic)

*Alert Rapid Relaxation Training Exercise (ART) © 1990 Robert Fried, New York, N.Y.

breathing. This is a skill that may take several weekly training sessions to acquire.

I have tried to program the instructions that follow in such a way as to make it possible for you to develop the same level of skill. But you are at a slight disadvantage: Instead of relaxing and following verbal instructions, you must read them first, remember them and, then, with eyes closed in some instances, follow them. So:

1. Sit comfortably in your favorite chair. Sit as far back in the chair as you can, so that the back of the chair supports your back. Your back should be more or less straight, forming a right angle with your thighs. Your legs should also be at a right angle to your thighs. Feet should be flat on the floor, four to five inches apart.

Open your jacket or vest, loosen your collar or tie. Loosen any tight belt or garment restricting abdominal expansion.

Place your hands in your lap and begin to let yourself slow down and relax. Imagine that the weight in your body is drifting to the bottom of your feet.

Caution: Always tense and relax muscles slowly. It does nothing to help you relax to "jerk" or "snap" muscles. And it is very easy to hurt yourself unless you proceed very gently.

2. Extend your legs forward, keeping your heels on the ground. Point your toes forward until you feel the tension in your calves and ankles. Hold the tension to a count of five: "One. . . two. . . three. . . four. . . . *five.*

Then relax slowly and gently.

Could you feel the tension? Good.

Repeat this procedure.

3. Bring your legs back so that your feet are flat on the floor, about 5 inches apart. Now press your feet down onto the floor as hard as you can—don't tip your chair backwards. Hold to a count of five.

Then relax gently.

Could you feel the tension in your calves? In your thighs? If you could, good.

Now repeat the procedure.

4. Imagine that there is a string encircling your body, around your abdomen (belly). Now push out your abdomen, slowly. . . as if you wished to break that string. Hold the tension to a count of five.

Then relax slowly and gently.

Could you feel the tension in your abdomen? In the small of your back? If you could, good.

This is a diaphragm stretching exercise. Contraction of your diaphragm pushed your abdomen out. That, parenthetically, is why we call diaphragmatic breathing "abdominal" breathing.

Since the diaphragm is also attached at the lower back, you may feel tension there also when contracting it. Did you? Good.

Now repeat this procedure.

5. Extend your arms, elbows slightly bent, and contract your biceps muscles, as hard as you can, to a count of five.

Then relax gently.

Could you feel the tension in your arms? Your shoulders? If you could, good.

Repeat.

6. Gently raise your shoulders as high as you can, keeping your head in a straight line with your back. Hold to a count of five.

Now relax *gently*.

Could you feel the tension in your neck and shoulders? If you could, good.

Repeat this procedure.

7. Close your eyes and squeeze your forehead by

frowning. Purse your lips as if you wished to kiss someone. Do this as hard as you can. Hold to a count of five.

Now relax gently.

Could you feel the tension in your forehead and
cheeks? If you could, good.

Repeat the procedure.

The exercise above is an active muscle relaxation exercise and varying versions of it are widely used to reduce
muscle tension and anxiety. Some practitioners prefer to
reverse the sequence, starting at the head and working
towards the toes. If you prefer that sequence, by all means
do it that way.

ABDOMINAL/DIAPHRAGMATIC BREATHING

The following is an abdominal breathing training exercise which I have used very successfully to correct rapid,
shallow chest breathing, and promote relaxation. It promotes reduced muscle tension, pulse rate, and blood pressure, and a general sense of alert well-being, relaxation
and comfort.

Since many of you who will try the following exercise
have not done anything like it before, I have broken down
the training procedures into several days, so that your
muscles will have time to adjust and become toned for this
task.

*It is generally a good idea to do deep abdominal breathing
exercises slowly at first, without straining the diaphragm. The
emphasis is on comfort.* You are not trying to add bulk to
muscles, like a weight lifter. You are actually trying to
*re*learn a skill that you once had quite naturally, as an
infant.

This is a different form of *aerobics*: You are trying,

here, to increase oxygenation of the body by increasing the efficiency of breathing. You do not need to plunge like a "health freak" into "pain as a measure of success." If you experience pain and discomfort, you are doing it *wrong*.

Day 1

Preparation:

Here also, you will have to read through all the instructions before beginning each exercise so that you can learn the steps and do them, where necessary, with your eyes closed.

Seat yourself comfortably in your chair. Sit all the way back so that your back is supported by the back of the chair.

Unbutton your collar. . . jacket. Loosen your tie, belt, or any other tight-fitting clothing.

Place your hands on your knees and pause for a moment.

How Do You Breathe?

Place your left hand on your chest, just over your breast bone. And your right hand over your abdomen (over your belly button).

Look at your hands as you breathe. What is the left hand doing? What is the right hand doing? Are they moving together?

Your left hand, over your chest, should not be moving as you breathe in and out. And your right hand, over your abdomen, should be moving *out* as you *inhale*, and *in* as you *breathe out* (exhale).

Check and make sure that you are doing this:

> *Breathe IN—Belly OUT*
> *Breath OUT—Belly IN*

Repeat three times, then stop.

Do you feel dizzy? If not, good. If you feel dizzy, you are overbreathing (hyperventilating). This means that you are putting too much effort into it, too early in the game. You are moving too much air out of your lungs too quickly. Make the motions a little more subtle: not so far out on inhale and not so far in on exhale.

You will soon improve if you do not *overpractice*. But if you feel dizzy, stop and rest a little while until the dizziness passes. The initial dizziness disappears after a few practice sessions. Rarely, it may not stop. *If you do not stop feeling dizzy after a few practice sessions, stop trying.*

Note: If your left hand is moving predominantly, or if both hands are rising and falling at the same time, you are breathing with your chest. Or, is the movement of your hands shallow and slow, or shallow and rapid? Make a note to yourself.

Close your mouth. Breathe through your nose only. Yes, in and out through the nose, from now on and forever! Do not breathe through your mouth. It tends to promote overbreathing (hyperventilation). Breathing through the nose is healthier for you. The nose prepares the air for you: It cleans it, warms and moisturizes it.

Breathing through the nose will also keep the nasal passages warm. Among other things, this will reduce your likelihood of catching a cold: Cold viruses are deposited in the nose. They begin to multiply when the temperature in that tissue reaches a certain narrow low temperature range. Breathing through the nose keeps it warm and moist.

Look at your hands: As you inhale, hold your chest and don't let it rise. Let the hand on your abdomen rise as the air "fills your abdomen."

In fact, the air is not filling your abdomen. That is why I put that in quotes. The air is filling your lungs, and when you can't raise your chest your lungs fill by contraction of the diaphragm: This pushes out your abdomen, giving the impression that it is filling with air.

If you are uncertain about what to do, try the following procedure: Place a book on your lap (spine up, so that it won't slide off). Now, without coordinating it with your breath at all, push the book out as far as you can with your abdomen.

When you inhale, and you are filling up with air, your abdomen should move out about as far as it did when you pushed the book. If you find that the book did not move out much, don't worry. If you are tense and tight, that is to be expected. You will improve with practice.

On exhale: Slowly—but never so slowly that it creates discomfort—pull your abdomen back as far as it will go, but do not let it raise your chest.

Good. Now don't stop. Don't pause; repeat the inhale and exhale procedure once more.

Rest for a moment.

BREATHING RHYTHM

You will find, after a few days of practicing just 3 to 4 minutes per day—don't do more, now—that your inhale and exhale will be of approximately the same duration. There should be no pause in breathing—not before or after inhale or exhale—just one smooth motion. Your breathing rate may range between 3 and 7 breaths per minute. If you continue to do this exercise, you may soon notice how good it feels.

The emphasis, then, is on comfort. You are doing a difficult exercise: Your diaphragm is a very large muscle and you are contracting it, then you are pushing it back in place with your abdominal muscles. This is heavy work. It is strenuous and you will benefit from the exercise only if you do it in moderation and do not permit the muscles to get tired. Exercising tired muscles does not improve them.

Now, once again: inhale. . . fill up. And, exhale. . . pull all the way back. Repeat this procedure three times, then stop. That's all for today.

If you do more than this, it may be counterproductive, and may result in diaphragmatic cramps. You may be a little dizzy; that will pass. You may have a slight tendency to overbreathe (hyperventilate) at first. Many of my clients do. It will pass and, with practice, it will disappear. So take my advice: Wait until tomorrow to continue.

Day 2

Prepare yourself for the exercise in the same way as you did yesterday: Sit back in your chair. Place your hands on your knees for a moment. Let yourself relax.

Close your mouth.

Place your hands on your chest and abdomen as you did yesterday. Once you get the knack, you can do it without your hands.

Now, looking at your hands, inhale, holding down your chest, and letting your abdomen "fill up." Then, exhale slowly, and pull your abdomen all the way back.

Repeat this procedure three more times.

That's enough for today.

Did you find it to be any easier? Did your abdomen move further out when you inhaled? Did the hand on chest remain more or less motionless? Can you pull your abdomen a little further in?

Notice that I recommend only very short exercise sessions the first few days. Your diaphragm and abdominal muscles need time to tone up.

Most persons who look to self-help may be at least a little compulsive, and will overdo everything, including breathing exercise. Restrain yourself, please. You'll see; it will come along much faster that way. You will not be fighting against sore muscles.

Day 3

Let's see you do the exercise without your hands. Prepare yourself in your chair, as you did yesterday.

Try it. Does your chest remain more still as you inhale, and is your abdomen moving outward? If it is, good. If not, go back to using your hands.

But, if you can, then proceed breathing in and out four times in a row—close your eyes.

Good!

If you still need to use your hands, then proceed, eyes closed, and imagine what your hands are doing.

Good.

That's it for today.

Day 4

Can you do abdominal breathing without your hands now? If you can, good. Then you may do the following exercise that way. Otherwise, keep your left hand on your chest and your right hand on your abdomen until you can do the exercise without the use of your hands.

You are, once again, seated comfortably back in your chair, with your hands resting on your thighs and, after reading this, you will close your eyes and. . .

Imagine that you are at the beach. It is midmorning, the sun is shining and warm, but not hot. Feel the warmth of the sun on your head. . . on your shoulders. . . on your arms.

The sky is clear and you are standing on the beach and looking at the ocean. The ocean is calm.

Do you have this scene in your mind? Can you picture it? When you set the beach scene, be sure to set a scene with which you are familiar: a place where you have vacationed, perhaps.

You may close your eyes once more, after adding the following to the beach scene: As you look at the ocean, in your mind's eye, begin abdominal breathing and as you

inhale, get a sense that you are breathing in ocean air, and
FILL UP YOUR ABDOMEN, saying to yourself:

"I feel awake, alert, and refreshed."

And as you breathe out, feel the tension in your body
flow out with your breath, as you say to yourself:

"I feel relaxed, warm, and comfortable."

Do this for four breaths, then stop.

After a few minutes of rest, repeat the procedure.
That's all for today.

Day 5

Repeat the procedure, as you did yesterday, adding
the following, eyes closed.

As you are standing on the beach, and looking at the
ocean, in your imagination, the sun is shining and warm,
but not hot. You can feel the warmth of the sun on your
shoulders, your head and your arms. And, the sky is clear
and the ocean is calm. . . .

As you breathe in, see the surf rolling up on the
beach, towards your feet. And as you breathe out, see the
surf rolling out again.

Continue for four consecutive breaths.

Can you picture this? If you can, good. Try it again,
for three consecutive breaths.

And now, with the action of the surf rolling in when
you inhale, say to yourself, *"I feel awake, alert, refreshed!"*
And, rolling out, as you exhale, say *"I feel relaxed, warm and
comfortable."*

Try it. If you don't get it right away, don't be dis-
couraged. It improves with very little practice.

Try four consecutive breaths, coordinating inhale
with the surf rolling up on the beach, and your saying to
yourself, "I feel awake, alert, and refreshed!" And, as the
surf rolls out, as you exhale, "I feel relaxed, warm, and
comfortable."

I would recommend the following to you, if you wish

to learn this exercise. Do it once during the morning, and once in the afternoon or evening—not more for the first week or two. And definitely do not do more than four to five breaths, each time, or "round."

If you do not strain your muscles, you may be amazed at how quickly you will become proficient at this type of breathing exercise.

After about 3 weeks, I usually recommend that you do the exercise in "rounds of 3":

Four or 5 breathing cycles, and a few moments' rest, followed by a second round of 4 or 5 breathing cycles, followed by a moment's rest, and finally, a third round of 4 or 5 breaths.

Always start the first round easy: not too far out on inhale, not too far in on exhale. Then, a little more with each progressive round. You may or may not wish to precede a breathing exercise session with the active relaxation exercises. That is up to you.

These are the initial daily breathing exercises that have helped many of my clients to overcome tension, anxiety, and the other psychosomatic and stress-related disorders listed above.

When you have mastered these exercises, you may progress to using them to overcome anxiety in specific situations:

1. Wherever you are sitting, adjust your posture as you would for the relaxation exercise, with your back against the back of the chair, your feet flat before you.

2. If you can, loosen your clothing.

3. Close your eyes, concentrate on abdominal breathing, and focus your attention on your nostrils: As you inhale, feel the cool, fresh air rushing into your nostrils. Experience that freshness. *Fill up*; and say to yourself, *"I feel awake, alert, and refreshed!"*

As you exhale, you may not feel the air exiting your

nostrils (it is at body temperature). And feel the tension and anxiety in your body flowing out with your breath, saying to yourself, "*I feel relaxed, warm, and comfortable!*"

Let me show you now how these breathing exercises may be integrated into a treatment program aimed at reducing your symptoms.

INTEGRATING DEEP-DIAPHRAGMATIC BREATHING WITH OTHER STRATEGIES TO CONTROL TENSION, ANXIETY, AND PHOBIAS

It is likely that you are now seeing some sort of "shrink" to either overcome your sense of failure at not becoming as socially and/or financially successful as you would have wished. Or because you are now paying in stress and physical symptoms, the cost of having achieved that success and of maintaining it.

Stress leading to anxiety, tension, headaches, etc. can be more or less successfully controlled with medication—antianxiety sedatives and tranquilizers. But, you may become dependent on them, and their abuse creates a whole new set of problems.

That is one of the reasons that relaxation training, especially employing methods derived from meditation, has been so widely accepted as an alternate form of stress and anxiety reduction—even among many traditional medical practitioners.

In my recent publication, "Relaxation with Biofeedback-Assisted Guided Imagery: The Importance of Breathing Rate as an Index of Hypoarousal," published in the journal *Biofeedback and Self-Regulation* (vol. 12, 1988), I show that the most important component in relaxation is the naturally occurring reduction in breathing rate that typ-

ically accompanies meditation. The breathing method described above is abstracted from meditation techniques
and refined to give you its essentials.

Thus, when you are doing the breathing exercise,
with or without the mental imagery, you are getting the
active ingredients of meditation—the "wheat," as it were. I
have taken great pains to refine it from the chaff.

There are two ways to use the breathing exercise: (a)
on a regular basis, two or three times per day, a triplet of
"rounds" with imagery to reduce the general stress level;
and (b) in counter-tension, anxiety, or phobia treatment,
where you may wish to use the second set minus imagery.

The use of breathing control in conjunction with
counter-anxiety or phobia treatment involves the use of
abdominal breathing before or during an anxiety attack, a
panic attack, or a phobic reaction, in conjunction with
"cognitive restructuring."

Cognitive restructuring may involve a number of different techniques. I frequently make use of "cognitive self-
statements" to counter the client's anxious thoughts:

I described such a strategy in an article, "The Role of
Psychophysiological Hyperventilation Assessment in
Cognitive Behavior Therapy," in the *Journal of Cognitive
Behavior Therapy* (vol. 3, 1989):

> J.F. . . . is a 27-year-old female agoraphobic who continued
> to manifest very subtle hyperventilation even after over-
> coming her phobias. [She] experienced her first panic attack
> in a New York City subway following her attempt to run
> after and catch a train. She thought at first that she was,
> somehow, dying and only later recognized her experience
> as anxiety. This spontaneous insight did not, however,
> help her to cope. Subsequently, she began to fear having
> panic attacks and to avoid places where she thought that
> they might occur, e.g. trains, airplanes, buses, auto-
> mobiles, elevators, at the dentist. She feared not being in

control and being away from a safe place and felt anxious whenever she left home.

The treatment strategy for J.F. was broad-based and typical of the therapy applied to agoraphobics and panic disorder patients. . . only a limited number of patients respond to the purely behavioral treatment. . . . In addition to breathing retraining, relaxation training. . . and biofeedback, J.F. was given cognitive therapy as well as in vivo coping desensitization.

J.F. experienced a fear of fear, commonly the case in agoraphobics. This fear included thoughts such as, "I'm going to die." "I'll lose control." "I can't stand this anxiety." "I'll have an attack and I won't be able to deal with it." "I'll be stranded, I'll faint or fall, and make a fool of myself." "This will never go away." She was taught to recognize how these thoughts lead to anxiety and how to replace them with coping self-statements such as "It's anxiety—not a heart attack." "It may be uncomfortable but it is not dangerous." "I can control it—it will pass—I won't faint: It's my breathing that makes me feel dizzy, so I'll use this feeling of dizziness as a reminder to breathe properly." "I'm not helpless, and people won't think I'm crazy."(p. 11)

Thus, a combination of breathing and coping self-statements helped this client to overcome her agoraphobia. There are many other instances when breathing may be used to counter anxiety and produce calm in the face of a phobic object or situation. For instance:

• As our symposium speaker listens to his introduction to the participants, his eyes are closed momentarily. He is doing abdominal breathing, and as he inhales, he focuses his attention on the quality of the air entering his nostrils and he is saying to himself:

"I feel alert and refreshed. I am in control. I have done this before and it will go very well!"

As he exhales, he is saying to himself:

"I feel relaxed and comfortable. The program will go well."

• Our airline passenger has closed her eyes and is now shifting to slow abdominal breathing as she reclines in her seat. As she inhales, she focuses her attention on the air entering her nostrils and is saying to herself:

"I feel awake and alert, and in control. It is my usual breathing that makes me anxious. Nothing will happen to me."

As she exhales slowly:

"I am relaxed and comfortable, in control."

Such an exercise can also be used in other situations: in a crowded elevator; when attending a stressful meeting; in a social setting; before engaging someone in a conversation and before, during, or after any situation that creates enough anxiety to cause discomfort or panic.

A "round" of 3 to 5 breaths may usually do it.

INTEGRATING BREATHING EXERCISES INTO A PROGRAM TO CONTROL BLOOD PRESSURE AND HEART DISORDERS

If you are in the care of a physician prescribing medication, you may have been advised also to control your weight, sodium intake, etc., and to get "stress management," perhaps counseling and "relaxation training."

It is apparent to everyone that you are usually keyed up and tense.

You are inclined to follow your doctor's instructions. Also, you have heard, or read somewhere, that meditation, relaxation, including "better breathing," have helped others, so you are willing to give it a try. You may often note that you seem slightly out of breath.

Your decision is actually quite sound. A British physician, S. Patel, writing for the *Lancet* over the past 15 years, has shown conclusively that many meditation methods are so effective in lowering blood pressure that a good percentage of clients may go off medication. Deep abdominal breathing is the active ingredient in meditation that lowers blood pressure.

The use of breathing to lower blood pressure is not new. A treatise, *The Cure of High Blood Pressure by Respiratory Exercises*, by Lothar Gottlieb Tirala, M.D., Ph.D., Professor of Medicine, University of Munich, was published in—are you ready for this—1928!

First and Second Week

To begin with, you will wish to track your pulse rate and blood pressure regularly. Do this when you are at rest.

You may observe your pulse rate and blood pressure with an automatic, self-inflating, *digital* device. They have unfairly been said to be imprecise. But the error, in my experience, tends to be less than that occurring when someone inexperienced uses the old-fashioned "cuff-and-stethoscope and fingers-on-the-artery" method.

Since blood pressure and pulse rate vary with tension and anxiety, you will wish to know what accounts for what you are observing: Is it "stress"? Is it nutritional? Is your sodium intake up, or potassium level down? Have you had a high tyramine-foods day? Either stress or foods will cause these things to happen.

For this reason, please turn to the suspect foods list, in the chapter on nutrition. Make a copy of the protocol form, one for each week, and begin to track these food-stuffs in your diet.

Mark your blood pressure, taken in the morning and in the evening, right on the form. If you have begun to eliminate the foods that contain substances promoting arterial blood vessel constriction or increased blood pressure, compare your resting blood pressure to that before nutrition changes.

Beginning Week Three

Now, add the breathing exercises, using the schedule set forth above.

When you have developed the skill of deep abdominal breathing so that you can do it effortlessly, you may also begin to do a round "prophylactically," (as a preventive measure):

- before a meeting;
- during or after a nerve-racking meeting or other event;
- when the bus is late. . . in a traffic tie-up;
- waiting on line at the bank;
- when the children are fighting among each other;
- when your neighbor's stereo volume is too loud;
- when the report due is not coming along smoothly;
- when the bank teller can't find your account;
- when the airlines reservations clerk announces that the "computers are down."

I am sure that you have no difficulty identifying the situations *in your life* that cause you to experience aggravation, tension, anxiety, and stress—that "make your blood boil." Identify and list them in a hierarchy, in descending order of their annoyance value, beginning with the most annoying:

1. _____
2. _____
3. _____
4. _____
5. _____
etc.

Get into the habit of doing a breathing round (4 breaths or so before, during, or after any such situation). Keep track of the foods, and of your blood pressure and pulse rate at least twice a day. It will help you to maintain the program when you see it succeed for you.

INTEGRATING BREATHING INTO A PROGRAM TO REDUCE MIGRAINE, RAYNAUD'S, AND IDIOPATHIC SEIZURE SYMPTOM FREQUENCY AND SEVERITY

Look carefully at the heading of this section. You will notice that the emphasis is on reducing symptom frequency and severity—on reducing suffering. There are very few conditions that are *directly* caused by improper breathing. *Many factors need to be present before a disorder emerges.*

By the same token, there are very few conditions that proper breathing will "cure." And I do not claim otherwise.

But, most disorders are significantly aggravated by improper breathing. And, most disorders are significantly ameliorated by restoring proper breathing. In fact, I use the second, short breathing exercise to raise my threshold for pain at the dentist and I almost never use an anesthetic.

It is helpful to track your blood pressure even if you do not have hypertension, because psychosomatic conditions tend to be aggravated by anxiety, by certain foods, and by allergy: Pulse rate increases in the presence of foods to which you may be "sensitive," or in allergy.

Hand temperature, in Raynaud's and migraine, indicates arterial blood vessel constriction. Track symptom frequency and severity for 2 weeks before beginning the control program (you may wish to make copies of the symptoms and foods checklist for your convenience).

If you suffer from Raynaud's syndrome, you may find it helpful to note your hand temperature (at the right index finger) before and after *each* breathing exercise. I recommend the home use of a simple digital thermometer with 1/10th degree F steps, ranging at least from 70 to 100° F, that can be purchased at any hobby shop or *Radio Shack*. Tape the little probe to your finger and wait for the temperature to stabilize.

When you have mastered abdominal breathing, you may note a rapid increase in hand temperature. Yes, just from the breathing change!

With advice from your physician or nutritionist, you may wish to reduce or eliminate foodstuffs from your diet, while tracking blood pressure, pulse rate (and, where appropriate, hand temperature), symptom frequency and severity, and, doing the breathing exercise. As noted earlier, *it is not advisable to simply eliminate foods from your diet* without consulting a professional expert—even if these foods obviously cause an allergic or other reaction.

A given food may be an important source of vitamins, nutrients, or minerals. And, eliminating it may require the substitution of an alternative source of these necessary components. Secondly, some experts hold that food sensitivity may act like an addiction, and eliminating it from the diet may result in withdrawal symptoms. These have been reported in connection with milk, sugar, wheat, chocolate, etc.

I make it a practice, where such sensitivity is suspected, to refer the client to Dr. Richard M. Carlton, the Manhattan-based physician with whom I collaborate.

Symptoms Checklist

Name: _____   Date: _____

Symptoms:

1) **Mild** ( ),   **Moderate** ( ),   **Severe** ( )

2) **Mild** ( ),   **Moderate** ( ),   **Severe** ( )

3) **Mild** ( ),   **Moderate** ( ),   **Severe** ( )

4) **Mild** ( ),   **Moderate** ( ),   **Severe** ( )

Frequency: _____/day; and during the last week: _____

Blood Pressure

Instructions: Indicate systolic blood pressure before vertical line, and diastolic after it, for each sample taken, each day. And indicate the pulse rate obtained with each blood pressure sample in the space below.

Example: 125 | 78

(82)

	Mon	Tue	Wed	Thu	Fri	Sat	Sun
Sample: 1)							
2)							
3)							
4)							
5)							

A NOTE ON BREATHING AND HAND
TEMPERATURE BIOFEEDBACK

There have been many recent media accounts of the use of biofeedback in the treatment of psychosomatic and stress-related disorders. What is biofeedback?

"Feedback" provides knowledge of results about the performance of a task. It may involve correction by using an instrument indicating how you are doing at learning to control an involuntary body function, such as pulse rate or blood pressure.

It has been used to retrain various damaged or otherwise impaired muscles and limbs in rehabilitation medicine and physical therapy, and has even been used to teach the deaf to form words by showing them when they are forming the proper tongue and palate configuration.

Biofeedback has been used to teach persons to relax by showing them the degree of muscle tension in various muscles, especially those in the forehead and in the shoulders. When muscles contract, they emit a very small electric current. An electronic instrument can be used to amplify and "feed back" this information converted to a tone, for instance, whose loudness or pitch corresponds to degree of tension. This is called *electromyographic* biofeedback.

The tone helps the trainee to know when trial-and-error adjustments lead to a lowering of tension.

A blood pressure cuff can be modified so that blood pressure change can be noted as a change in the pitch of a tone rising and falling with corresponding change in blood pressure.

Biofeedback is indicated when the behavior being learned is covert: muscle relaxation, artery dilation, etc. These cannot be observed readily.

You are not equipped to control blood pressure voluntarily. And even though you may ultimately experience pain from continuously contracted muscles, you usually are not aware that you are "tense." You do not experience the diameter of your blood vessels. But how can you tell if you are narrowing your arteries?

When arteries constrict, they limit blood flow in surrounding tissue and there is usally a corrresponding change in *skin temperature*. Skin temperature is the temperature measured at the surface of the skin, unlike *core temperature*, inside the body.

But of course you would intuitively expect your hand temperature to be warmer in a warm room than in a cool one. Thus, hand temperature can only be an approximation of the degree of blood flow because it will also depend on room temperature.

So, let's look at some simple guidelines. At room temperature, about 70° F, you would expect hand temperature to be above about 85° F. Anything less suggests tension, stress, anxiety, or something else—maybe Raynaud's.

In Raynaud's (primary or secondary), migraine, hyperventilation, anxiety, panic attacks, and phobias, idiopathic seizures, and angina, we frequently observe unusually cold hands. Sometimes, even astonishingly cold: I have seen one young lady with hand temperature at 76° F in a room at 78° F!

These people will, laughingly, tell you that they are famous for having the coldest hands anywhere: "My husband always says, "Charlotte, don't touch me with your hands or feet when we go to bed!'"

Temperature biofeedback is frequently suggested to control these conditions. Self-regulation increase in hand temperature, one of the more common forms of biofeedback, is based on the assumption that learning to increase hand temperature improves blood flow through the hand and, therefore, through the body as a whole. This assumption, though not accurate in its details, is not, however, without considerable merit and research support. And it has been shown to be very helpful in many cases. I have used it regularly with my clients, but with a twist, as you will see.

The typical procedure in temperature biofeedback is to provide you with a thermometer that has an attachment at the end of a wire that can be taped to one of your fingers. Room and finger temperature are noted and you are then given minimal instructions to increase your finger temperature. Typically, learning progresses by trial and error, which you may spontaneously recognize to correspond to muscle relaxation.

Here comes the twist—the breath connection: Arterial blood vessel diameter and, therefore, blood flow, are also related to the amount of carbon dioxide in your blood. If you are hyperventilating, you are reducing CO_2 level and your arteries will constrict.

And so it stands to reason that if you breathe properly you will correct blood CO_2, and the conditions that impaired circulation tend to promote. And as the correction takes place, you should be able to observe hand temperature increasing.

This is very precisely what my clients observe during breathing retraining. Here is a simple way that you can do it yourself:

ABDOMINAL BREATHING AND HAND TEMPERATURE

A finger temperature indicator card is provided with this book. It has a small oval temperature sensor. If you misplace it, you may obtain another one from FUTURE HEALTH, P.O. Box 947, Bensalem, PA 19020 at nominal cost.

Step 1. With a standard wall thermometer, note the room temperature. Write it down. Do not proceed if the room temperature is below 70° F, or if you recently came in from the cold and your hands haven't adjusted yet.

Step 2. Place your right index finger on the oval sensor on the card for about 10 seconds. Note the finger temperature and write it down.

Step 3. Do the abdominal breathing exercise of your choice.

Step 4. Repeat Step 2. Did your hand temperature go up? By how much? Write it down.

As you repeat this exercise, you may note that your hands will warm more rapidly with practice.

THE BREATH CONNECTION—AN INTEGRATIVE APPROACH

Tension, Anxiety, and Stress

These disorders are characterized by chronic muscle tension and pain, anxiety and apprehension. They may include depression, "burnout," and vague somatic symptoms, especially referred to the chest and heart.

Many of the symptoms of the hyperventilation syndrome are present, including sighing respiration and shortness of breath; inability to catch one's breath is also frequently reported, as well as chronic fatigue, inability to concentrate, and vague "cardiac" symptoms, such as palpitations.

Hand Temperature

Instructions: Record each sample of your hand temperature, taken at the right index finger.
Example: (84.5) [degrees Fahrenheit]

	Mon	Tue	Wed	Thu	Fri	Sat	Sun
Room temp: ____							
Sample: 1)	( )	( )	( )	( )	( )	( )	( )
Room temp: ____							
2)	( )	( )	( )	( )	( )	( )	( )
Room temp: ____							
3)	( )	( )	( )	( )	( )	( )	( )
Room temp: ____							
4)	( )	( )	( )	( )	( )	( )	( )
Room temp: ____							
5)	( )	( )	( )	( )	( )	( )	( )

1. *Breathing*. At least two rounds of deep abdominal breathing with imagery, each day: one mid-morning, the other in the early evening. Each round should last not more than 3 to 5 minutes.

A set of breathing rounds without imagery, when severe tension is experienced. The round should not exceed five breaths.

2. *Monitoring*. Blood pressure and pulse rate monitoring is recommended as well as monitoring foods.

3. *Nutrition*. Tyramine should be reduced or eliminated because it may increase pulse rate and "palpitations."

Anxiety Phobias

These disorders are characterized by anxiety that may involve a specific situation, object, or thought; or it may be more or less nonspecific, i.e., "free-floating." The attacks may be gradual or rapid in onset, and may entail a severe anxiety reaction with rapid shallow breathing, hyperventilation, trembling, sweating, fear, appprehension, and foreboding of doom or disaster.

1. *Breathing*. At least two sets or rounds of abdominal breathing with beach imagery per day—mid-morning and early evening, as indicated above; 3 rounds of 4 to 5 deep abdominal breaths, with beach imagery, separated by 2 to 3 minutes of rest.

A deep abdominal breathing round (4 to 5 breaths), without imagery, with positive self-statements such as *"This will pass quickly when I regulate my breathing"*; *"Nothing will really happen to me"*; *"It is not my heart, but my breathing that makes me feel this way,"* before, or during, an exposure to the triggering event.

2. *Nutrition.* Tyramine and serotonin-containing foods will lower the threshold to an attack and, by increasing natural arousal, worsen anxiety. It is difficult to slow things down that are speeded up by ideas, when the body is independently speeded up. So monitor common foods, especially sugar, wheat, corn, milk, and MSG. You may be surprised to find that you feel worse on the days when you consume these foods.

Raynaud's Syndrome, Migraine, Idiopathic Seizures

These disorders obviously do not form a homogeneous grouping, but are so combined because of their dependence on factors affecting the arterial blood vessels, the blood, and oxygen delivery to body and brain tissues. The common factor, arterial constriction and spasms, differentiates them only with respect to the site of the arteries involved, and has been elaborately described to be a function of low oxygen (hypoxia) in previous sections.

In Raynaud's disease there are varying degrees of constriction of the capillaries in the fingers and toes, somtimes giving the extremities a blotched purplish and whitish appearance.

If you have this condition, you know that it is painful and that hands and feet are usually cold, especially in the winter. Anxiety as well as "migraine foods" will cause aggravation of the condition.

In migraine, nausea and vomiting, and/or sensory disturbances of vision, hearing, or smell, may be the only symptoms, or these may precede pain in the head or abdomen. Arterial constriction followed by dilation is thought to be responsible for the pain.

Idiopathic seizures may take many forms: petit mal,

grand mal, psychomotor seizures. In many cases, they involve loss of consciousness, loss of postural control, and specific or gross muscle convulsions.

In some cases, temporal lobe seizures, for instance, may occur as severe, therapy-resistant mood disturbances, frequently with strong suicidal tendencies.

1. *Breathing.* A concerted effort should be made to shift permanently to abdominal breathing when at rest. And, especially to control any spontaneously initiated hyperventilation, because Raynaud's disease, migraine, and seizures are very sensitive to the constrictive effects of low blood carbon dioxide.

Migraine and seizures sufferers frequently have so called "premonitory" signals or symptoms. These may be sensations or hallucinations. In migraine and seizures, the premonitory symptoms are often thought to be a benign warning. That may be an inaccurate description.

Premonitory symptoms are symptoms of the attack at a lower level of severity. If you can prevent a worsening of the condition, at that level, the attack can frequently be averted.

I have treated a number of persons with migraine and idiopathic epileptic seizures—one even with organic seizures—who were able to avert or abort migraine or seizures if they began deep abdominal breathing as soon as they experienced the premonitory signs.

Consequently, I also recommend that a set of three abdominal breathing rounds, 4 to 5 breaths with *no* imagery, with 2 to 3 minutes rest between rounds, be used when "premonitory" symptoms appear.

You may note that if you do this properly, your hand temperature will increase considerably.

2. *Nutrition.* Elimination of "migraine foods" has been very helpful to many of my clients. Watch out for the amino acids tyramine, tyrosine, serotonin, and tryp-

tophan, found in many common foods. And bear in mind that the first successful treatment of seizure conditions was nutritional.

The Ketogenic diet has a very respected history, though it is little used now. One of the earliest and best descriptions of it may be found in Helmholtz and Goldstein, *American Journal of Psychiatry* (vol. 94, 1938). This article summarizes 15 years of experience with its use with children.

Watch especially sugar, red meat, wine, wheat, milk, corn, licorice, spinach, MSG, fried foods. And remember, hypoglycemia is well known to increase the frequency and severity of these conditions. Lower salt intake.

3. *Monitor* hand temperature as a good indicator of threshold. As has been noted, I have seen clients in these disorder categories whose hand temperature was well below room temperature. You may notice, if you suffer any one of these conditions that your hand temperature "tells the tale."

If you are able to eliminate tyraminergic foods from your diet without impairing nutrition you will notice very quickly that your typical hand temperature will increase considerably. As you note the increase in hand temperature, you should also begin to see a decrease in frequency and/or severity of your symptoms. Careful tracking of symptoms will show you that objectively.

Then, when you begin to add abdominal breathing to your routine, you may notice a further increase in average hand temperature and a further decrease in symptom severity and frequency.

Panic Attacks, Agoraphobia

Panic attacks and panic disorder with agoraphobia are so closely linked to hyperventilation that they are thought by many clinicians to be indistinguishable. This point is underscored in a publication by J.R. Marshall, professor of psychiatry at the University of Wisconsin Medical School. The article is entitled "Hyperventilation Syndrome or Panic Disorder—What's in the Name?" (*Hospital Practice*, vol. 22, 1987). The condition is characterized by breathing difficulty such as, "Can't catch my breath," "Can't get enough air" (dyspnea), palpitations, chest pain, and so on. . . that is, the criteria given in the DSM-III (see Chapter 8).

It should be pointed out that an important aspect of the panic attack is that it is generally tied to the notion of imminent peril, such as a heart attack, stroke, or the likelihood of asphyxiation—fear of dying.

1. *Breathing.* Because of the relationship between panic attack and "dyspnea"—"Can't catch my breath!"—I recommend that an attempt be made to make abdominal breathing habitual when at rest. This is not easy. First, you need to learn deep diaphragmatic breathing so that you can do its more subtle form on a regular basis.

To accomplish this goal, I suggest that you proceed as indicated above and do at least two sets of rounds, with imagery, each day.

Secondly, try to set a goal for yourself of remembering to shift to diaphragmatic breathing for at least one or two breaths (without imagery), not more, each time that you think of it, during the course of the day.

Reward yourself for remembering by saying to yourself, "Good! I remembered."

Do a set of rounds whenever you feel the beginning of an attack: As you do the breathing, say to yourself, "*It is not my heart. It is my breathing that makes me uncomfortable.*" "*As soon as I get my breathing under control, this attack will end.*" "*I can control it with my breathing.*"

And remember, a panic attack never lasts very long anyway. Time yours and see for yourself. They are self-limiting. And as your breathing improves, you may observe that the frequency and duration of attacks will diminish.

2. *Monitor* wheat, milk, sugar, coffee/tea, chocolate, etc.

Tension Headache, TMJ/Bruxism

These conditions are part of the muscle tension pattern that characterizes the way that some persons react to the stresses of their life.

Tension headache is frequently caused by the uneven contraction of muscle groups in the right and left side of the shoulder and neck region near the head. TMJ, or "temporomandibular joint syndrome," is the pain in the jaw region associated with chronic contraction of the jaw muscles. Bruxism, for anyone who has ever wondered why his/her dentist bills were so high, is the grinding of teeth during sleep.

1. *Breathing.* Breathing exercises are one of the most effective ways of relaxing and reducing muscle tension. For conditions that involve principally gross or skeletal muscles, you may find the use of the muscle relaxation exercises helpful as a prelude to doing the daily breathing exercises.

I also recommend that you use the muscle relaxation exercises at times of the day, at home or in the office, if possible, when tension is high, coupled with a set of breathing rounds without imagery.

For TMJ and bruxism, I also recommend frequent self-monitoring. This helps you to "tune in" to yourself. Just like the hyperventilation-related disorders, it is important to become conscious of the undesirable condition.

You probably are not aware that you are tensing muscles; consequently, you may not think to relax them. So it is important to *think* about these things periodically and to ask yourself, "Am I clenching my jaw?"

If you do clench your jaws as part of your tension pattern, I also recommend a "long-lost" (but fortunately rediscovered—don't ask me where) yoga position called "the village idiot." It consists of sitting in a stoop-shouldered position, hands loosely at your sides, head limply forward, mouth slightly ajar and lower jaw slack.

Try this for about 1 minute, each time that you are aware that you are clenching your jaws.

2. *Nutrition*—no special recommendations.

3. *Other.* It has been my experience that some cases of TMJ, even those so designated by your dentist, are in fact not due to stress-related tension. There are many instances when they are undetected dental or orthodontic problems, some involving the more or less natural realignment of the jaws as teeth shift to the midline—a universal naturally occurring maturational phenomenon.

Asthma, Emphysema

Although asthma and emphysema are breathing disorders, they present quite distinctly different treatment problems. In emphysema, there is an organic change in the lung structure such that there are, in the end, fewer alveoli and, therefore, a reduced gas transfer surface. In asthma, there is an impairment of air flow into the lungs.

1. *Breathing.* In addition to the daily breathing exercises, my asthma and emphysema clients have benefited

from deep abdominal breathing, especially when their condition is aggravated by higher levels of pollens or industrial air pollutants which promote or aggravate bronchial constriction. The reason for this is that abdominal breathing is more efficient than chest breathing.

By breathing abdominally, more air (greater volume) moves in and out of the lungs with each breath. By breathing exclusively through the nose, air is cleaned and prepared for the lungs.

It is important to remember also that hyperventilation may lead to rapid diaphragmatic fatigue. Consequently, by increasing the efficiency of breathing, diaphragmatic fatigue can be avoided.

I have seen clients develop the ability to breathe comfortably as slowly as 1 or 2 breaths per minute, in a few dozen training sessions. In 3 cases, it is less than 1 per minute. And, the amount of air they breathe per minute may be somewhat greater than when they breathe "normally"! This is very helpful to "voice" students.

Typically, the *amount* of air breathed each minute does not change much as a consequence of slower breathing rate. The volume of air breathed increases proportionately as the breathing rate drops to 4, 3, or less, per minute.

It can be very helpful, when you have certain kinds of breathing impairments, to be able to breathe so smoothly. It helps air flow way down into the smaller airway passages of the lower lobes of the lungs, when it flows slowly and gradually. Vortex currents are reduced at the entrance to these increasingly smaller airway passages. These vortex currents, by analogy, cause air molecules to act like cars all trying to enter a highway at the same time, thus impeding orderly traffic flow.

2. *Monitor*—in asthma, pulse rate and hand tempera-

ture as indicators of arterial constriction and the action of allergens and/or tyramine foods. Action hormones and vasoconstrictive amines adversely affect asthma sufferers. They promote bronchial constriction, vasospasm of bronchial arterioles, and edema (fluid swelling). In fact, *I make it a practice to think of asthma sufferers as having migraine*, and apply all the migraine treatment lore to them.

3. *Nutrition*. I recommend that asthma sufferers monitor their diet as though they were migraine sufferers. They should be aware that in addition to milk, sugar, wheat, tomatoes, eggplant, licorice, nuts, and alcohol, a major U.S. hospital survey found that 80% of children suffering from asthma were extremely sensitive (allergic) to chocolate.

4. *Other*. They were also shown, parenthetically, to be surprisingly sensitive to their own dandruff and to cockroaches. The common house roach, as has been mentioned, is one of those creatures said to have an "exoskeleton." This means that its outsides are its skeleton. It will shed this skeleton, as it outgrows it, and pieces may be found airborne, in carpeting, on furniture slipcovers, or whatever surfaces it traverses in your home. An asthma attack may be triggered by inhaling such roach skeleton debris.

It is a good idea to keep this in mind if you suffer asthma attacks. Keep your home roach-free. . . and wash your hair with an antibacterial soap or shampoo. Dandruff is caused by a scalp bacteria—*pitirosporum ovale*. Very small mites that live in your hair and eyebrows feed on dandruff flakes.

As these shed their exoskeleton, just as roaches do, fragments fall into your face, and are inhaled through the nose and mouth. Now there's a bizarre and dangerous breath connection for you.

Diabetes, Gastrointestinal Disorders

Gastritis, ulcers, colitis, ileitis, and irritable bowel syndrome are considered to be strongly influenced by stress. And diabetes can be added to this category. That is, there is no evidence that these conditions are *caused* by stress, or are psychosomatic; yet they are thought to be strongly *aggravated* by stress or emotion.

1. *Breathing.* Clients with these disorders are usually referred to me for "relaxation training" and "stress reduction." The reason for this is that most physicians are aware that the stress hormones have an adverse effect on these conditions. Consequently, they may recommend either beta-blockers or behavioral methods in accordance with their orientation.

Daily sets of breathing rounds, preceded by the muscle relaxation exercises, may be supplemented by the use of the exercise without imagery several times during the day. This takes, all in all, about 15 minutes or so out of the day.

2. *Nutrition.* Each of these conditions has special nutritional requirements which are beyond the scope of this book. But I should like to mention that it has been very helpful to keep in mind that:

(a) Chromium, obtainable as a dietary supplement in health-foods stores, taken under the direction of your physician, helps to stabilize the *glucose tolerance factor* (GTF) in diabetes and hypoglycemia. It may tend to reduce the dependence on insulin, so watch out.

(b) Any digestive problem resulting in malabsorption syndrome may result in significant potassium loss that will aggravate the condition further. Potassium has been shown to be essential in regulating digestion.

(c) Many forms of digestive disorders, including gastritis, are due to folic acid deficiency, and in some cases to *insufficient* stomach acidity.

(d) In some instances it has helped my clients who suffer from irritable bowel syndrome to make a concerted effort to slow down when they eat: they simply eat too fast.

Insomnia

Insomnia may be either the inability to fall asleep, or it may be frequent waking during the night, with an inability to fall asleep again.

1. *Breathing.* Insomnia is often the result of the inability to relinquish daytime tensions and concerns by nighttime. If you suffer from this debilitating condition, you may benefit from relaxation. Do the daily combination of muscle relaxation exercises and breathing exercise with imagery.

Using abdominal breathing to help sleep. When you have mastered deep abdominal breathing by practicing the daily exercises for a few days or weeks, and you can do them easily and smoothly, without the need to monitor chest and abdomen with your hands, you may proceed as shown below.

This exercise may be done sitting in your home, at the office, while traveling, or reclining in bed at night. It is a relaxation exercise which is not intended to produce *alert* relaxation. Although you would do it in bed if you intend to use it to help you to fall asleep, it can be done equally well sitting up. But let me illustrate its use as an aid to slumber. It goes something like this.

Here also, you will have to read the instructions from beginning to end so that you can do them with your eyes closed. Then, as you are reclining in bed, make yourself comfortable, let the tension drain from your body, and begin to concentrate on abdominal breathing:

Inhale. . . fill up. Good.

Now, as you exhale, say to yourself, "I'm letting the tension out of my forehead." And focus your attention on your forehead. And pull back your abdomen gently, on exhale. That's good.

Inhale.

As you exhale, say to yourself, "I'm letting the tension in my forehead flow out with my breath." As you focus your attention on the tension in your forehead, feel it flowing out with your breath.

Inhale.

As you exhale, say, "I'm letting the tension out of my face. I'm letting my jaw relax." And focus your attention on your face and jaw.

Inhale. . . fill up. That's good.

As you exhale, say to yourself, "I'm letting the tension in my face and jaw drift out with my breath." And feel the tension flowing out with your breath.

Next, exhale.

And as you exhale, say to yourself, I'm letting the tension out of my neck and out of my shoulders. I'm letting my shoulders down." And focus your attention on your neck. . . your shoulders.

Then inhale.

And as you exhale, say to yourself, "I'm letting the tension in my neck and my shoulders flow out with my breath." And get a sense that you can feel the tension in your neck and shoulders flow out with your breath as you exhale.

Next, inhale.

And as you exhale, if you are lying in bed, first imag-

ine that the weight in your arms is drifting to their underside, i.e., the part of your arms resting on the bed. And,
focus your attention on your arms and your hands, and
say to yourself, "I'm letting the tension out of my arms
and out of my hands and my arms feel heavy."

Inhale fully. Good.

Exhale and say to yourself, "I'm letting the tension
flow out with my breath," and as you focus your attention
on your arms and hands, feel it flow out.

Inhale.

Exhale and, if you are lying in bed, first get a sense
that the weight in your body is drifting to the underside—
the side in contact with the bed—and say to yourself, "I'm
letting the weight in my body drift to the underside of my
body."

Inhale.

Exhale and say to yourself, "I'm letting the tension in
my body flow out with my breath." And get a sense that
the tension in your body is flowing out with your breath.

. . . Good night.

If you are doing this exercise in a sitting position, your
feet are flat on the floor before you. And instead of "I'm
letting the weight in my body drift to the underside. . ."
substitute, "I'm letting myself sink further back into the
seat, letting the seat support my weight, and I'm letting
the weight in my body drift to the bottom of my feet."

2. *Nutrition.* There are many substances that will contribute to restlessness, and some that will help you to fall
asleep. Stimulants such as sugar and caffeine will promote
sleeplessness; so will tyramine in foods, chocolate, and
tea, coffee, and colas (which contain caffeine). They promote rapid heart rate, palpitations, etc. Many also contain
salicylates (in additives and coloring) which contribute to
hyperactivity in some children (see the list in chapter 9).

Some foods contain substances that actually promote sleep: tryptophan, found in abundance in milk and turkey, for example, helps you to fall asleep. Bear in mind, however, that milk is mucogenic (promotes mucus) and may cause snoring or promote hyperventilation during sleep by blocking the air passages of the nose. It is always a trade-off. Even though it is a "nutrient" substance, readily available in health food stores, you really should not self-prescribe tryptophan (many persons do). Among others, it may promote headaches in those so predisposed.

THE BREATH CONNECTION

Stress-related and psychosomatic disorders have in common mechanisms reflected in breathing—*the breath connection*. And I have found that relaxation training centering on slow, deep abdominal breathing has been enormously helpful to most of my clients, whose complaints and symptoms span a wide range of stress-related and psychosomatic disorders. I recommend it, together with other treatment strategies, including nutrition, to strengthen the ability of your body to fight back.

ILLUSTRATIVE CASE: S.N.

Mr. S.N. is a 32-year-old single man, employed in the fashion industry. He is of average height and weight. As he entered my office, his gait and posture suggested weariness, perhaps even depression. His handshake was weak and his hand was cool.

He reported suffering from "panic attacks" which occurred principally when he travelled. The disorder is in quotes here because I did not agree with his assertion. His description was better suited to anxiety attacks with a mild agoraphobia. The attacks did not have many of the characteristics of typical panic attacks.

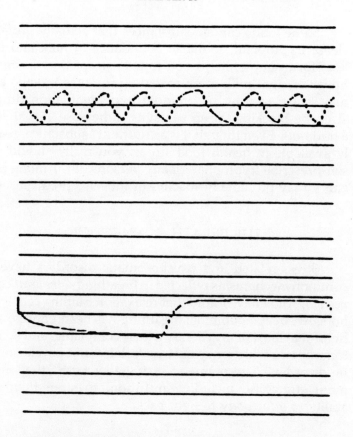

Twenty-second breathing samples. (Top) rate, before training: 21 breaths per minute; (bottom) rate, after training: 3 breaths per minute.

He expressed some doubt at first about how the breathing exercises would help him with his symptoms. I explained the relationship between anxiety and tension and told him that breathing training would facilitate a "relaxation response" that would help him to reduce and even abort his anxiety attacks.

It is possible to obtain a tracing of breathing patterns using an electronic gas analyzer coupled to a computer. The tracing is called a "capnogram." It is obtained by inserting a slender tube, about 1/4 in.

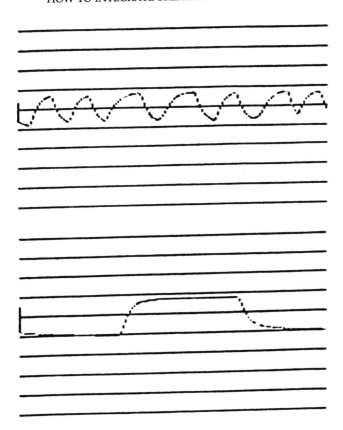

Twenty-second breathin° samples. (Top) rate, before training: 21 breaths per minute; (bottom) rate, after training: 4 3/4 breaths per minute.

into a nostril. The computer analyzes exhaled breath and the result can be seen as a 20-second sample in the figure on the preceding page.

The top graph shows the breathing pattern before training began: Breathing rate is 21 per minute, and CO_2 is 4.82%. After the third weekly abdominal breathing training session, rate drops to 3 breaths per minute as seen in the bottom graph, with CO_2 at 4.72%.

Since the tracing represents a 20-second time interval, breathing rate can be determined by simply multiplying the breathing cycles by 3: the trace rises with inhale, and drops with exhale.

On the fourth session, S.N. reported that his anxiety was considerably reduced and that he could control his attacks on public transportation by switching to abdominal breathing. After the 5th session, he had one session every two weeks, and after the 9th session, he felt confident that he could continue on his own.

ILLUSTRATIVE CASE: L.V.

Mr. L.V. is a 41-year-old married securities broker with three children. His medical history reveals nothing out of the ordinary. He drinks "occasionally at social gatherings," does not smoke, but, though he "watches" his diet and exercises regularly at a health club, he suffers moderate hypertension.

Initially, his breathing rate was 21 breaths per minute [see preceding figure, top graph], and 5.84% CO_2. The latter is significantly elevated, indicating that even while sitting in my recliner, he was spinning his wheels rapidly. His blood pressure was 130/95.

He quickly learned deep abdominal breathing and when coupled with "beach imagery," was able to bring his breathing under control in 15 minutes. Breathing rate dropped to 4 3/4 per minute [see bottom graph] and CO_2 normalized to 4.94%; blood pressure dropped to 112/83.

Mr. L.V. comes in every few weeks to check his progress and practice his breathing exercise under my supervision. His blood pressure continues to decline and is, now, in the 130/80 range.

CHAPTER 11

Music and Breath: A Sound Connection

INTRODUCTION

One of the most challenging tasks in breathing retraining is to get people to exhale fully. Asthmatics, for instance, give the impression of holding some air reserve in anticipation of future need; and persons with hyperventilation do not seem to have the ability to contract the diaphragm fully. It therefore becomes a continuous struggle to get the proper exhalation so that the next breath will be fuller.

In order to improve breathing, I have adopted a combination of instructions, biofeedback, and imagery, and have recently added music to the training procedure, with notable results.

Although many therapists report using music as an adjunct to relaxation, the conventional wisdom teaches us little about its actual effects on us.

I have *noted* references to the bodily effects of music in *offbeat* publications (bad as they are, both puns are intended): Numerous studies report that various forms of music relieve tension, anxiety, and pain, and lower muscle tension, pulse rate, blood pressure, and increase endorphin release.

The less conventional scientific publications report the use of music in helping the mother-to-be to relax during "birthing," and to reduce the experience of pain in all sorts of chronic cases, especially intractable cancer. Pioneering this work is a group at the Kaiser Permanente facility in California.

Among the pieces most widely cited in that context are the "New Age" compositions of Steven Halpern, including the well-known "Anti-Frantic Alternative," "Crystal Suite," and "Crystal Cave," *Sound Rx*, which have been used widely as relaxation music; Kitaro, "Silk Road," *Canyon Records*, and the various "Environments," including "Slow Ocean," *Syntonic Research, Inc.*

These are all fine pieces, and there are others that are comparable. But there is nothing about them that helps us to understand how they relax us.

DRUGS, MEDITATION, AND THE AMERICAN YOUTH MOVEMENT

The 1960s saw the birth in the U.S. of a popular youth movement that focused its interest on "mind-expanding" hallucinogenic drugs such as LSD and marijuana. This interest in the *inner experience* kindled interest in meditation and music because they affect consciousness. It also quickly came to the attention of science.

Fueled by studies of the heart and brain waves in the yogic meditative state by the noted French neurologist Gasteau, subsequent studies, especially those of the Japanese neurophysiologists Kasamatsu and Hirai (*Psychologia*, 1969:12), showed that bodily changes reliably occur with meditation. Among these are:

- muscle tension decreases
- breathing becomes deep, slow, and rhythmic
- pulse rate decreases
- blood pressure drops
- brain wave patterns show a predominance of alpha (8 to 18 cycles/sec) activity

It was also noted that this state is relaxing, "feels good," reducing tension and anxiety. But, more startling, its long-term effects were beneficial for persons who suffer from anxiety and stress-related disorders—especially cardiovascular disease including hypertension.

Within a few years, there was a great interest in meditation because it was felt by some persons that it helped them to *transcend* common daily life, while for others it reduced anxiety, muscle tension and blood pressure. But the trend to meditation soon took on the characteristics of a fad, and various "gurus" emerged to lead meditation cults. The cultists eventually dwindled as other, newer cults emerged to take the place of meditation.

Nevertheless, the scientific meditation studies had a permanent impact and their legacy became the *relaxation techniques* currently in use by clinicians. There are several forms: Benson's *Relaxation Response* (Avon, 1975) is one of the better known.

These techniques are, for the most part, combinations of various elements of the original TM or Zazen methods which have been abbreviated to reduce the amount of time required to practice them. Their universal aim is to focus the practitioner away from the cares of the day, by focusing on breathing, muscle relaxation, and pleasant mental imagery. In many instances, this occurs against a background of music—especially "New Age" music.

THE EFFECT OF MUSIC ON THE MIND AND THE BODY—THE ROLE OF MUSIC IN INDUSTRY

Many factories and offices now "pipe in" music for the benefit of their employees. It is said to make them happier, work harder, have fewer accidents, fewer absences, and feel less tired at the end of the day.

Most research indicates that the majority of employees like music at the workplace. About 10% dislike it. But most studies of music in the workplace focus only on its effect on work output. The employee who appears happier, has fewer absences, is less tired at the end of the day, and has a greater work output in the short run may, however, be the first to suffer stress, psychosomatic disorders, and reach burnout.

Furthermore, the effects of music depend on the nature of the music and the complexity of the work. In complex tasks requiring a high degree of skill and concentration, attending to music would not improve job performance. That is why most industrial workplace settings pipe in innocuous music of the Musak type.

There is no evidence that music promotes creativity, stress reduction, or wellness in the workplace. It is in place because some people like it, while others do not object to it.

MUSIC, RELAXATION, AND OTHER FUNCTIONS

There are reports of other studies of the mental and physical effects of music in scientific publications: various forms of music relieve tension, anxiety, and pain. But we know relatively little about *how* we perceive music and *how* it affects us.

DOES MUSIC AFFECT HUMAN BEHAVIOR?

In an interesting address to the *Music Research Foundation Symposium*, at the New York Academy of Sciences, Taylor and Paperte (*Journal of Esthetics*, 1958:51–58) state that:

> Music cannot be separated from perceptual, symbolic, and personal processes—particularly emotional and physiologic—if one is to understand how music induces and modifies human behavior. . . . (p. 251)

The authors also provide other insights. First, emotions evoked by music reside in the individual, not in the music. Second, music, because of its abstract nature, may bypass intellectual control and contact lower centers of the brain directly.

Third, though music may act *indirectly* on emotions by arousing associations and images in the intellect, its structure (rhythm and tempo) may evoke covert as well as overt movement which also give expression to emotion. This expression may be without symbolic or latent content and is, therefore, joyful and nonthreatening.

Curiously, covert movement, and simple motor actions, such as tapping in accompaniment to music, have been reported to improve mental ability.

But the most significant finding in their report is that the main effect of music is principally either *stimulating or relaxing*.

A number of recent books detail the effects of music. Steven Halpern, in his book *Sound Health* (Harper & Row, 1985), reports that music may show a paradoxical effect. Subjective reports of persons listening to Lizst's *Liebestraum*, No. 3, reported it to be "highly relaxing, soothing and meditative," even though their physiological reactions to the music showed otherwise.

Three conclusions can be drawn from Halpern's findings. First, externally imposed rhythm is rarely as relaxing as the personal internal rhythm. Relaxation will happen at the psychological and physiological level when the body can express its own inner nature and "harmony."

Secondly, relaxation may vary in depth. Some types of classical music can produce light relaxation which may show none of the physiological characteristics of deep relaxation. Most people can't tell one from the other but its long-term effects may be different.

Third, "neutral" compositions, those that do not bring forth images, found predominantly among "classical" and "New Age" compositions, seem to allow the body and mind to move into a mental pattern where the listener seems able to visualize a personal therapeutic imagery and utilize mental self-healing capacities.

Lingerman, in *The Healing Energies of Music* (Theosophical Publishing House, 1983), cites specific examples of what music can do:

- increase physical vitality
- relieve fatigue and inertia
- pierce through moods, uplift feelings
- calm anxiety and tensions
- focus thinking, clarify goals
- release courage and follow-through
- deepen relationships and enrich friendships
- stimulate creativity and sensitivity
- strengthen character and constructive behavior
- expand consciousness of God and horizons of spirituality

Different instruments seem to affect different aspects of the self:

- physical body: brass, percussion, electronic music
- emotions: woodwind, strings
- mental: strings
- soul: harp, organ, wind chimes, high strings

Music for the body:

- Elgar, Pomp and Circumstance
- Schubert, Marche Militaire
- Copland, Rodeo

Music for feelings and moods:

- Brahms, Piano Concerto No. 1
- Handel, Harp Concerto
- Pachelbel, Canon in D
- Bruch, Scottish Fantasy

Music for clear thinking:

- J.S. Bach, Brandenburg Concertos
- Baroque string music of Telemann, Vivaldi, Albinoni, Corelli, etc.

Music for meals and good digestion:

- Vivaldi, lute concertos
- Mendelssohn, string trios
- Mozart, Concerto for Flute and Harp

Music to help you sleep:

- Barber, Adagio for Strings
- Debussy, Clair de Lune

Dr. Randall McClellan, in *The Healing Forces of Music* (Amity House, 1988), makes a number of relevant points: There is presently *no* scientific explanation for why we respond to music in the first place.

While the auditory nerve stimulates the *hypothalamus* (the seat of emotion in the brain), and the hypothalamus also stimulates the *frontal cortex* (responsible for the intellectual interpretation of the sounds), it also sends impulses to the *thalamus*, triggering the "thalamic reflex" which is noted as rhythmic foot-tapping, swaying, nodding the head, etc.

The thalamus also influences metabolism, through its action on the *limbic system*, which is basic to biological function. It controls waking/sleeping cycles, hormone release, pulse rate, blood circulation, etc.

McClellan cites the work of Hevner, and of Helen Bonny, a noted music therapist. Bonny's work (with Savary, Harper & Row, 1975) centers on recognizing the value of music to enhance, prolong, and experience one's personal mood on a deeper level.

Bonny selected a wide variety of compositions, mostly from Western "classical" tradition and catalogued the selections according to their compatibility to eight mood groups:

1. Solemn   5. Humorous
2. Tragic   6. Joyous
3. Tender   7. Dramatic
4. Tranquil   8. Majestic

Kippner (cited in Altshuler, *Music and Medicine*, 1948) defines various states and levels of consciousness and indicates the way that music may affect that state:

State of consciousness	Characteristics	Role of music
Dream	Part of sleep cycle	Unexplored
Sleep		Can induce, prevent, or terminate
Hypnogogic	Between sleep and wakefulness	Not known
Hypnopompic	At end of dream cycle	Not known
Hyperalert	Activities demanding concentration	Not known
Lethargic	Fatigue, depression	Can relax, lift mood
Rapture	Intense feeling, emotion	Can induce, intensify
Hysteria	Negative mood, anxiety	Can calm
Fragmentation	Psychosis, dissociation, stress	Can prevent, or lift
Regressive	Age-inappropriate	Not known
Meditative	Minimal thought, brain alpha waves	Primary use of music in many cultures
Trance	Alert concentration on a single stimulus, chant	Tradition in almost every culture
Reverie	Dreamlike state	Can induce
Daydream		Major use of music
Stupor/coma	Suspended consciousness	No known effect
Stored memory	Past event not immediately available to consciousness	Can release
Expanded states	Drug-, hypnosis-induced	Can facilitate
Normal state	Logical, rational, thinking, goal-directed	Can cause return to, help to sustain, lift out of

Thus, music may serve to help:

- explore one's inner self
- develop self-awareness
- clarify personal values
- release blocked-up psychic energy
- enrich group spirit
- bring about deep relaxation
- foster religious experience

There are two types of spiritual music; one leads to a *trance* state, the other to the *meditative* state.

Trance most commonly results from repetitive rhythmic patterns sounded simultaneously over long periods of time. Trance is utilized by societies where shamanistic rituals dominate spiritual experience. Drums typically play a significant role in the procedure.

Music for meditation, on the other hand, affects the mind first, and the body second. It creates an atmosphere conducive to stillness and inner contemplation. It is quieter and slower; melodic phrase may last as long as the inspiration phase of breathing. *Its purpose is to slow and deepen breathing*, altering perception of time by focusing us on the present moment.

Contemporary American meditative music is derived chiefly from Eastern music, especially that from India as popularized by Ravi Shankar in the 1960s. It is the most common basis for relaxation-therapy adjunct music presently used in the U.S. It possesses some of the following characteristics:

- Melody: Older types used only three tones. Newer type uses up to seven diatonic tones, and melody progresses by steps with few "skips."

- Duration of phase: Equal to one breath.
- Loudness: Moderate to soft.
- Rhythm: Smooth and flowing with no sudden rhythmic changes.
- Tempo: Slow to moderate pitch change.
- Silence: Periods of silence, equal to one breath.
- Tonal quality: Flutes, strings, and voice.
- Texture: Simple (Western music is frequently too complex, and arouses emotions).
- Emotional content: Not intended to express personal emotional content. Emphasis on transpersonal peacefulness and inner joyousness.

The meanings, associations, and emotions experienced in music are shared by members of a culture. Others may learn to appreciate it, but they will not likely share associations to it. But there is reason to assume that there may be some elements in both Eastern and Western music traditions which transcend tradition: Characteristics of certain Western music create a dynamic energy in which a "sense of pressing forward" leads to anticipation sweeping us along to the inevitable "resolution" and "release."

McClellan proposes a number of *pan-cultural* music healing characteristics. Here are some of them:

- Pulse: At or below heart rate (72/minute) for calming and reducing tension.
  Slightly above heart rate (72–92/minute) for energizing.
  Triple meters slow breath more effectively than double meters.
- Rhythm: Smooth and flowing at all times for integrating internal body rhythm with energy flow.
- Drones: Without pauses have meditational and calming effect.
- Pauses: When at slow pulse rates, harmonize and inte-

grate internal body rhythms, breath and heart rate. At
fast rates, can lead to a frenetic state. Pauses can produce
a trance in the listener.

- Melodies: Slow and sustained for meditational purposes;
  pitch sequences primarily by step; at heart pulse rate or
  slightly faster for energizing purposes; tones drawn from
  the modes of five, six, and seven tones, Predominantly
  diatonic and asymmetrical. Avoid too many cadences.

- Dynamics: Very soft to moderately loud, depending on
  the composer's intent; no violent contrasts of loud and
  soft; change in dynamic levels should be slow and gradual, never sudden.

- Harmony: Used sparingly, if at all; when used, harmony
  should be modal and diatonic; harmony should be re-
  stricted to triads; avoid sevenths and ninths as they are
  too thick; movement of chord changes should be extremely slow.

- Duration: Minimum of 15 minutes of steady music; 20 to
  45 minutes optimum duration.

- Texture: Drone plus maximum of two voices for calming
  purposes. Voices should be widely spaced from each
  other.

- Tone Quality: Generally the softer quality instruments;
  most common ensemble, flute, strings and voice; others,
  pure organ tones (no vibrato), synthesizer when made to
  sound like organs, or other acoustic string and wind instruments.

- Resonance: Time should be sustained from four to eight
  seconds using either natural or electronic reverberation
  for calming purposes. Minimum reverberation for faster
  tempos when intention is to energize.

- Phase Structure: Smooth and flowing; one phase should
  last for the duration of one slow expiration of the breath
  as a minimum length when the intention is to calm. (pp.
  183–84)

Other pan-cultural characteristics of music are the
physiological and brain changes that some selections can
be shown to produce.

THE EFFECT OF MUSIC ON LEARNING

According to *Your Emotions and Your Health* (Rodale, 1986):
"Listening to music while studying is also very calming," says Dr. D. Schuster, Professor of Psychology, Iowa State University (p. 453).

"Reviewing material while listening to baroque music—music that has approximately one beat per second, such as Bach, Handel, Vivaldi—helps keep you in a relaxed state of mind," states Dr. O. Caskey, a psychologist with the El Paso School District (p. 454).

Speaking about his own musical compositions, some of them to the baroque beat, designed as counter-stress measures, Dr. Steven Halpern states that ". . . music brings you to a balanced brain state so that you're able to absorb, retain and recall information more easily. . . . It improves your creativity" (p. 454).

Dr. Charles Schmid of San Francisco recommends the slower movement of some baroque works to relax and enhance learning, including the Pachelbel Canon in D, the Mozart Piano Concerto No. 21, and the Albinoni Adagio in G.

THE EFFECT OF MUSIC ON THE AUTONOMIC NERVOUS SYSTEM

That music has a calming or exciting influence on the hearer is common everyday experience. . . . (But) do we realize that we enjoy music not so much for what it is but for what it does? The accelerated breathing rate, the increased blood pressure, the heightened bodily tonicity, the feeling of power and the reserve of strength make us supermen as we react to music. Blood composition, blood chemistry, blood distribution, blood pressure are all influenced by music. Equally important and extensive respiratory changes also take place under musical stimulation. Without these physiological reverberations music would be quite ineffectual, physically and mentally. (p. 162)

So says Prof. J. Kwalwasser of Syracuse University (*Exploring the Musical Mind*, Coleman-Ross, 1955).

But the autonomic nervous system reaction to music is not so simple as that described above, according to Harrer and Harrer, in *Music and the Brain* (Critchley et al. eds., Wm Heinemann, 1977). Employing the most modern and up-to-date recording equipment, they studied the nature and extent of these bodily changes and reported the following:

1. The automatic/physiological (autonomic) response to music depends on (a) individual constitutional factors such as age, sex, life-style, physical fitness, health; and temporary states such as those induced by alcohol, coffee, etc.; (b) emotional factors; and (c) attitudes towards music, its role in one's life, attitude towards the musical selection.

2. The physiological system most affected by music depends on (a) individual patterns: in some persons, respiratory changes predominate, while in others it is cardiovascular; (b) type of music: dance music and marches tend to result in motor responses while others may induce respiratory or cardiovascular changes.

3. There are significant differences between the listener and the performer.

Studies on Herbert von Karajan, conducting Beethoven's Leonora Overture No. 3, showed that his highest pulse rate did not occur at the point of maximum physical effort, but during those passages with the greatest emotional impact for him—those he later singled out as being the most profoundly touching. At these moments, pulse rate doubled.

4. Autonomic Reactions

(a) *Cardiovascular system.* Pulse rate increases in response to music.

In short selections, a decrease below resting baseline is seldom detected. An increase in pulse rate may be equally likely to be an expression of pleasure or disapproval. Pulse patterns are fairly consistent when the same piece of music is repeatedly played to the same person. Syncopated rhythms may produce extrasystole.

It is sometimes possible to "drive" (increase or decrease) pulse rate by dynamic changes in music volume, or change in rhythm. Relaxing and pleasure-charged passages, and sometimes the ending of a piece, may give rise to changes in pulse rate synchronously with respiration rhythm.

Vasoconstriction and vasodilation have also been observed in response to music.

(b) *Respiration.* Changes in frequency and depth of respiration occur with concomitant changes in the relationship between inhale and exhale—towards rhythmic or arrhythmic.

Individual response to music is highly stable and reproducible with repetition of the same piece of music. Intraindividual consistency corresponds to attitude towards the musical piece. In conventional Western/classical music, intraindividual differences are less significant than for other types of music.

In musical selections with prominent accelerations or decelerations of rhythm, there is a tendency to primary pulse synchronization in some persons, while others show synchronization of breathing rhythm. This suggests that it is possible to differentiate persons as primarily "circulatory" or primarily "respiratory" reactors.

(c) *Motor (muscle) activity.* During perception of music, there is *differentially* increased muscle activity. Music goes to the legs:

Muscle *action potentials* increase sharply in the legs but only slightly in the forehead. A reverse effect is found when doing mental arithmetic tasks: Muscles of the forehead (frontalis) tighten, while muscle in the legs relax.

In a study of persons listening to Bach's Brandenburg Concerto No. 1, pulse rate increased at the beginning and continued at a raised level. At the end of the selection, pulse rate oscillations occurred synchronously with respiration, indicating an alteration in respiratory regulation.

Respiration accelerated at the beginning, coupled with decreased breathing (tidal) volume, which increased again later on in the performance. At the end of the piece, respiration dropped to half of peak rate. Results were reproduced with repetition of the performance.

Increased muscle activity, pulse, and respiration which occur in response to the musical selection are expression of a generally raised level of activation: *But this activation is qualitatively different from the activation associated with stress: It involves muscle groups opposite to those active during mental tasks.*

When a person is asked to squeeze an *ergometer*, a device used to measure strength of hand grasp, while listening to music, the strength of the grasp is invariably reduced significantly. This is further indication that the "activation" of motor responses, pulse rate, and respiration, indicates a qualitative change in the "pattern" of responses.

What we learn from this is that listening to music may be similar in its effects to doing mild exercise to relieve tension:

Exercise is physically activating and may even be strenuous, yet its effect, over all, is to relax and reduce physical and mental tension.

But there are yet other aspects of music experience that contribute to its salutary effects:

It has been hypothesized that another physiological effect of music is the brain's increased release of endorphin, its own natural form of morphine—the "feel good" medicine—produced by meditation and running. Its release into the bloodstream is reported to produce a dreamy and extremely pleasurable sensation.

BRAIN FUNCTIONS

No discussion of the effects of music is complete without an examination of right-brain function.

According to many neurophysiologists, the right (brain) hemisphere is generally regarded as playing only a minor role in most persons. Since we are principally verbal beings, and language is a predominantly left hemisphere function, we tend to emphasize left hemisphere activities, especially those revolving around speech communications.

In clinical and scientific studies involving persons whose left hemisphere has suffered damage, it has become clear that while speech is impaired, musical ability is not. These studies have given a new perspective to the function of the right hemisphere.

In the evolution of the human brain, from that in creatures believed to be little differentiated from their ape ancestors, the gradually increasing requirement for communication and information processing and storage "contributed" to gradual hemisphere specialization: the analytic and sequential functions of language on the "dominant" left hemisphere (97% of population), and synthetic, spatial integration, and holistic relations on the right.

Nonhuman animals, no matter how complex their communication, do not show hemisphere specialization. Thus, the left hemisphere specialization is a function of the complexity of the human world. It is precisely that complexity that is said to lead to the mental and physical stress that is injurious in the long run.

Although the perception of music appears to involve sequences, a left hemisphere function, the evidence points to holistic recognition—like an image that is recognized as a whole rather than as a composite of its parts. And imagery is an important relaxation strategy.

The evolution of Western music may be thought to point to a gradual shift of the focus of music processing by the brain from the "minor" hemisphere in baroque or classical music, to the major hemisphere in today's avant-garde music.

When stimulated by music, the right hemisphere of the brain is stimulated. Stimulated means that blood flow increases to that area, resulting in increased metabolism. By increasing the stimulation to a given portion of the brain, neurophysiologists tell us, we increase its function, or role.

Increased blood flow and metabolism in specific areas of the brain are always related to increased activity in those areas. Increased right hemisphere blood flow and metabolism are invariably observed in the deep meditative state that has proven so beneficial in relaxation and in hypertension treatment.

Stimulating the right side of the brain is, in the words of Dr. Steven Halpern, an "anti-frantic" strategy.

The right/left hemisphere synchronization, which I

have personally observed many times in my clients during deep relaxation, indicates reduction of dominance of the left side—involved in anxiety.

I have used music extensively in teaching abdominal breathing in connection with the treatment of stress-related and psychosomatic disorders, and I will try to translate that experience into a format which you can use, and, I hope, enjoy.

Once again, you will have to read through the instructions and memorize them so that you can apply them in a relaxed state, with your eyes closed, while listening to music.

The pieces that I like best are Daniel Kobialka's "Timeless Motion," and "Path of Joy," *Li-sem Enterprises*, especially the numbers "Pachelbel Kanon," and "Jesu, Joy of Man's Desiring." I use these music pieces to accompany abdominal breathing. With alert "healing," or "alert energy," I like to use Jean Michel Jarre, "Oxygene," *Polygram Records*.

With "beach imagery," I use two tape recorders and softly, barely audibly, superimpose ocean waves on one of the Kobialka pieces.

Let's try it. Here is what you might do:

HOW TO. . .

Let's assume that you have been doing the exercises and that you now can sustain deep abdominal breathing without effort, and without getting dizzy, for at least 5 to 10 breaths.

Please sit back in your comfortable chair, or recliner, loosening your collar and belt, etc. Close your eyes and focus your attention at your nostril. Try this for 3 breaths.

Good.

Did you feel how cool and dry and refreshing your breath feels as it enters your nostrils?

Good.

Now try it again. concentrating on that sensation of "cool, and dry, and refreshing."

Now play the Kobialka "Pachelbel Kanon" at a reasonable sound level—not too loud or too soft. And close your eyes and once again focus your attention at your nostrils and the sensation of breathing in cool, dry, fresh air.

Good.

Round 3: Repeat the above, but after about the second deep breath, imagine that you are breathing in the music. Imagine that you are not listening to, but breathing in the music and fill up every space in your body with the music that you are inhaling. When you exhale, slowly pull your abdomen as far back as you can, letting the tension in your body flow out with your breath. Then, repeat the inhale procedure. Do this for about 4 or 5 breaths.

How do you feel?

Many of my clients find this to be an extremely helpful and enjoyable procedure.

You can also combine it with beach imagery by imagining that you are at the beach, listening to the music, and imagining that you are breathing in the music as you are watching the ocean waves. If you have two sources, you may wish to superimpose ocean wave sounds on the music.

There are some instances when a more alert state of relaxation is desired. In that case, I use the "Oxygene" piece, with ocean wave sounds superimposed, and my instructions are:

"As you inhale, imagine that you are breathing in the music and that it is carrying energy into your body. Feel the energy "percolating" all through your body. And as you exhale, feel the tension bubbling out with your breath."

I also use the "Pachelbel Kanon," or "Jesu, Joy of Man's Desiring," with or without superimposed ocean sounds, when doing the relaxation sequence, "I'm letting the tension out of my forehead. . . ." given in Chapter 10.

The music and sound selections that I have listed here are those that appeal most to me and to my clients. I have also used "Celtic Harp," and other pieces. You will want to experiment and find what pleases and relaxes you best.

THE EFFECT OF MUSIC ON ABDOMINAL BREATHING

I have used the pieces mentioned above with numerous clients. With very few exceptions, they have reported to me that they like it and that they find that it helps them to relax more quickly.

It invariably slows down the breathing cycle. This means that the volume of air increases with each breath, and that less work is being done to move air in and out of the lungs. This promotes relaxation.

THE BREATH CONNECTION—CONCLUSION

It has, at times, been tough reading this book: We have covered much information and many ideas. Let me summarize some of them for you.

First, *psychosomatic disorders* must, in the end, be defined as encompassing all disorders which are either "caused by" or affected by mental or emotional factors.

Now, since stress is an emotional factor, it stands to reason that the class of stress-related disorders and psychosomatic disorders must, at the very least, overlap.

These overlapping categories of disorders include just about everything from anxiety and panic attacks, to phobias, migraine, sleep disorders, hypertension, muscle, neurological, gastrointestinal, and a host of other disorders, as outlined in this book.

Secondly, you are not *responsible*, in the ordinary sense of that word, for having acquired one or more of these. You could not, at will, acquire a disorder to which you do not have a predisposition, by virtue of genetic inheritance.

That means, that if there is absolutely no history of allergies in your family, the chance that you will have one is slim indeed. That holds also for migraine, if there is no evidence of vascular disease in your family.

No matter how emotionally upset you become, you cannot readily produce a disorder which does not run in your family in one form or another.

Thirdly, stress-related and psychosomatic disorders result from an increase in the likelihood or severity of conditions to which you are predisposed when you make unreasonable demands of your body, such as stress in the form of sustained arousal, or poor nutrition.

Finally, some forms of breathing can cause both psychosomatic disorders and sustained stressful arousal. When stressful arousal is sustained by these forms of breathing, stress-related and psychosomatic disorders may increase in frequency and severity.

A program including sound medical advice, nutrition, and exercises which focus on restoring physiological calm and order through deep diaphragmatic breathing with imagery and music may be very helpful in reducing the frequency and severity of the symptoms of your disorders and, it is hoped, ultimately getting rid of them for good.

Thus, while you may not be responsible for acquiring your disorder, you can take responsibility for controlling it.

Deep abdominal breathing, as taught in this book, has been shown to be an important component in a program to control stress-related and psychosomatic disorders and music has a profoundly salutary effect on breathing. It helps to increase ventilation, and seems to help reduce the effort or work required by the body to gain air.

Listening to music is also a fun way to practice breathing. And I hope that in addition to finding these exercises helpful that you also enjoy doing them.

Index

Acidosis, metabolic, 70–71, 123, 232
Action hormones: *See also* Adrenaline; Noradrenaline
  in asthma, 266
Adrenaline, 39, 144, 155
Advertising industry, 102
Aerobic exercise, 52, 65, 235
Aerophobia, 184–188
Agoraphobia, 85, 174, 184
  breathing therapy, 244–245, 258
  case example, 271–274
  hyperventilation and, 76, 261–262
  vitamin B_6 and, 139
Air
  atmospheric, composition of, 64–65
  expelled from lungs, 62, 65
  end-tidal, 65
Airplane phobia: *See* Aerophobia
Alcoholic beverages, as tyramine source, 126, 128
Alert and Rapid Relaxation Technique, 33, 230
Allergic reactions, 67
  food-related: *See* Dietary factors
Altitude, as aerophobia cause, 185–188

Alveoli, 64
Amines, vasoactive, 124, 203, 266
Amino acids, migraine and, 260–261
Anemia
  breathing rate, 70
  folic acid deficiency and, 227
  hyperventilation and, 70, 227
  iron-deficiency, 137
  nutritional deficiency and, 141
  prevention, 139
Anger, 40, 169
Angina
  calcium and, 175
  cold hands in, 254
  hyperventilation and, 161
  hyperventilation challenge and, 78
  tyramine and, 123
Anorexia, 227
Anoxia, 65, 201
Antianxiety drugs, 243
Antibody production, 133
Anticonvulsants, as migraine therapy, 203
Antidepressants, 122
Antihypertensives, 104
Anxiety: *See also* Anxiety-related disorders

Anxiety (*cont.*)
  anticipation of future and, 43
  breathing as indicator of, 111, 181
  breathing/cognitive restructuring
    therapy, 243–246, 256, 258
  breathing patterns, 168
  breathing rate, 169
  cold hands in, 254
  death-related: *See* Fear, of death
  definition, 99
  dietary factors, 119–120
  hyperventilation and, 76, 171–172,
    180
  hypocapnia and, 171
  individual nature of, 107
  left-brain dominance in, 295
  meditation and, 279
  music and, 277
  neurocirculatory asthenia and, 85
  psychosomatic disorders and, 81
  relaxation techniques, 176–177,
    243–246
  respiratory neurosis and, 168
  spirogram, 169
  threshold, 172
Anxiety-related disorders, 81–84
  case examples, 188–191
  dietary factors, 141–146
Aorta, in vasodilation, 158
Aortic arch
  circulatory system regulation by,
    157
  receptors, 59, 155
  vasodilation and, 158
Arachidonic acid, 205
Aretaeus, 196
Argon, 65
Aristotle, 100
Arousal, 40
  sexual, 63
Arrhythmia
  cardiac, 154, 162
    hyperventilation and, 77
    hyperventilation challenge and, 78

Arrhythmia (*cont.*)
  cardiac (*cont.*)
    magnesium deficiency and, 138
    potassium deficiency and, 227
    respiratory sinus rhythm, 156
Arteries
  blood flow, 153
    blood pressure and, 156–158
  constriction: *See* Vasoconstriction
  diameter: *See also* Vasoconstriction;
    Vasodilation
    autonomic nervous system con-
      trol of, 157, 158–159
    carbon dioxide control of, 158,
      159, 255
  dilation: *See* Vasodilation
  in epilepsy, 195–196
  in hypocapnia, 173–174
Asphyxiation, 173
Aspirin, as prostaglandin inhibitor,
  205
Asthenia, neurocirculatory, 38, 85,
  167, 180
Asthma, 67
  breathing therapy, 264–265, 277
  dietary factors, 134–135, 266
  hand temperature in, 265–266
  hyperventilation and, 76–77
  inhalants and, 124, 135
  psychoanalytic theory of, 38
  pulse rate in, 265–266
  tyramine and, 123–124
  vitamin B_6 therapy, 124
Atmungs-Pathologie und Therapie
  (Hofbauer), 177
Attitude, role of, 228–230
Auditory nerve, 284
Autogenic training, 214–215
Autonomic nervous system
  arterial diameter control by, 157,
    158–159
  bodily function regulation by, 60
  music and, 289–293
  parasympathetic, 39, 40, 60, 114

Autonomic nervous system (*cont.*)
  sympathetic
    arousal and, 40
    bodily function regulation by,
      39, 60
    breathing and, 169
    heart stimulation by, 155
    in Raynaud's disease/syndrome,
      210
    tyramine effects, 123
    in vasoconstriction/vasodilation,
      157–158

Baroreceptor, 59
Behavior
  music and, 281–289
  stereotyped, 103, 104
Behavioral medicine, 28–30
Benadryl, 92
Berger, Hans, 209
Bernard, Claude, 157–158
Beta-blockers, 204, 267
Beverages, tyramine-containing, 124,
  126, 128, 129
Biofeedback, 99
  as behavioral medicine, 28, 30
  definition, 253
  electromyographic, 253
  hand temperature regulation with,
    215–218, 253–255
Blood
  acid-base balance
    breathing and, 173
    buffer mechanism, 66
    carbon dioxide and, 66, 137
    definition, 77
    hemoglobin and, 66–67
    hyperventilation and, 9, 42, 67,
      76
    metabolism and, 66, 184
    potassium and, 138
  acidity of, 174; *see also* Blood, acid-
    base balance
  oxygenation, 64, 65, 228

Blood circulation: *See* Blood flow
Blood flow
  alveolar, 64
  arterial, 153, 156–158
  in brain, 174
    breathing rate and, 152
    in hyperventilation, 174, 176
    in meditation, 294
  factors affecting, 152–153
  during fight-or-flight reaction, 39
  hand temperature and, 215–218
  hyperventilation and, 9, 174, 176
  in vasoconstriction, 173
Blood pressure, 149–150; *see also* Hy-
    pertension
  antidepressants and, 122
  arterial blood flow and, 156–158
  baroreceptors and, 59
  breathing and, 158
  breathing therapy, 246–249
  diastolic
    definition, 155
    measurement, 157, 252
    normal, 157
  dietary factors, 247
  heart and, 154–156
  hyperventilation and, 151–154,
    158, 159–160
  hyperventilation challenge and, 92
  measurement, 156–157, 247, 252,
    253
  music and, 278, 279
  normal, 149, 157
  in stress, 150
  systolic
    definition, 155
    measurement, 157, 252
    normal, 157
  tyramine and, 126
Blood pressure cuff, 157, 247, 253
Blood volume, 154
Body–brain interaction, 30–31
Book of Genesis, 55
Bradykinin, 206

Brahman, 55
Brain
arterial diameter control in, 158–
159
blood flow, 174
breathing rate and, 152
in hyperventilation, 174, 176
in meditation, 294
evolution, 43–44, 293–294
hemispheric specialization, 293–
295
in hyperventilation, 123
in hypocapnia, 174
lactic acid production by, 184
in music perception, 284
vascular bed of, 159
Brain function, music and, 293–295
Brain waves
discovery, 209
in epilepsy, 207
hyperventilation challenge-related,
195
in migraine, 202
music and, 279
relaxation, 202
seizure, 202
sensory motor rhythm (SMR),
216–217
Bread, as tyramine source, 126–127
Breath holding, 39, 42
Breathing, 55–71
abdominal/diaphragmatic
for aerophobia, 187
for agoraphobia, 244–245, 258
for anxiety, 243–246, 256, 258
for asthma, 264–265, 277
benefits of, 228
for blood pressure, 152, 246–249
contraindications, 231–232
for diabetes, 267
for emphysema, 264–265
for epilepsy, 207, 249–252
for gastrointestinal disorders,
267

Breathing (cont.)
abdominal/diaphragmatic (cont.)
hand temperature and, 255–256,
257
with imagery, 230–232, 244
for insomnia, 268–270
inspiration/expiration ratio, 67–
68, 168
lung ventilation in, 68–69
for migraine, 249–252, 260
with music, 295–297
for panic attacks/disorders, 258,
262–263
for phobias, 243–246, 258
prophylactic, 248–249
for Raynaud's dis-
ease/syndrome, 249–252
for schizophrenia, 32, 168
for stress, 256, 258
for tension, 243–246, 256, 258
training exercise, 235–243
abnormal, 30–33, 66–68; see also
Dyspnea; Hyperventilation;
Tachypnea
clothing-related, 70
psychological factors, 180–182
blood pressure and, 158
chest, 58, 64, 67, 69–70
conditioning and, 216–218
control, 59–60
cyanide-related stimulation, 211–
212
diaphragmatic: See Breathing, ab-
dominal/diaphragmatic
function, 173
hypertension and, 130
as life, 55–56
music and, 286, 288, 291–292
observation of, 57–58
pulse rate and, 156
reverse, 58
rhythm of, 7, 67–68
shallow, 66, 67
surfactant, 64

Breathing mode, 67
Breathing patterns
  of heart attack patients, 162
  individual nature of, 56
  in neuroses, 168–169
  sex differences in, 169
Breathing rate
  brain blood flow and, 152
  breathing volume and, 65–66
  in depression, 170
  emotional factors, 169–170
  in grief, 170
  hyperventilation and, 42
  measurement, 58
  music and, 279
  normal, 65, 68, 149
  in relaxation training, 243–244
  in stress, 150
Breathing retraining: See Breathing,
  abdominal/diaphragmatic
Breathing therapy: See Breathing, ab-
  dominal/diaphragmatic
Breathing volume, breathing rate relationship, 65–66
Breathlessness: See Dyspnea
Bronchi, 61, 63
Bronchiole, 61, 63
Bronchitis, chronic, 76–77
Bruxism, 263–264
Bulimia, 227
Bumex, 92
Burrhole, as headache therapy, 197–198
Buspar, 92

Caffeine
  as insomnia cause, 270
  as migraine cause, 132–133
Calcium
  cardiac arrhythmia and, 154
  deficiency, 138
  depression and, 138
  excess, 137–138
  hypocapnia and, 175
  muscular hyperactivity and, 175

Cannon, W. B., 38–39
Capillary abnormalities, 210–211
Carbon dioxide: See also Hypocapnia
  acid-base balance and, 66, 76
  arterial diameter control by, 158,
    159, 255
  biofeedback regulation of, 217
  end-tidal air content, 65
  hyperventilation and, 173
  ischemic heart disease and, 79
  normal levels, 79
  panic attacks and, 182
  syncope and, 159
  transport by blood, 60, 64, 153
Carbon monoxide, atmospheric air
  content, 64–65
Cardiac output: See Heart, work output
Cardiovascular disease: See Heart
  disease
Cardiovascular system
  breathing and, 151
  hyperventilation effects, 88, 89, 90,
    151–164
    blood pressure, 151–154, 158,
      159–160
    syncope, 159–160
  music and, 291
Cardizem, 92
Carlton, Richard M., 120, 144–146,
  250
Carotid sinus, 59, 157, 158
Carroll, Lewis, 197
Catastrophe theory, 135–136
Catlin, George, 61
Cheese
  as salicylate source, 206
  as tyramine source, 124–125, 127,
    128
Chemoreceptor, 59, 173
Chest pain: See also Angina
  in hyperventilation, 160–161
Childbirth, music during, 278
Children

Children (cont.)
  hyperactivity, dietary factors, 119–
      120, 131, 205, 270
  ketogenic diet, 261
  migraine, 132–133, 134
    therapy, 203
  respiratory sinus arrhythmia,
      156
Chocolate
  as asthma cause, 124, 128
  as insomnia cause, 270
  as tyramine source, 125, 126
Chopin, Frederic, 197
Chromium
  deficiency, 123
  glucose tolerance factor and, 267
Chronic obstructive pulmonary dis-
    ease, 67, 76–77, 170
Chvostek's sign, 83, 84
Circulatory disease: See also Heart
    disease
  tyramine and, 126
Clothing, as hyperventilation cause,
    70
Cockroach, exoskeleton, 124, 135,
    266
Codeine, with empirin, 93
Coffee
  as insomnia cause, 270
  as tyramine source, 124, 126, 128
Cognitive behavior therapy, 99
Cognitive restructuring, 243–246,
    256, 258
Colitis, 267
Communication, brain hemispheric
    specialization and, 293–294
Conditioning, 99, 101–102
  breathing and, 216–218
  counter-, 113
  energy expenditure and, 102–103
  Pavlovian, 39–40, 101–102
  psychosomatic disorders and, 44
  stress-related disorders and, 101–
      115

Consciousness, music and, 284–286
Convulsions: See Seizure disorders
Coping strategies
  disease and, 47
  hyperventilation and, 181
Copper, 138
Coronary artery disease, 42
Coué, Emile, 213
Counterconditioning, 113
Creativity, music and, 280, 289
Cure of High Blood Pressure by Respira-
    tory Exercises, The (Tirala) 152,
    247
Cyanide, as breathing stimulant,
    211–212

DaCosta's syndrome, 85, 180
Dandruff, 266
Daydreaming, 285
Death, fear of, 170, 174
Deductive reasoning, 43–44
Depression
  breathing rate, 170
  calcium and, 138
  dietary factors, 119–120
  dyspnea and, 170
  hyperventilation and, 170
"Depressive delusion of imminent
    death," 170
Desensitization, 113
Diabetes
  breathing therapy, 267
  dietary factors, 267
  glucose tolerance factor and, 267
  insulin-dependent, 232
  metabolic acidosis and, 70–71, 123,
      232
  tyramine and, 123
Diagnostic and Statistical Manual of the
    American Psychiatric Association
    (DSM-III), 178–180, 183
Diet
  ketogenic, 136, 261
  oligoantigenic, 133

Dietary factors, 119–146
  in anxiety, 119–120
  in asthma, 134–135, 266
  in blood pressure, 247
  in childhood hyperactivity, 119–
    120, 131, 205–206, 270
  in depression, 119–120
  in epilepsy, 134–135, 250
  in gastrointestinal disorders, 267,
    268
  in hypertension, 121–130, 141
  in insomnia, 270–271
  in migraine, 119–120, 122, 130–
    136, 203–204, 250, 260–261
    in children, 132–133, 134
  in oxygen transport, 133–134
  in panic attacks, 143–146, 259, 263
  pulse rate and, 249
  in vasoconstrictive disorders, 122–
    124
Digestion, music and, 283
Disease: See also Illness; names of
    specific diseases
  coping strategies, 47
  personality factors, 47
Disorientation, 174
Diuretics, 104
Dizziness, 78, 92, 159, 174
Double-blind study, 100
Drugs: See also names of specific
    drugs
  effectiveness, 100
  hallucinogenic, 278
  as hyperventilation cause, 91–93
Dyspnea, 130
  in depression, 170
  in hyperventilation, 88
  in obstructive lung disease, 170
  in panic disorder, 178, 262
Dysponesis, 28, 172

ECG: See Electrocardiogram
EEG: See Electroencephalogram
Effort syndrome, 38, 85, 167, 180

Electrocardiogram (ECG), 154
  during hyperventilation, 161–162
Electroencephalogram (EEG)
  during migraine, 202
  during syncope, 159
Electrolytes, 154, 155, 227
Emotion
  breathing and, 56–57
  breathing rate and, 169–170
  hyperventilation and, 172
  music and, 281, 283, 290–291
Emphysema, 67
  breathing therapy, 264–265
  hyperventilation and, 76–77
Empirin, with codeine, 93
Endorphins, 278, 293
Energy conservation, physiological,
    102–103
Epilepsy, 206–210; see also Seizure
    disorders
  age factors, 207–208
  arterial constriction and, 195–196,
    207, 209
  brain cell dysfunction and, 206–
    207, 208
  breathing therapy, 207, 249–252
  capillary abnormalities and, 210–
    211
  dietary factors, 134–135, 250
  historical background, 208
  hyperventilation and, 77, 134–135,
    140, 207, 208–210
  idiopathic
    breathing therapy, 249–252
    cold hands in, 254, 261
    dietary factors, 134–135
    hyperventilation and, 77
    tryptophan and, 131
    tyramine and, 123
  incidence, 207
  inhalants and, 135
  magnesium deficiency and, 138, 140
  migraine and, 133, 135, 195–196,
    203, 207

Epilepsy (cont.)
   as psychosomatic disorder, 195
   seizure classification, 208
   temporal lobe, 231
Ergometer, 292
Ergotamine, 104
Ergot derivatives, 104, 201
Evolution, of brain, 43–44, 293–294
Evolution theory, of psychosomatic
   disorders, 43–44
Exercise
   aerobic, 52, 65, 235
   for cardiovascular fitness, 155–156
   for tension relief, 292–293

Fainting: See Syncope
"Falling disease"; see Epilepsy
Fat, dietary, as tyramine source, 125,
   127
Fatigue, diaphragmatic, 265
Fear
   of death, 170, 174, 177, 180
   of flying: See Aerophobia
   nervous system function in, 103–
   104
Fensterheim, Herbert, 91
Fibrosis, interstitial, 67
Fight-or-flight reaction, 38–39, 43,
   44, 114, 121
Flying, fear of: See Aerophobia
Folic acid deficiency, 139, 227, 268
Food additives, 132–133
Food allergy: See Dietary factors
Food coloring, 132–133, 206
Freud, Sigmund, 177–178, 197
Frontal cortex, in music perception,
   284
Fruit
   as salicylate source, 206
   as tyramine source, 125, 126, 127,
   130
   as tyrosine source, 131
Frustration, prolonged, 40
Future, anticipation of, 43

Galen, 196, 208
Gastritis, 267, 268
Gastrointestinal disorders, dietary
   factors, 267
Glucose, 114, 183, 184
Glucose tolerance factor, 267
Grief, 170

Habit, psychosomatic disorders and,
   111–112
Hallucinogens, 278
Halpern, Steven, 278, 281–282
Hand temperature, 152, 257
   in asthma, 265–266
   biofeedback control, 215–218, 253–
   255
   diaphragmatic breathing and, 255–
   256
   in epilepsy, 254, 261
   handwarming techniques, 214–215
   in migraine, 152, 215–218, 249–
   250, 254, 259, 261
   in Raynaud's syndrome, 215, 216,
   249–250, 254
Headache: See also Migraine
   tension, 263–264
   trephination for, 197–198
   tryptophan-related, 271
Heart: See also Cardiovascular system
   blood pressure and, 154–156
   contractions, 154, 155
   description, 154
   stroke volume, 151, 155–156
   work output, 151, 160
Heart attack patients, breathing patterns, 162
Heart disease
   biofeedback therapy, 30
   breathing rate and, 70
   coronary artery disease, 42
   hyperventilation and, 70
   hyperventilation challenge and, 92
   ischemic, 79
   meditation and, 279

Heart disease (*cont.*)
  relaxation therapy, 30
  tyramine and, 126
Heart rate
  factors affecting, 155–156
  music and, 287, 288
Helium, 65
Hemicrania, 196
Hemigraine, 196
Hemoglobin
  acid-base balance and, 66–67
  hypocapnia effects, 174
Henry VIII, King, 226
Himmler, Heinrich, 197
Hippocrates, 208
Histamine
  migraine and, 133, 204
  nasal mucus lining response, 63
  Raynaud's disease/syndrome and,
    210, 211
  storage, 137
Histamine blocking agent, 104
Homeostasis, 40, 60
"Honeymoon nose," 63
Hood, Thomas, 57
Hyperactive reflex, 82, 84
Hyperactivity
  childhood, dietary factors, 119–
    120, 131, 205–206, 270
  muscular, 175
Hyperkinetic syndrome: *See* Hyper-
    activity, childhood
Hyperpnea, 159
Hypertension
  biofeedback therapy, 30
  breathing and, 130
  breathing rate and, 70
  dietary factors, 121–130, 141
  hyperventilation and, 70
  incidence, 152
  magnesium deficiency and, 138
  nutritional deficiency and, 141
  potassium deficiency and, 227
  psychoanalytic theory of, 38

Hypertension (*cont.*)
  relaxation therapy, 30
  tyramine and, 122, 123, 126
Hypertensive crisis, 122
Hyperventilation, 49, 75–95
  acid-base balance and, 9, 42, 67, 76
  agoraphobia and, 76, 261–262
  anxiety and, 76, 171–172, 180
  associated disorders, 76, 91
  asthma and, 76–77
  blood flow and, 9, 174, 176
  brain oxygen content and, 188
  breathing rate and, 42
  breathing therapy, 277
  carbon dioxide in, 173
  cardiovascular effects, 88, 89, 90,
    151–164, 160–163
    blood pressure, 151–154, 158,
      159–160
    syncope, 159–160
  causes, 76–77
  characteristics, 77–79, 80
  clothing-related, 70
  cold hands in, 254
  coping strategies and, 181
  definition, 68, 75
  in depression, 170
  diagnostic problems, 84–91, 94
  electrocardiogram, 161–162
  emotional factors, 172
  epilepsy and, 77, 134–135, 140,
    207, 208–210
  Freud's interpretation of, 177–178
  gastrointestinal effects, 88, 89, 91
  as hysteria, 85
  incidence, 80
  iron deficiency and, 137
  medication-induced, 91–93
  migraine and, 180, 202–203
  musculoskeletal effects, 89, 90
  neurologic effects, 88, 89, 90
  panic attacks and, 76, 174, 178–
    180, 182–184, 261–262
  personality factors, 181–182

Hyperventilation (*cont.*)
  phobic behavior and, 170–171,
    174, 180
  prevention, 172
  psychological disorders and, 172–
    173, 176–178
  psychological effects, 90
  respiratory effects, 89, 90
  seizure disorders and, 136
  symptoms, 86–91
  syncope, 149–150, 159–160
  tyramine and, 123
  vasoconstriction and, 123, 202
  vitamin B_6 and, 139
Hyperventilation challenge, 91–92,
    196
  contraindications, 78–79, 92
Hyperventilation Syndrome, The
    (Fried), 11–12
Hypocapnia
  in anxiety, 171
  definition, 173
  effects, 173–184
    on arteries, 173–174
    on hemoglobin, 174
    on muscles, 175
    on nervous system, 175–176
Hypochondriac, 82, 227–228
Hypoglycemia, 70, 201, 261, 267
Hypothalamus, 39, 284
Hypothyroidism, 227
Hypoxemia, 65
Hypoxia
  altitude-related, 186–188
  chronic: *See* Hypoxemia
  definition, 65, 183, 201
  graded, 183
  hyperventilation and, 172–173
  migraine and, 201–203
Hysteria, 38
  hyperventilation and, 49, 85, 177
  music and, 285
  as respiratory neurosis, 168

Ileitis, 267
Illness: *See also* specific types of ill-
    ness
  bodily adjustments to, 59
  predisposing factors, 45–47
    life events, 45–47
  psychosomatic components, 100
Imagery, 279
  with diaphragmatic breathing,
    230–232, 244
  music and, 282, 294, 295, 296
Inhalants, 265
  asthma and, 124, 135
  epilepsy and, 135
  migraine and, 135
Insomnia, 268–271
  breathing therapy, 268–270
  dietary factors, 270–271
Inspiration/expiration(I/E)ratio, 67–
    68, 168
Institute for Rational Emotive
    Therapy (IRET), 28
International Center for the Disabled
    (ICD), 141, 144
Iron, dietary, 137
Irritable bowel syndrome, 267, 268
Ischemia, 79

Jefferson, Thomas, 197
Job performance, music and, 280
"Junk food," migraine and, 132–133

Kabandi Katyayana, 56
Kaiser Permanente, 278
Ketogenic diet, 136, 261
Kinin, 206

Lactic acid, 184
Language
  brain hemispheric specialization
    and, 293–294
  development, 43
Learning, music and, 289

Life events, illness and, 45–47
Limbic system, 284
Lind, James, 225–226
Linnaeus, Carolus, 100
Lister, Joseph, 100
LSD, 278
Lubar, J., 207
Lum, L. C., 51, 78
Lung
  airway passages, 61–63
  as external organ, 8
  minute volume, 65–66
  in abnormal breathing, 66
  in anxiety, 171
  in diaphragmatic breathing, 68
  structure, 63–64
  tidal volume, 66
  ventilation in, 8

Magnesium, 137–138
  cardiac arrhythmia and, 154
  deficiency, 138, 141
  in diabetes, 123
  in epilepsy, 140
Malabsorption syndrome, 267
Manganese, 138
Marijuana, 278
Marplan, 122
Meat, as tyramine source, 124–125,
    126, 127, 128, 129
Meditation, 243, 278
  for blood pressure control, 246–
    247
  bodily changes during, 278–279
  music and, 285, 286
  transcendental, 32, 279
  Zazen methods, 279
  Zen, 56
Medulla, in circulatory system reg-
    ulation, 157, 158
Memory, music and, 285
Mental ability/concentration, music
    and, 281, 283

Metabolic disorders, chest breathing
    and, 69–70
Metabolism, 58
  acid-base balance and, 66, 184
  aerobic, 183
  anaerobic, 182, 183–184
  homeostasis and, 60
Methane, 65
Migraine, 196–198
  anxiety and, 195
  breathing therapy, 249–252, 260
  capillary abnormalities in, 210–211
  causes, 201
  control, 214
  dietary factors, 119–120, 122, 130–
    136, 203–204, 250, 260–261
    in children, 132–133, 134
  epilepsy and, 133, 135, 195–196,
    203, 207
  hand temperature in, 152, 215–
    218, 249–250, 254, 261
  historical background, 197–198
  hyperventilation and, 180, 202–
    203
  incidence, 197
  kinins and, 206
  low brain oxygen in, 201–203
  nasal mucus lining in, 63
  prostaglandins and, 205–206
  research, 196–197
  seizure disorders and, 197
  stress and, 195
  symptoms, 198–200, 260
  tension and, 195
  tryptophan and, 131
  tyramine and, 123
  vasoconstriction in, 216, 259
  vasodilation in, 259
Milk
  allergic response to, 119
  asthma and, 123–124
  as tryptophan source, 203, 271
  as tyramine source, 125, 128

Mind Power and Privileges (Olson), 213–214
Minerals, dietary, 136–137; *see also* specific minerals
Minute volume: *See* Lung, minute volume
Mite, 266
Monoamine oxidase, 122, 126
Monoamine oxidase inhibitor, 122
Monogesic, 93
Mood, music and, 283, 284
Motor activity, music and, 281, 292–293
Mouth, function, 61
Muscle
    action potentials, 292
    in hypocapnia, 175
    motor activity, music and, 281, 292
Music, 275–297
    abdominal breathing and, 295–297
    autonomic nervous system and, 289–293
    behavioral effects, 281–289
    brain function and, 293–295
    emotion and, 281, 283, 290–291
    as endorphin inducer, 293
    learning and, 289
    meditative, 285, 286–287, 288
    Musak, 280
    "New Age," 278, 279, 282
    pan-cultural characteristics, 287–288
    physical effects, 277–278
    psychological effects, 277–278, 280–288
    as relaxation therapy, 292–293, 295–297
    in the workplace, 280
Myocardium, oxygen supply, 160
Myxedema, 227

Napoleon Bonaparte, 197
Nardil, 122

Nausea
    age factors, 200
    hypoglycemia and, 201
    migraine and, 198, 200, 259
Neon, 65
Nervous system: *See also* Autonomic nervous system
    in hypocapnia, 175–176
Neurasthenia, 39, 177; *see also* Asthenia, neurocirculatory
Neurosis
    anxiety, 85, 87, 173, 210
    breathing measurements, 168–169
    breathing patterns, 168–169
    cardiac/cardiovascular, 38, 180
    respiratory, 168
    spirometry, 167–168
Neurotransmitters, 212
"New Age," music of, 278, 279, 282
Niacin, deficiency, 227
Nitrogen
    atmospheric air content, 64
    end-tidal air content, 65
Noradrenaline, 39, 155
Nose
    mucus blanket, 62–63
    respiratory function, 61–62
    structure, 61–62
Nutrient deficiency: *See also* specific nutrient deficiencies
    stress and, 140–141
Nutrition: *See* Dietary factors
Nutritionist, 120

Obstructive pulmonary disease: *See* Chronic obstructive pulmonary disease
Oligoantigenic diet, 133
Olson, A. B., 213–214
Operant conditioning, 44
Orientation, 114
Osteoporosis, 138

Oxygen
  atmospheric air content, 64
  end-tidal air content, 65
  excess, 65
  hemoglobin interaction, 174
  low: *See also* Hypoxia
    as aerophobia cause, 185–188
    metabolism and, 183–184
    transport, 8, 60, 152–153
    alveolar, 64
    dietary factors, 133–134
    psychosomatic disorders and, 52
Oxygenation, 65, 228

Pain relief, with music, 277, 278
Panic attack/disorder
  breathing therapy, 258, 262–263
  cold hands in, 254
  dietary factors, 143–146, 259, 263
  flying-related: *See* Aerophobia
  hyperventilation and, 76, 174, 178–
    180, 182–184, 261–262
  lactic acid and, 184
  symptoms, 88, 178–179, 182–183
  vitamin B_6 and, 139
Parahydroxyphenylacetic acid, 126
Parry's compression test, 197
Pasteur, Louis, 100
Pavlovian conditioning, 39, 40, 101–
  102
Pellagra, 227
Penfield, W., 202, 209
Personality factors
  in disease, 47
  in hyperventilation, 181–182
pH: *See also* Blood, acid-base balance
  definition, 77
Phobia: *See also* Aerophobia;
    Agoraphobia
  breathing/cognitive restructuring
    therapy, 243–246, 258
  cold hands in, 254

Phobia (*cont.*)
  hyperventilation and, 170–171,
    174, 180
  relaxation techniques, 176–177
Physicians' Desk Reference, 87
Pippalada, 55–56
Pitirosporum ovale, 266
Placebo study, 100
Platelet aggregation
  amines and, 203
  thromboxane and, 205
  tyramine and, 123
Platelet aggregation factor, 203, 204
Pollutants: *See also* Inhalants
  asthma and, 124
  atmospheric air content, 65
Potassium
  cardiac arrhythmia and, 154
  deficiency, 138
  malabsorption syndrome and, 267
Prasna Upanishad, 55
Prehistoric peoples, trephination
    practiced by, 197–198
Primaxin, 93
Productivity, music and, 280
Prostaglandins, migraine and, 205–
    206
Psychoanalytic theory, of psycho-
    somatic disorders, 37, 38
Psychological disorders, hyperven-
    tilation and, 172–173, 176–178
Psychological effects, of music, 277–
    278, 280–288
Psychological factors/symptoms
  in breathing disorders, 180–182
  in hyperventilation, 176–178
Psychophysiological disorders, 12, 52
Psychosomatic components, of ill-
    ness, 100
Psychosomatic disorders, 37–52, 80–
    84, 99
  anxiety-related, 81–84, 141–146,
    188–191

Psychosomatic disorders (cont.)
  common types, 47–49
  conditioning and, 44
  definition, 37
  evolution theory of, 43–44
  fight-or-flight theory of, 38–39
  general adaptation theory of, 39–41
  habit and, 111–112
  multifactor theory of, 44–47
  oxygen delivery and, 42
  predisposing factors, 179
  psychoanalytic theory of, 37, 38
  somatic weakness theory of, 42
  stress and, 112
Pulse oximeter, 186
Pulse rate, 149–150
  in asthma, 265–266
  breathing and, 156
  dietary factors, 249
  measurement, 153–154, 247, 252
  music and, 278, 279, 287, 290–291, 292
  normal, 149, 154
  in stress, 150
  tyramine and, 258
Pyridoxal-5-phosphate, 140
Pyridoxine: See Vitamin B$_6$

Qui, 56

Radial artery, 154
Rational emotive therapy (RET), 28
Raynaud's disease/syndrome, 210–212
  breathing therapy, 249–252
  control, 214
  dietary factors, 250
  hand temperature in, 215–218, 249–250, 254, 259
  tyramine and, 123
  vasoconstriction in, 216, 259
Receptor
  of aortic arch, 59, 155

Receptor (cont.)
  baroreceptor, 59
  chemoreceptor, 59, 173
Red blood cell, in respiration, 8
Reflexes
  hyperactive, 82, 84
Relaxation techniques, 176–177, 113
  behavioral medicine and, 28
  benefits of, 114
  breathing rate in, 243–244
  healing characteristics, 287–288
  meditation-related, 279
  music-related, 281–282, 286, 277, 295–297
  training in, 232–235
Resentment, 169
Respiration, 59–60
  music and, 292
  oxygen/carbon dioxide exchange in, 8
  sighing, 78, 80, 172, 178
Respiratory disorders: See also specific respiratory disorders
  breathing rate and, 70
  hyperventilation and, 70, 76–77
Respiratory system, components, 60
Rickets, 138
Rosett, Joshua, 78

"Sacred illness": See Epilepsy
Salicylates
  as hyperactivity cause, 205–206, 270
  food sources, 205
Salt: See also Sodium
  as electrolyte, 155
Schizophrenia
  breathing therapy, 32, 168
  capillary abnormalities in, 211
  cyanide therapy, 211–212
Scott, Walter, 57
Scurvy, 225–226
Secondary gain, 51, 227
Sedatives, 243

Seizure disorders
    classification, 208
    dietary factors, 136
    hyperventilation and, 176
    hyperventilation challenge and, 92
    idiopathic, types of, 259–260
    magnesium deficiency and, 138
    migraine and, 197
    premonitory symptoms, 260
    sensory motor rhythm brain waves
        and, 216–217
    therapy, 136, 214
Self-hypnosis, 214–216
Self-regulation, 30, 99, 214
Selye, H., 39–41
Sensor, 59
Serotonin
    migraine and, 203–204, 260–261
    tryptophan and, 203–204
Shakespeare, William, 56–57
Shamanism, 286
Shankar, Ravi, 286
Shavasan, 32
Shut Your Mouth (Katlin), 61
Sighing, in respiration, 78, 80, 172,
    178
Skin temperature: See also Hand tem-
    perature
    arterial constriction and, 254
Sleep
    music and, 283, 285
    tryptophan and, 204, 271
Snoring, 271
Social Readjustment Rating Scale, 46,
    47
Sodium, 138, 154
Somatic weakness theory, of psycho-
    somatic disorders, 42
Sound Health (Halpern), 281–282
Speech, 293
Spirogram, 167–168, 169
Staphylococcus, 63
Starch, as tyramine source, 125
Sterman, M. B., 207

Stereotyping, of behavior, 103, 104
Stress
    breath-holding response, 42
    breathing therapy, 256, 258
    calcium loss and, 227
    diaphragmatic contraction in, 66
    as nutrient deficiency cause, 140–
        141
    potassium loss and, 227
    psychosomatic disorders and, 112
Stress-related disorders, 227
    conditioning and, 101–115
    meditation and, 279
Stress Without Distress (Selye), 39–40
Stroke volume: See Heart, stroke vol-
    ume
Studies on Hysteria (Freud and
    Breuer), 177
Suicidal tendencies, seizure-related,
    260
Svetasvatara Upanishad, 56
Syncope, 77, 159–160, 174

Tachycardia, sinus, 160
Tachypnea, 130, 171, 177
Tea
    as insomnia cause, 270
    as tyramine source, 124, 126, 128
Temporomandibular joint syndrome
    (TMJ), 263–264
Tension
    breath-holding response, 42
    breathing/cognitive restructuring
        therapy, 243–246, 256, 258
    breathing rate, 169, 169–170
    exercise and, 292–293
    as headache cause, 263
    muscular, 28
    music and, 277–278, 279, 292–
        293
    prolonged, 40
Thalamic reflex, 284
Thalamus, 284
Thermometer, digital, 216, 250, 255

Threat, body's adjustment to, 223
Thromboxane, 205
Thyroid disorders, 227
Tidal volume, 66, 68
TMJ: *See* Temporomandibular joint
    syndrome
Tolstoy, Leo, 57, 197
Torr, 79
Trachea, 61, 61–62, 63
Trance state, music-related, 285, 286
Tranquilizers, 243
Transient ischemic attack (TIA), 79
Trephination, 197–198
Tryptophan
    agoraphobia and, 140
    epilepsy and, 131
    migraine and, 131, 260–261
    panic disorders and, 140
    serotonin and, 203–204
    as sleep inducer, 204, 271
Turbinate, 62
Tyramine
    action mechanism, 122
    antidepressants and, 122
    asthma and, 123–124
    dietary sources, 124–130
    hypertension and, 122, 123
    hyperventilation and, 141
    insomnia and, 270
    migraine and, 131–132, 260–261
    panic attacks and, 259
    platelet aggregating factor and,
        204
    pulse rate and, 258
    Raynaud's disease/syndrome and,
        123
    as sympathomimetic substance,
        121
    vasoconstriction disorders and,
        122–124
Tyrosine, 124
    dietary sources, 130–131
    migraine and, 260–261

Ulcer, 267
Unconditioned response, 44
Unconsciousness: *See also* Syncope
    hyperventilation-related, 176
Upanishads, 55, 56

Vagus nerve, vagal tone and, 155
Vascular disease: *See also* Heart dis-
    ease
    tyramine and, 126
Vascular system
    arterial: *See* Arteries
    definition, 153
    self-regulation, 213–214
Vasoconstriction
    asthma and, 266
    blood flow effects, 173
    of brain arteries, 176
    carbon dioxide and, 255
    epilepsy and, 207, 209
    of extremities, 173
    hyperventilation and, 123, 202
    hypocapnia and, 173–174
    music and, 291
    Raynaud's disease/syndrome and,
        259
    regulation, 157, 158
    skin temperature and, 254
    tyramine and, 122–124
Vasoconstrictor, as migraine therapy,
    201
Vasoconstrictor nerve, 157
Vasoconstrictor reflex, 158
Vasodilation
    bradykinin and, 206
    migraine and, 197, 201
    music and, 291
Vasodilator nerve, 157–158
Vasodilator reflex, 158
Vegetables
    as tyramine source, 125, 126, 127,
        128, 129
    as tyrosine source, 131

Vertigo, 174
Visken, 93
Vitamin(s), 139–140
Vitamin B$_1$, deficiency, 139
Vitamin B$_3$, deficiency, 139
Vitamin B$_6$
  as asthma therapy, 124
  deficiency, 139–140, 141
  as seizure disorder therapy, 136
Vitamin B$_{12}$, deficiency, 139
Vitamin C
  deficiency, 141, 225–226
  recommended daily allowances
    (RDA), 139
Voltaren, 93
Vomiting, migraine-related, 259

Water vapor
  atmospheric air content, 64
  end-tidal air content, 65
Watson, J. B., 102
Wheat, allergic response to, 119
Woolf, Virginia, 197
Workplace, music in, 280

Yeast, as tyramine source, 125, 126,
  127, 129, 130
Yoga, 30, 32

Zen, 32, 56
Zinc
  deficiency, 141
  function, 137